Flying Cars,
Amphibious Vehicles
and Other
Dual Mode Transports

Flying Cars, Amphibious Vehicles and Other Dual Mode Transports

An Illustrated Worldwide History

GEORGE W. GREEN

McFarland & Company, Inc., Publishers

Jefferson, North Carolina, and London

LIBRARY OF CONGRESS CATALOGUING-IN-PUBLICATION DATA

Green, George W., 1921–
Flying cars, amphibious vehicles and other dual mode transports :
an illustrated worldwide history / George W. Green.
p.   cm.
Includes bibliographical references and index.

ISBN 978-0-7864-4556-1
softcover : 50# alkaline paper ∞

1. Flying automobiles — History.   2. Motor vehicles,
Amphibious — History.   3. Work cars (Railroads) — History.
4. Ground-effect machines — History.   I. Title.
TL684.8.G73   2010   629.04'6 — dc22   2010017290

British Library cataloguing data are available

Front cover: top Transition by Terrafugia, Inc. (courtesy of Terrafugia,
Benjamin Schweighart); bottom Aquada amphibious sports car
(courtesy Gibbs Technologies, Ltd.); background ©2010 Shutterstock

Manufactured in the United States of America

*McFarland & Company, Inc., Publishers
Box 611, Jefferson, North Carolina 28640
www.mcfarlandpub.com*

To Pauline, Norma and Mary,
"My Treasure Trinity"

Contents

Acknowledgments

While dozens of individuals and organizations have made this book possible, I must mention particularly the dedicated ongoing commitment and assistance of Timothy Bogar, without whose help the project could never have been completed.

Others include George Balf, Ralph Dunwoodie, Tashi Georgoff, Charlie Gorey, John Perala, Leonard Opdycke, Lionel Salisbury, Jake Schultz, John Spragge, Molly Swart and Eugene Turner.

Introduction

A dual purpose vehicle is one that is intentionally designed and purpose-built or converted for two distinct functions in the one unit. Various descriptive terms are used for them, such as two-way vehicle and at one time hybrid, but the latter is now pretty well restricted to describing power source, not use.

It wasn't long after the motor car came on the scene that people realized that "if one is good, two is better" in utilization options.

Farmers began to depend on their vehicles as an expedient source of power. Power take-off (PTO) involves putting a drive belt on a rear wheel and using the vehicle's power to run machines, churn butter, saw logs, pump water, fill a silo or generate electricity. Much more recently a company envisioned converting the 8-ft-long DaimlerChrysler Smart Car into a riding lawn mower equipped with lasers instead of blades.

Various pairings of the land-water-air domains have resulted in a surprising array of logical vehicle permutations:

- Road-Air Vehicles
- Amphibious Vehicles
- Road-Rail Vehicles
- Water-Air Vehicles
- Water Submersible Vehicles
- Road Submersible Vehicles
- Rail-Water Vehicles

One dimension beyond duals is limitless triphibious vehicles, embracing all three possible variables.

The advent of these vehicles is really not surprising, as they obviously reflect our multitasking culture. Our fast-paced, frenetic lifestyle demands a multifunctional tandem tempo, although the "one-man band" concept is not without problems.

The vehicle listings obviously could have been arranged in several different logical ways: by country of origin, inventor/designer, or vehicle name. I chose to arrange the entries by decade because it seems to be the best approach to the great diversity of designs. This chronological approach facilitates referencing, highlights trends and brings into sharp focus important developments.

Examples are the great number of roadable aircraft and flying cars that emerged in the 1940s after the end of World War II and the rash of amphibious ATVs that came out in the 1960s. Wars have stimulated research in dual vehicles and governments get much more interested in them when conflicts are imminent.

The amount of space allocated to each vehicle reflects its unique configuration, distinctive design features, specifications and performance data, general characteristics and improvements over time.

The listings are selective rather than exhaustive, but they yield an overall picture of the role of dual vehicles in the transportation system.

It is interesting to note that some categories, like flying cars, fall in the conceptual realm — only a relative few have even flown and most languish in garages, patent office files or museums, a pattern of utter futility so far. More viable inventions like amphibious vehicles and hovercraft in contrast have achieved full marketing acceptance worldwide.

The question now is, have all dual combinations been exploited? By no means. With today's technological advances, we can expect to see new pairings that reflect the limitless imaginations of inventors.

CHAPTER I

Road-Air Vehicles

To the engineering mind with a creative bent the intriguing technological challenge of a flying land vehicle or a roadable aircraft is apparently irresistible.

Such bizarre mobility has always provoked fascination in both peace and war. Normally to traverse the world you are required to choose one particular method of travel, but multimodality expands your options, providing an exciting new range of possibilities.

The nomenclature is very wide and vehicles of this type are variously referred to as combination, dual capacity or mode, convertible, multimodal, composite, inter-media, hybrid, unconventional, etc.

Since the first patent for a flying car, said to have been issued to Felix Longobardi on December 3, 1918, more than 375 different designs worldwide are estimated to have been advanced, ranging from the relatively crude to the ultra-sophisticated.

Here is a rough breakdown of the percentage of designs by decade.

1900–1909	1%
1910–1919	1%
1920s	6%
1930s	13%
1940s	21%
1950s	8%
1960s	15%
1970s	8%
1980s	7%
1990s	10%
2000s	10%
	100%

Note the big bulge in the 1940s right after World War II ended and the current resurgence.

This steady stream of the ultimate "off-road" vehicle is amazing, since probably fewer than 6 percent have ever been off the ground. And the stark reality is that none have so far reached full marketing maturity and gone into quantity production over an extended period.

However, despite this record, today more than 40 individuals and organizations are actively engaged in soliciting investors and deposits on future orders of vehicles in various stages of development and testing. This unmistakably testifies to a current interest worldwide.

"Consider a landing strip as you consider a driveway," advised *House and Garden* magazine early in 1945.

In preliminary drafts of the 1944 Highway Construction Act, Congress called for roadside landing strips alongside all major highways.

There is no recognized ongoing compendium or clearinghouse for elusive flying vehicle data, only sporadic magazine articles, technical papers, and internet offerings. Patent application records perhaps provide the most information. Incidentally, more than 3,000 patents are issued from Washington every week, covering all types of applications; but remember that patents only protect a particular design, not all conceivable designs.

This book covers the saga of the flying vehicle by providing a detailed chronological account of a complicated series of events stretching over 100 years.

There are two basic designs for these vehicles:

- A roadable aircraft is a vehicle primarily intended for use as a practical light airplane and secondarily intended as a licensed motor vehicle with the wings folded or removed, carried or towed.
- A flying land vehicle is primarily intended for surface use and is provided with a flying module (wings, tail and propeller) and other equipment and modifications to enable it to fly. The module may be folded and stored, carried on the vehicle or on a trailer.

Foldable wings, of course, are standard on shipboard aircraft.

Integrated roadable aircraft have all of the components for flight and road travel incorporated into the vehicle.

Modular flying cars have one set of components for flight and another for driving. Modules are combined or separated when converting.

In both approaches the original unit must be revised, redesigned and reengineered.

Rotary-winged VTOL aircraft that use the thrust of air to lift straight up are also adapted for highway use with necessary modifications and equipment.

Vehicle designers usually contend that their concepts are intended for a rather wide variety of logical, related uses:

- Commuter travel
- Intercity business trips by sales representatives and professionals.
- Recreation and vacations, camping and boating
- Sports, hunting and fishing
- Flying clubs
- Air taxis
- Escort services (no, the *other* kind)
- Agriculture and ranching: crop dusting and spraying, seeding, fertilizing, plant pollination, weed control, fence patrol, cattle counting and sheep herding
- Mining
- Prospecting
- Exploration crews
- Oil and gas drilling
- Surveys
- Parcel delivery to rooftops
- Aerial photography
- Advertising
- Radio and TV traffic updates and event coverage

- Law enforcement, particularly border patrol narcotics surveillance and interdiction
- Fire patrol
- Emergency medical ambulance rescue service
- Hobby flying
- Military and paramilitary operations such as reconnaissance

As with any other mechanical invention, designers carry their projects forward in a sequence of logical steps: preliminary concept, creative rough designs, working drawings on paper and/or the computer, scale models, test and production prototypes, testing, patent applications, certification, license, prospectus, brochure, etc.

The following car makes have either been considered or actually used as bases for flying vehicles: AMC (Gremlin, Javelin), Buick, Cadillac, Chevrolet (Camaro, Vega), Datsun, Dodge (Challenger), Ford (Maverick, Pinto), Honda, Jeep, Lotus, Mercedes-Benz, Oldsmobile, Pontiac (Firebird), Porsche, Simca, Studebaker, Subaru and Volkswagen.

Several methods of marketing flying vehicles have been advanced:

- Outright purchase
- Lease
- Rental
- Group purchase with shared ownership

Some designs are intended to be sold as kits or plans for the home-built, do-it-yourself market. Also flight modules adaptable to a variety of cars might be offered for lease to airports.

While the vast majority of projects have involved independent, individual inventors, there are some notable exceptions. Partnerships include such well-known names as Whitaker-Zuck, Nye-Poisson, and Gerhardt-Horn, as well as father and son teams like William and Russell Parrish. In some cases design consultants, professional developers and business promoters have come into the picture later to advance the vehicle in the civilian or military market, lending expertise the inventor may lack.

From time to time several major automotive or aircraft manufacturers have participated in relatively brief forays into flying vehicles, as have industrial design studios such as that of Norman Bel Geddes. The traditional "Big Three" (General Motors, Ford and Chrysler) have reported interest as did Studebaker and others.

It has also been suggested that it would make a lot of sense for a consortium of automotive and aircraft interests to get together, along with related groups.

On the aircraft side we list both U.S. and foreign organizations, some of which have gone to the extent of fashioning prototypes: British Aerospace, Convair, General Dynamics, Avco, Boeing, Consolidated Vultee, Ling-Temco, Hughes, Lockheed, Samsung, Southern and Volante.

Even a few forward-thinking automobile dealers on the West Coast have given flying cars a close look.

When it comes to countries of origin for designs the U.S. clearly dominates in total numbers of different inventions and patent applications, followed by France, Italy, Russia, Israel, Great Britain, Canada, Japan, Romania, Germany, the Netherlands and Switzerland.

History

Historical forerunners of the flying vehicle are legion in ancient myths, fables and legends:

- 2200 B.C.: A three-horse-drawn chariot bore the Chinese Emperor Shun towards the heavens while others in boxy carts propelled by vaned wheels fluttered about.
- 1500 B.C.: King Kai Kawas of Persia had his chariot taken aloft by four swans.
- Fourth century A.D.: The first concept of rotary-wing aviation came from the Chinese. A book called *Pao Phu Tau* tells of the "Master" describing flying cars (fei chhe) made from wood from the inner part of the jujube tree with ox-leather straps fastened to returning blades that set the machine in motion (huan chein i yhi chhi chi). This is the first recorded evidence of what we might understand as a helicopter. The technology needed to create a helicopter had not been produced yet but the concept of rotary-wing aviation had unquestionably been developed. In 1907 the French pioneer Paul Cornu lifted a twin-rotored helicopter into the air entirely without assistance from the ground. In 1924 French pioneer Etienne Oehmichen became the first to fly a helicopter a kilometer in a closed circuit, taking 7 minutes and 40 seconds, to be followed in 1936 by the introduction of the German Focke-Wulf 61, the first practical helicopter.
- 1772: Canon Desfarges built a winged carriage, the Voiture Volante.
- 1781: Jean-Pierre Blanchard's Vaisseu Volante was designed to be lifted and propelled with paddles.
- 1808: While Sir George Cayley is usually acknowledged as the "father of the airplane" for his design with fixed wing and true tail assembly, it is conceivable that he could also be considered the "father of the flying car." His aerial carriage or coachman's carrier was a glider, with a body remarkably like an open boat with wheels. In two tests it served as an over-the-road carriage up to a point and then as a glider, rumbling down a hillside to gain sufficient speed to become airborne before floating across a small valley in Yorkshire, England.
- 1842: William Samuel Henson in England patented designs for an aerial steam carriage which included a description of all parts of a modern airplane except ailerons. It could easily have passed for a flying car on the basis of its appearance. It had an enclosed body for crew and passengers and was to be driven by a steam engine and pusher propeller mounted behind and above a fixed fabric wing that conceivably was removable. Unfortunately it failed its flight test in 1847.
- 1848: Henson's partner succeeded in building a model of a steam-powered airplane which flew about 120 ft.
- 1875: At the Crystal Palace, London, inventor Thomas May demonstrated his Aerial Steamer, a monoplane with two large propellers driven by steam. There was no pilot and the craft never really flew, but it did rise about 15 cm (6 in.) off the ground while following a circular track.
- 1900: Albert Robida's view of the skies of the future included flying taxis.
- 1900: A French novelty company produced a series of trading cards which predicted life in the year 2000 including flying cars.

Media

The media continue to be lavish in depicting flying vehicles, whether in newspapers or magazines (editorial matter, news articles, cartoons, advertising and comics like *Buck Rogers* and *Non Sequitur*) or on the radio, television or the internet.

In the late 1940s Texaco Oil included flying cars in advertisements for Sky Chief Brand gasoline.

Mr. Boffo (Joe Martin, *Neatly Chiseled Features*).

Flying cars featured on the cover of *Air and Space*, January 1996.

In addition references to flying cars may be found in books and motion pictures and in the work of artists and industrial designers like Norman Bel Geddes, who in the 1930s predicted a roadable flying sedan featuring retractable wings.

References also turn up in displays and exhibits (fairs, expositions, auto dealer shows, conventions, fly-ins, Olympic Games) and in parades. Notable was the Futurama exhibit

Flying cars featured on the cover of *Air and Space*, September 2000.

of GM at the New York World's Fair of 1939-1940. Honda had a float in the 2008 Rose Bowl Parade with a periodically morphing, levitating pickup truck that changed into a spaceship.

Provocative names for airborne automobiles have usually focused on the air, sky, birds or the vehicle's flying ability. Unfortunately the media have proved careless about reporting nomenclature, often treating individual proper names as confusing generic terms like skycar, aircar and simply flying car.

The Gernsback Airmobile of 1955 was envisioned by Hugo S. Gernsback, editor-publisher in the 1930-1940 period of many popular pulp magazines on science fiction and other similar topics. His vehicle was a narrow, two-wheel, gyro car, powered by atomic-electrical energy, that used telescopic, retractable stabilizers (wings) and had a retractable tail. A counter-gravitational field was to be created around or below the Airmobile, which meant that you could levitate it at will.

Moulton B. Taylor's Aerocar was operated by radio station KISN in Portland, Oregon, in the 1960s for traffic updates. It flew for "Operation Air Watch." Bob Cummings also used it in his CBS television show.

Several television shows have featured flying vehicles: *Star Wars, Star Trek, The Jetsons, Captain Kangaroo, You Asked for It, I've Got a Secret, To Tell the Truth, What's My Line,* and others. *Monster Garage,* hosted by Jesse James, has built an exotic experimental flying sports

Jesse James flying sports car (courtesy Discovery).

car. Paul Moller has had his Volantor on at least three different television shows, including *Invention* on the Discovery channel and also on Korean TV.

One major auto manufacturer is currently running a television commercial showing how driving its cars will let you fly over traffic. This premise may not be as farfetched as it seems, since new technologies, new regulations and advancements in computer design are changing the possibilities.

Fanciful books abound on the topic of flying vehicles.

The Penetralia in 1856 by clairvoyant Andrew Jackson Davis predicted that "aerial cars will move through the sky from country to country." Interestingly enough, in addition to his foretelling the coming of both the airplane and the car, he predicted prefabricated concrete buildings. In more detail he predicted the "internal combustion engine, carriages and traveling saloons on country roads — sans horses, sans steam, sans any visible power, moving with greater speed and safety than at present. Carriages will be moved by a strange and beautiful and simple admixture of aqueous and atmospheric gases — so easily condensed, so simply ignited and so imparted by a machine somewhat resembling our engines as to be entirely concealed and manageable between the forward wheels of these land-locomotives."

Prophetic visionaries like Jules Verne in France, H. G. Wells in England and Leonardo Da Vinci in Italy predicted in their books scientific fantasies in the sky.

In the 1920s and the 1930s popular children's author Oliver B. Capelle wrote a series of stories about Uncle Nat Denny, Buster and Sally, featuring their adventures with the Magic Flying Auto. These appeared in *Children's Playmate* magazine.

In the 1930s both Victor Appleton and Victor Appleton II (pseudonyms) featured in their Tom Swift series of books for boys Tom's prolific vehicle intentions and exploits, including fantastic flying cars such as the Triphibian Atomicar.

In 1968 James Bond author Ian Fleming saw his other great creation brought to the big screen, *Chitty Chitty Bang Bang*, an imaginary flyable car restored by the eccentric Professor Potts. In the 1964 book Fleming describes the car as a five-ton, pre–1914 Mercedes with a six-cylinder Maybach aero engine originally built by Count Zborowski. It was supposedly capable of speeds over 100 mph. Mud flaps front and rear became dragon-like wings that enabled it to soar through the air. Fleming's fascination with cars runs through the Bond books — Chitty could float on water and fly, feats which the Bond producers repeated, with different cars, in *The Spy Who Loved Me* (1977) and *The Man with the Golden Gun* (1974). Several cars were used in the filming of the movie. The car used for the hovercraft scenes was lighter since some of it was constructed from aluminum instead of brass. It also had its engine taken out for the flying scenes so that it would be light enough to hang from a helicopter. The car used in most driving shots was built by Alan Mann in Hertfordshire in 1967 and was fitted with a Ford 3000 V-6 engine and automatic transmission.

The 1930 musical *Just Imagine* saw cars in the sky over New York City by 1980, and in 1940 the late comedian Jack Oakie, expertly playing the part of tyrant Benito Mussolini in Charlie Chaplin's film *The Great Dictator*, proudly related his plans for a land-sea-air combination vehicle to support his buddy Adolf Hitler.

In 1964 Dr. William R. Bertelsen put together his ninth version of his Aeromobile, the Model 250, for Universal Picture's tour to publicize its movie *The Brass Bottle* about Aladdin's Lamp.

Ian Fleming's book *Chitty Chitty Bang Bang* focused on an imaginary flying car of the same name (© 1964 and renewed 1992, from *Chitty Chitty Bang Bang* by Ian Fleming, illustrated by John Burningham. Used by permission of Random House Children's Books, a division of Random House, Inc.).

In 1974 a special flying version of American Motors' Cassini Matador played a spectacular role in the James Bond thriller filmed in Thailand, *The Man with the Golden Gun.*

In 1985 *Back to the Future* with Christopher Lloyd and Michael J. Fox came out, featuring a souped-up version of the DeLorean car as a time machine. In the first sequel, at least one 21st-century car was shown with ducted fans that could fold up for parking and down for flight.

Some other notable films featuring flying vehicles have appeared. In the movie *Blade Runner* a 21st-century roadable aircraft had a ducted fan in the fuselage in the rear and two tiltable ducted fans located out front. *The Absent-Minded Professor* and *Meet the Robinsons* also included flying vehicles.

In February 2002 *The Flying Car Movie* was aired on the Jay Leno *Tonight Show*, a short film by Kevin Smith.

In looking to the future of roadable aircraft and flying vehicles it is probably best to list the advantages and disadvantages for such programs. This yields a perspective over some 375 different designs in the past 100 years.

Advantages

- A number of successful flights have occurred, at least one cross-country.
- Related seaplanes, skiplanes, hovercraft, and pilotless planes have been successfully produced.
- A significant number of energetic designer organizations and individuals are currently soliciting investors and deposits on future orders.
- Congested roads are crying for relief; taking to the skies is imperative.
- All-terrain vehicles would allow personal or business commutes to otherwise inaccessible places such as steep mountains and would allow amphibian-type performances in creek areas.
- Historical interest has already been displayed by substantial number of major automobile and aircraft manufacturers.
- Aircraft Crashes Record Office reports 136 air crashes worldwide in 2007, one of the safest years in aviation history.
- Vehicles have a wide variety of logical intended uses, over 20 identified so far.
- The vehicles could provide a new sport for competition.
- Options are open for renting, leasing and group purchase.
- There is a virtually untapped home kit market (scratch building).
- The potential government market is significant: military (part of proposed *Star Wars* initiative), law enforcement and intelligence operations, etc.
- Media coverage would increase.
- Ownership could be recognized as a unique status symbol.
- A flying car can be used significantly more often as a car than an aircraft only would be. It could extend subdivisions to a radius of 300 miles and more than double the practical door-to-door automobile range to 100 miles in one hour.
- Vehicles could operate out of proposed mini airports 600 ft. long that could be

located at supermarket parking lots, golf courses, business parks or any reserved section of two-lane road that is two blocks long.
- Established pilots have potential as an initial prime market.
- The availability of computer-aided design (CAD) would facilitate development.
- Advanced technology can allow vehicles to fly in predetermined patterns along three-dimensional highways in the sky, guided by supercomputers linked to GPS satellites and geostationary systems.
- Vehicles lend themselves to novel marketing techniques like toy model kits, weather vanes, hangar art and home décor.
- There is a propensity for multiple vehicles in U.S. households; 35 percent have at least three according to Experian Automotive.
- Honeywell forecasts a 40 percent rise in demand for civil helicopters in the next five years.
- The advent of these vehicles could bring back life to small, less crowded local airports, some of the most underutilized infrastructures (nearly 6,000 public-use local airports in U.S. alone).
- The aerospace industry is booming.

Disadvantages

- The inventor mentality obviates cooperative efforts among designers.
- It is difficult to recruit sales talent to complement the technical expertise of the inventor for generating professional sales literature and publicity and a viable outcome from a practical marketing plan.
- Inherently insurmountable problems are possible: mechanical, image, etc.
- Relatively few designs so far have been carried beyond drawings, models and even prototypes, which often end up in museums and inadvertently solidify their concept vehicle status.
- There have been some spectacular crashes.
- Substantial expenditures would be required to build very compact, elevated skyports, preferably 30–40 ft. above existing freeways, with all tall signs and utility poles relocated.
- Definitive marketing research findings are scattered and proprietary.
- There is a transitory record of desultory, sporadic government interest for military or civilian applications.
- There is no ongoing, active trade association, publication or website devoted to coordinating information and disseminating it.
- In a very narrow view of the market potential, some feel that it is much more logical to provide a plane owner with an automobile than to furnish a motorist with an aircraft.
- The number of student pilots now is about a third less than in 1990, as is the number of private pilots, most of whom are in their 50s, 60s, 70s and 80s, largely due to neglected recruiting, advertising and publicity activities.

Problems

A careful look at all the formidable difficulties involved with these types of vehicles is in order.

Mechanical

The structural challenges are obvious when trying to match a car and an aircraft. The direct combination of conventional automobile and aircraft features is impossible as there is insufficient compatibility and dual usefulness for much copying of features. The development of systems having some similarity is possible and leads to suitable compromises, while maintaining the integrity of the two units.

Specifically, the problems are center of gravity and balance and weight (too heavy for the air and too light for the road); aerodynamics to yield road clearance; complicated and unfamiliar combined controls and instruments; unreliable belt drive systems; undersized tires; fragility; excessive noise; lengthy conversion time; limited fuel availability and rapid consumption rate; cluttered, cramped interior; undersized passenger compartment and small luggage space; poor visibility; lack of safety; hard starting; hard handling, especially three-wheelers; difficulty climbing; and lane width limitations.

Service

The channels of distribution and maintenance and service outlets are untried.

Financial

The sales price is anticipated to be very high, and even rental and lease rates or kits would be expensive. The same is true for insurance (auto and aircraft liability, auto body and aircraft hull coverage). It could be difficult to qualify for research grants and the cost of development would be high.

Regulatory

Rules would issue from international, regional and local organizations (governmental, safety, ecological, etc.). It might be necessary to attain multiple licenses. A ban on home-built kits in residential neighborhoods is possible. The FAA is tightening rules on prefabrication and the amount of assistance being given. There are now 30,000 amateur-built aircraft certified in the U.S.

Image

Unfortunately, there is a sizable contingent of the public that makes fun of these vehicles. The mere mention of a "flying car" seems to provoke immediate derisive appellations such as strange, dowdy, odd, ridiculous, frivolous, toy, trivial, curious, fiasco, dangerous, weird, bizarre, science fiction, absurd, unrealistic, impractical, and irrelevant. This throws the whole idea into the realm of science fiction.

Designers are criticized as suffering from a relentless obsession or as having a pie in the sky mentality. This criticism is probably not surprising, as it is directed at one of the most unsuccessful activities in the technological world, one which literally "never got off the ground."

Has any other single category of vehicle patent application ended up more in the Washington "graveyard?" This has led to its current status as a stepchild in the demimonde of experimental aviation with perhaps the lowest patent productivity level.

Anyone who considers these vehicles far-fetched should consider that the prestigious California Institute of Technology in 1999 endorsed the theory that the pyramids in Egypt were raised by large kites. The hieroglyphics call them "invisible gods in the sky." Nothing is impossible.

Many aircraft experts agree that the concept of a flying car is viable. Perhaps that is why hope springs eternal in the human breast for the never-say-die cadre of designers. Maybe these designers simply want to leave a heritage or legacy of having invented a flying car. Here the profit motive is sublimated.

Do flying cars and roadable aircraft have a future? Only time will tell. The many advances in aviation, science and related technologies, combined with man's limitless imagination, are elements to keep inventions going.

Can the world be changed by a new technology? It has happened before. The dream lives on. Dennis Bushnell, chief scientist for NASA at its Langley, Virginia, research headquarters, has been quoted as saying he is "certain that the car has had its day and that the skycar is the future."

This book is intended as a tribute to all those audacious designers who "see tomorrow."

1900–1909

Back in the late 1800s in Romania, Trajan Vuia while still a young student designed and built a scale model of a flying machine called a winged automobile. This was a three-wheeled velocipede on which was assembled a metal frame set vertically, at its upper part being clamped a wing, direction rudder, engine and propeller.

He endured scoffing and ridicule mixed with envy when he went to France in 1902, after earning his doctor's degree from the Budapest Polytechnic school.

Then on March 18, 1906, he tested his modular monoplane prototype Vuia I near Paris. It was about the size of early Santos Dumonts.

This four-wheel carriage had steel tube construction and a triangular framework with no tail, rudder amidships and a tractor propeller built by Victor Tatin. A bicycle was the basis for the fuselage and pilot. It was to have been pedal-powered but was then retrofitted with a motor.

Fixed umbrella wings could be wrapped and packed like an umbrella.

SPECIFICATIONS

Engine . . . . Flat boxer, Serpollet-type
Span . . . . 22.96 ft.
Chord . . . . 6.5 in.

"Yeah, the road does feel smoother . . . Why do you ask?"

A 1986 cartoon from *Model Aviation Magazine* (courtesy *Model Aviation Magazine*).

Wing surface	62 sq. ft.
Wing weight	48.5 lb.
Total weight	531 lb.
Propeller diameter	7.87 ft.
Tires	Balloon

He went on with refinements to produce Vuia II in 1907.

A full-scale model of Vuia I is on display at the National Military Museum of Romania and at the Musee de l'Air.

It is said that Wilbur Wright worked on a flying car design in 1909 and that his father, Bishop Milton Wright, observed, "It is only given to God and angels to fly." This statement came just before the brothers made man's first powered flight in Kitty Hawk in 1903.

1910–1919

From 1910 to 1925 Rene Tampier in France built several different models of integrated roadable aircraft.

Rene Tampier's l'Avion Automobile in Paris in 1921 (courtesy Francois Jousset).

On October 23, 1921, in Paris he drove his l'Avion-Automobile and on November 7 he took to the air. This biplane, 12 ft. tall and 25 ft. long, had four wheels conventionally placed, the front ones steerable and the rear axle equipped with a tiny differential. The fuselage and tail section remained rigid but the wings folded along each side. Cranks were used to fold them into a horizontal and longitudinal position. A second pair of rubber-tired wheels dropped into place.

On the ground it was powered by a small, 10-hp, four-cylinder, water-cooled, auxiliary gasoline engine and in the air by a 300-bhp, eight-cylinder Hispano-Suiza V-12 engine.

It had a foldable steering gear and while on the road the pilot/driver would steer facing the reverse of his flying position, looking over the fuselage and tail. The rotating propeller pushed the vehicle down the road.

Ten folding wing units could fit where one regular aircraft was parked. Conversion took less than an hour but problems emerged due to the vehicle's height and bulkiness.

SPECIFICATIONS

Span (flying position) . . . . 42.6 ft.
(wings folded) . . . . 7.9 in.
Length . . . . 27.9 in.
Wing area . . . . 344 sq. ft.
Total weight . . . . 2860 lb.
Load/sq. ft. . . . . 8.3 lb.
Load/hp. . . . . 9.5 lb.

Metz-Air-Car advertisement in a 1911 issue of *The Automobile Magazine.*

Air speed was 112 mph and ground speed 15 mph.

Tampier tried unsuccessfully to interest the army in testing it for military uses.

In a 1911 issue of *The Automobile* magazine, the Metz AirCar was offered in a modest, two-inch, illustrated advertisement. The brief copy read: "Bleriot type aeroplanes complete or in the knock-down. Motors 30, 60 and 120 HP; propellers and all component parts. Everybody may fly. Manufacturers of Metz Runabouts — lightest and most economical automobile in the world. We want live, progressive dealers everywhere. Metz Company, Waltham, Mass."

In 1915 William N. Parrish and his son Russell announced plans for their Aero-Automobile to carry seven passengers in a body resembling that of a touring car. When operated on the road the wings were to be folded into the body.

In 1916 Glenn Hammond Curtiss, aviation pioneer, aircraft designer, engine mechanic and motorcycle rider, designed his Autoplane/Autolandplane Model 11, a modular, modified triplane, combination airplane and custom-made touring car, called an "aerial limousine."

The three-seat car portion stood on four little rubbertired, standard wire aircraft wheels, the front two steerable. The body was aluminum-framed with celluloid windows. The circular radiator, which provided water cooling for the engine, was placed in front of the hood. Adding to the automobile-like appearance was the thermometer cap of the radiator and the starting crank.

Glenn Hammond Curtiss, designer of the Autoplane (courtesy Glenn H. Curtiss Museum, Hammondsport, NY).

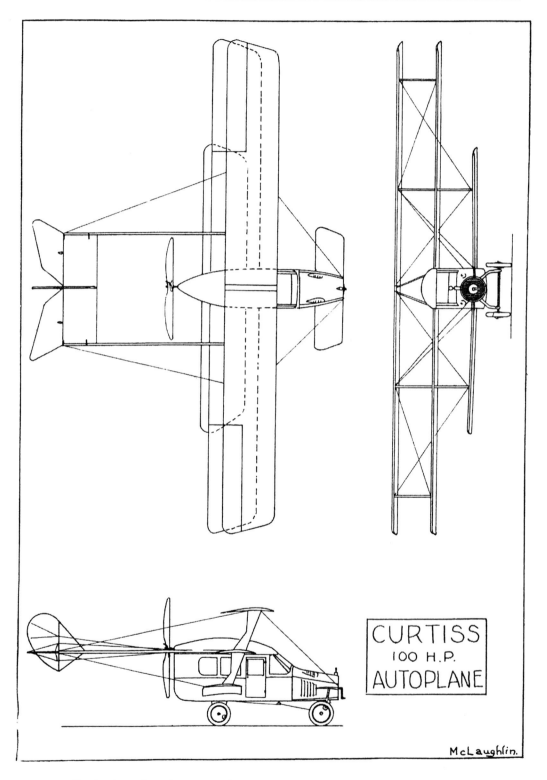

Curtiss Autoplane (courtesy Glenn H. Curtiss Museum, Hammondsport, NY).

Top and above: Exterior and interior views of the Autoplane designed by Glenn Hammond Curtiss (both photographs courtesy Glenn H. Curtiss Museum, Hammondsport, NY).

It was powered on the ground by a four-blade pusher propeller at the rear roof, driven by a shaft and then through belts or chains. There was an eight-cylinder, 100 bhp Curtiss OXX engine up front under the hood which drove the rear wheels through a gearbox and shaft. Twin boom outriggers held the tail section (stabilizers, elevator, fins and rudder).

The removable sets of three wings from a Curtiss Model "L" consisted of a small canard set over the four wheels and a contemporary staggered triplane arrangement over the cabin area. The flight units (wings and boom-mounted tail) detached from the car by nuts and bolts with lots of rigging guy wires.

The vehicle boasted a luxurious, plush interior in a velvet-curtained, leather-lined compartment with tapestries and brocaded upholstery, as well as arm chairs and ceiling light.

The car could carry a pilot-chauffeur in the front cockpit and two passengers in back.

SPECIFICATIONS

Span, upper two planes . . . . 40 ft. 6 in.
Span, bottom plane . . . . 23 ft. 4 in.
Chord, upper two planes . . . . 48 in.
Chord, bottom plane . . . . 42 in.
Gap between planes . . . . 39 in.

Autoplane on exhibit at the Pan American Aeronautical Exposition. Left to right: Rear Admiral Bradley A. Fiske, Henry Woodhouse and F.L. Faurotè (courtesy Glenn H. Curtiss Museum, Hammondsport, NY).

SCIENTIFIC AMERICAN

THE FLYING LIMOUSINE ON THE GROUND AND IN THE AIR—[See page 303]

March 24, 1917

Munn & Co., Inc., Publishers
New York, N. Y.

Price 10 Cents

Autoplane on the cover of *Scientific American*, March 24, 1917.

Stagger .... 11 in.
Height overall .... 10 ft.
Length .... 27 ft.
Area .... 390 sq. ft.
Fuel .... 30 gal.

PERFORMANCE

Speed .... 45–65 mph
Range .... 3 hr.
Road speed .... 45 mph
Climb .... 200 ft. in 10 min.
Useful load .... 710 lb.
Load per sq. ft. .... 5.67 lb.
Load gross .... 2,210 lb.

A prototype went on display during February 8–15, 1917, in New York City at the Pan-American Aeronautical Exposition at the Grand Central Palace.

Curtiss made a very short flight in it in 1919 and then World War I claimed his attention.

1920s

From 1920 to 1925 Virgil B. "Fudge" Moore's Autoplane Company in Southern California attempted to develop a market for hybrid vehicles named Road Runner. There were

models for an Aerial Taxi, a Navy Special Military Scout, a Salesman's Special and an Aerial Truck, all with streamlined bodies. The designs were so scaled that planes could be constructed in various sizes with corresponding motors and could be adapted to any special condition which might be met.

The Aerial Taxi was designed to carry a pilot, two passengers and 500 lb. of baggage. In the air it was a biplane with a rigid body and watertight fuselage, carrying the motor, controlling cabin or cockpit, passenger cabin, luggage compartment, lavatory and other special installations. The

Road-Runner logo for the Autoplane Company of Virgil B. "Fudge" Moore (courtesy Autoplane Co.).

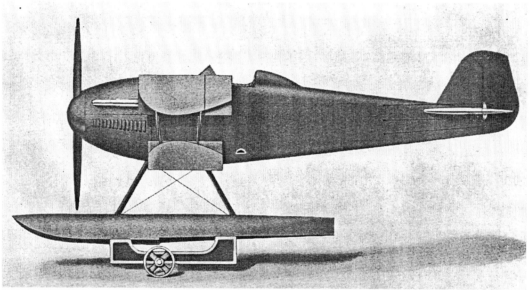

Top: Moore's Autoplane Aerial Taxi model. *Bottom:* Moore's Autoplane Navy Special model (both photographs courtesy Autoplane Co.).

pilot's cabin was forward of the passenger compartment and was entered by a door in the forward end. The passenger cabin was insulated and comfortably upholstered with temperature and ventilation controls, along with collapsible seats. Large plateglass windows were all around. It could be converted into a bedroom at night and was accessible from the ground. Both cabins were walled off with asbestos-covered, fire-proof sheet metal.

The instruments and engine controls were conveniently arranged and there was a self-starter on the motor whose power when applied on the road was transmitted to the rear axle through a clutch, selective transmission and differential. A separate clutch controlled the application of the power to the propeller to enable its disengagement. It stopped in a horizontal position and served as an ornamental bumper. A wheel operating upon a shaft

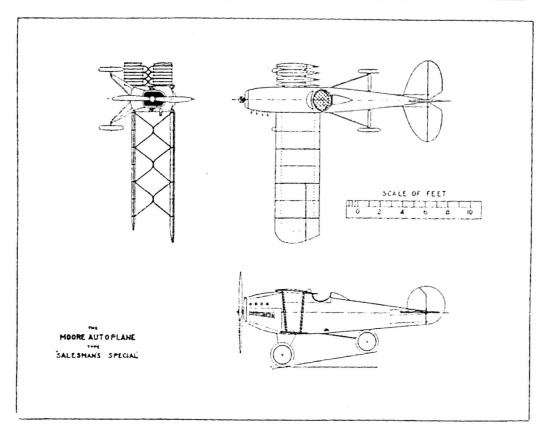

Moore's Autoplane Salesman's Special model (courtesy Autoplane Co.).

leading across the fuselage, when rotated, generated the power to fold and unfold the wings. Speed was 120 mph and the plane had fuel sufficient to fly 1,000 miles. It was designed to be transformed into a mailplane or truck.

The Salesman's Special carried only the pilot and minimal baggage.

The one-ton Aerial Truck was designed for such commercial purposes as freight or mail. It also had a speed of 120 mph and could carry fuel sufficient for 1,000 miles.

The Navy Special Military Scout was intended for combined military and aeronautical training as well as use as a sportsman's seaplane. It had folding wings, yielding an overall width of less than 7 ft., and was equipped with dual floats beneath the fuselage. While it did not have regular automobile features, it did possess special facilities for taking off from the deck of a ship.

Incidentally, Moore apparently had quite a flair for grandiose promotion. On June 8, 1925, he mailed out a 12-page, 8 × 11 in. illustrated packet extolling the virtues of the Road Runner Autoplane. Among the 1,000 recipients was the president of the United States! At one time he claimed that the Japanese government had tried to buy his designs, and, failing, had attempted to obtain his secrets through spies. He had worked previously for the E. B. Heath Aerial Vehicle Company in Chicago and he also operated a group known as the Scientific Research Association. Part of the funding behind the Autoplane came from the El Centro, California, Chamber of Commerce.

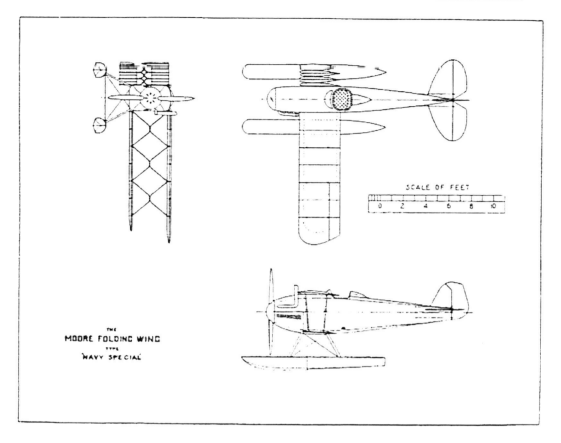

Moore's Autoplane Navy Special model (courtesy Autoplane Co.).

In 1921 Jerry Hall designed the l'Automobile Volante, a low-slung speedster with a propeller in the front and double wings.

In 1925 an airplane automobile was demonstrated in France. A propeller shaft ran from the fuselage to a transmission which turned the rubber-tired front wheels with their brakes and steering mechanism. The power to drive the plane on land was furnished by a small auxiliary engine. Its conversion into an auto took less than half an hour.

In 1926 Else H. Tubbe designed a single-engine, roadable airplane with a pusher propeller and three wheels.

In 1927 Marcel Leyat in France designed a roadable monoplane, l'Auto Avionette L-19.

In 1928 Anton Jezek designed a four-wheel combined automobile and airplane with a single engine and a tractor propeller.

VIRGIL "FUDGE" MOORE

Los Angeles, California,

June 8,   192 5

Hon. President of United States,
c/o White House,
Washington, D. C.

Honorable Sir:

    The enclosed booklet will explain to you a new creation
and invention that has been undergoing secret tests and development stages for the past number of years. Many foreign
countries are desirous of obtaining these patent rights, and
I am very anxious to have our own United States Government
adapt them first.

    In order that I may get this before our Government prop-
erly, I believe it necessary that I receive about 1000 letters
from prominent and progressive men of our country. I have
received to date over 250 letters from Aeronautical Engineers
and others who have looked over the blue prints, working
drawings and have viewed the experiments, and who have acknowledged the fact of its practicability. I have no stock
for sale and these letters are not for the endorsement of any
promotion proposition.

    What I need now is a letter stating in your own words,
just what you believe a machine of this type that will perform
the duties claimed for it to do, will mean to Commercial Aviation. If you will kindly favor me by doing this it will be
highly appreciated.

                            Address this letter to Virgil
Moore, c/o Scientific Research Asso-
ciation, 404-5-6 Insurance Exchange
Building, Los Angeles, California,
the Inventor and Patentee.

                              Sincerely yours,

THE AUTOPLANE
A COMBINED AUTOMOBILE AND AEROPLANE

VBM:LS
Enc.

Letter in promotional brochure for Autoplane 1925 (courtesy Autoplane Co.).

1930s

In 1930 the Weyman Lepere Aeromobile was introduced in France. It was a high-winged monoplane two-seater. The Renault engine was a six-cylinder, in-line, air-cooled and supported above the hull in the Rohrback-Dorner-Saro manner. With a sheet-metal front, the steel-tube fuselage was covered with fabric.

In the extreme nose was a side-by-side cabin with a large door on each side, a wide rectangular front window, a skylight, one set of controls and a seat similar to that of an ordinary motor car. The rudder was operated by pedals very similar to clutch and brake pedals.

Two Dunlop airwheels were mounted on normal undercarriage members with spiral springs on the shock-struts, and two smaller ones were mounted on rigid axles forward as an anti-capotage device. A tail-wheel was also fitted.

All surfaces, including the wings, were wire braced on the top and bottom, and the main wings had lift and landing wires supporting them at two points, one nearly halfway out along the span and another nearer the tips. They consisted of stranded cables bound to the edges of streamlined wooden fairings. The airscrew was mounted behind the uncowled engine as a pusher.

The air and landing speeds were low.

The vehicle was obviously a deliberate attempt to imitate a motor car and was meant to be flown the way one drives a car.

In 1930 William H. Nelsch designed a single-engine aircraft with three wheels, a tractor propeller and complete roadability.

In 1931 William Bushnell Stout, an automotive and aircraft designer, began to work on a series of experimental, integrated sky cars in his Stout Engineering Laboratories. When he sold his company to the Consolidated Vultee Aircraft Corporation (Convair) he remained in charge of the Stout Research Division from 1943 to 1945.

While there he announced the 1,500-lb. Skycar IV or Tri-Car, whose great advance was a wing control system which eliminated the necessity of ailerons, elevators and rudders. It was designed by George G. Spratt, an engineer in the division (his father, Dr. George A. Spratt, had been experimenting with this type of wing as early as 1903).

The wing stood on four articulated struts above the cabin and was controlled by a single stick inside. It could be tilted to any angle up and down for ascent and decent, moved sideways to bank and turn, and even rotated. All directional controls were in this single wing. It made Skycar IV simple to fly and the wing, which was the only part that had to be removed to make the craft roadable, detached in five minutes.

Otherwise it had four-wheel landing gear, a pusher prop in its stubby tail and an inverted, air-cooled, in-line, four-cylinder Michigan Rover engine that developed 75 bhp.

The aircraft could go 100 mph in the air and 70 mph on the road.

Stout predicted the flying automobile in the following article which appeared in the December 8, 1934, issue of *Automobile Topics*:

William Bushnell Stout with model of Stout Skycar (from the Collections of the Henry Ford).

AVIATION AND AUTOMOBILE ENGINEERING

"Aviation and automobile engineering are coming closer and closer together and eventually they will meet," observes W. B. Stout, president of Stout Engineering Laboratories. "When they do, automobiles will fly or conversely airplanes with their wings shed or folded temporarily, will run through the city streets. This day is coming just as surely as we now have radio, television and other accomplishments which 25 years ago appeared just as impossible.

"One of the truest signs of this converging of the airplane and the automobile is the extent

William B. Stout in Convair Model 103, also known as the Spratt-Stout Model 8 Skycar (National Air and Space Museum, Smithsonian Institution, NASM Videodisc No. 2001-3218).

to which each of the two industries is drawing upon the other in current practice. In the early days aviation drew heavily in man-power and ideas from the automobile industry. Today the pendulum is swinging the other way. The marked influence of aviation design on automobile design may be seen in some of the following features — such as, the ability of the automobile engine to run wide open under full load for days at a time — the greater horsepower per pound of weight in both powerplant and complete vehicles — the employment of large reserve horsepower — the use of alloy steel, aluminum and other metals which provide strength with lightness — balloon tires, Duco from wing dope, aluminum heads, etc.

"In some of the up-to-date cars, such as Ford and Terraplane, the car has one horsepower for every 24 to 28 pounds of weight. Airplanes of the normal cruising type have a horsepower for every 10 to 15 pounds of weight. When the power-weight ratio of the automobile comes down to the power-weight ratio of the plane, little remains except the matter of compensating design to prevent the automobile from flying. In other words, when that time comes engineering knowledge will have caught up with the problem and it becomes a mere matter of adaptation. Adaptation or ingenuity never lags far behind engineering knowledge.

"The aviation industry, on the other hand, has one big thing to learn from the automobile industry and that is how to manufacture good performing engines cheaply. If you buy an engine for your private airplane it costs you almost $100 per horsepower. If you buy an automobile engine for your automobile it costs you $2 per horsepower. The difference is in volume of sales.

"Now that the automobile engine is capable of running under sustained loads for the same length of time the airplane engine can run, there is no need for such a wide discrepancy. It would not be too big a step to imagine that if this quantity discrepancy continues to exist the automobile manufacturers may be building aviation engines adapted from car engines. In other words as far as performance is concerned aviation and automobile engineering are beginning to meet. Eventually there must be a readjustment of design to bring the output of the two types of engines closer together.

"The coming automobiles will borrow heavily from aviation as regards streamlining, vision, marked reduction in weight, greater use of aluminum and other light alloys, greatly increased power-weight ratio — getting down to something like 15 pounds per horsepower — and I would not even be surprised to see something like an airplane landing gear used in place of the present type of automobile spring suspension. After all, the independent springing or knee action that we have heard so much about is just a step in this direction."

In addition to the Skycar Stout created a series of unusual machines: the rail plane; a gas-driven railroad car; a collapsible house trailer; and a spacious, rear-motor vehicle he called the Scarab.

In 1932 Caudron-Renault in France developed the Aviocar, a monoplane with folding wings. It had a retractable wheel at mid-fuselage. The power to drive on land was furnished by a one-cylinder auxiliary gasoline engine that was mounted on the tail and pushed the vehicle.

In 1933 the Bureau of Aeronautics of the U.S. Department of Commerce sponsored a competition for a cheap safety-integrated aircraft capable of being driven on highways as a roadable autogiro. There were initially seven bidders but ultimately only five groups were chosen to produce under contract experimental aircraft prototypes for the government to study and test. A rotary wing craft that would fly 100 mph and be able to land and take off from a 30-ft. square area, together with the potential compactness of stored rotor blades as opposed to airplane wings, proved very attractive to experimenters. These vehicles are considered the precursors of the helicopter.

The most outstanding models were the PA-19 and the AC-35. The direct-control AC-35 operated on several road adventures. It had a welded steel structure. The pilot and one passenger sat side by side in an enclosed cockpit and 40 lb. of luggage could be accommodated. It had an overall length of 24 ft. with 17-ft. blades folded back, a height of 8 ft. and a width of 7 ft., weight of 1,350 lb., tread of 64 in., and a wheelbase of 114 in. The engine was a seven-cylinder, radial air-cooled Pobjoy 135 bhp which developed 90 hp at 3,500 rpm. Bore and stroke were 3.03 by 3.42 in. The engine was provided with louvers for cooling. A shaft ran forward from the engine to reduction gearing (approximately 3.5 to 1) which drove the propeller. To render it roadable the rotating blades were folded and pointed back over the tail. The propeller was disconnected from the engine by a dog clutch and locked in a vertical position so that it could not be rotated by the wind velocity. It was driven through the single rear wheel by a conventional clutch and bevel gearing and steered through the front landing wheels, which were activated by the brakes. The front prop was not removable. Air speed was 115 mph and it could throttle down to as low as 20 mph. Sufficient fuel and oil could be carried for 3.5 hours of cruising and fuel economy was 20 mpg. On land speed was 25 mph. It was designed to take off without wind, on short runways less than 150 ft. long.

Test pilot James G. Ray, vice-president of the Autogiro Company of America, returning from the National Air Races at Cleveland in 1935, landed by the roadside at Blandburg, Pennsylvania, and drove with rotor blades folded ten miles over the highway to Tyrone, Pennsylvania. At this point, safely beyond the highest ridge of the Alleghenies, he drove into a small roadside field, unfolded his rotor blades and took to the air; by following the Juniata Valley out of the mountains he completed his trip to Philadelphia.

Extensive publicity was given to his Washington, D.C. exploit. He landed in a small,

Pitcairn AC-35 Roadable Autogiro (National Air and Space Museum, Smithsonian Institution, No. 85-16410).

downtown park just north of the Department of Commerce Building and two blocks from the White House. He then drove down the street to the front entrance of the Commerce Building, where he formally delivered the vehicle to Eugene L. Vidal, director, who was the father of author Gore Vidal.

In 1960 Skyway Engineering Company tried to revive the AC-35 and proposed to go into production in 1962, but the plan did not materialize.

The Pitcairn PA-19 Cabin Autogiro model was offered by the Pitcairn Autogiro Company. New features included the tilt-adjusting rotor and cantilever arrangement of wings, landing gear and tail surfaces. It had a welded steel tube structure and no brace wires. The side trusses were of large diameter tubes and the top, bottom and panel bracing aft of the cabin section was formed by diagonal tension tubes. Attachment fittings had exceptionally large bearing surfaces. The fixed window framing was of all-steel construction and the upholstery was luxurious. A control column with a swingover wheel for dual control was used. The fixed wings were entirely of cantilever design in three sections. The detachable outboard wing panels were of monospar construction. The ailerons were large and had a specially shaped leading edge in front of the line of the ball bearing hinges. An independent tripod-type landing gear was used under each end of the steel center section of the wing. Semi-balloon wheels were used and the wheel track was 12 ft. The elevators were of steel tube construction. The engine was a Wright R-975 E-2, delivering 420 hp at 2,150 rpm. Provision was made to allow easy modification for the Pratt and Whitney Wasp Jr. T-3-A engine. A direct electric starter and generator were standard equipment and the two aluminum fuel tanks were slung below the cabin floor. The front tank contained a six-gallon emergency supply.

The full-load performances were with a Hamilton-Standard propeller:

Rotor diameter . . . . 50 ft. 7½ in.
Length overall, with rotor . . . . 35 ft. 9 in.
Length overall, without rotors . . . . 25 ft. 9 in.
Height overall . . . . 13 ft. 9½ in.
Weight empty . . . . 2,675 lb.
Weight three passengers . . . . 510 lb.
Weight of baggage . . . . 80 lb.
Payload . . . . 590 lb.
Weight of gasoline (90 gallons) . . . . 540 lb.
Weight of oil (8 gallons) . . . . 60 lb.
Weight of pilot . . . . 170 lb.
Total useful load . . . . 1,360 lb.
Gross weight . . . . 4,035 lb.
High speed . . . . 120 mph
Cruising speed . . . . 100 mph
Landing speed . . . . 0 mph
Rate of climb to 1,000 ft . . . . 850 ft./min.
Takeoff distance without wind . . . . 260 ft.

It is now on display in the Smithsonian Air and Space Museum.

In 1934 Daniel Vieria designed a single-engine autoairplane with a tractor propeller and three wheels.

In 1934 Mrs. Phoebe F. Omlie, a research liaison officer at the CAA in Washington, built a model roadable aircraft at the request of the Bureau of Air Commerce. Back in 1921 Omlie had been a wing-walker and parachutist.

The aircraft had a wingspan of 47 in., fuselage approximately 10 × 4.5 in., tail surface 15 in. long, three-wheel landing gear and a pusher propeller. It was painted dark blue and yellow.

She constructed it at the Langley Memorial Research Laboratories of the National Advisory Committee for Aeronautics for conference work to prove the safety of the tricycle landing gear. It was loaned to the Pink Palace Museum by the CAA in 1940.

In 1934 three possibilities for transforming aircraft were advanced in France, proposing retractable road wheels in aircraft and autogiros for ground travel.

In 1935 Joseph Marr Gwinn, Jr., a World War I aviator and former Consolidated Vultee employee, started the Gwinn Aircar Company and came out with a small, modular, two-place, side-by-side cabin biplane 16 ft. 3 in. long.

Its airframe had wood-frame wings and a semi-metal fuselage, made up of seven subassemblies bolted together to form a complete structure. Two different engines were used in two prototypes, a 90-hp British Pobjoy Niagara radial engine and a 130 hp Niagara radial engine.

The wings, with a span of 24 ft. and length of 16 ft., consisted of four panels, each 3 ft. 6 in. × 10 in. in size. They were bolted to fittings on the fuselage so that they could be removed and stored. It took two people to carry one panel. Power could be supplied to the wheels when the vehicle was used on the road. This required disconnecting the propeller gear box and hooking up the hydraulic system that supplied power to the wheels.

The plane had tricycle landing gear, no rudder, and a simplified instrument panel. The pilot operated the controls, patterned after those of the automobile, with a steering wheel in conjunction with the pedals. The accelerator regulated takeoff, landing and cruising.

It also boasted a heater, glove compartment, ashtrays, sun visor, tool compartment and radio. Top speed was 120 mph, cruising speed 109 mph, range 495 miles, fully loaded weight 1,600 lb., and useful load 550 lb. It carried 150 lb. of fuel (25 gallons), 45 lb. of baggage, and a pilot and passenger.

A prime objective of the design was to prevent spin and stall. A prototype was successfully flown in 1937 and CAA certification followed the year after.

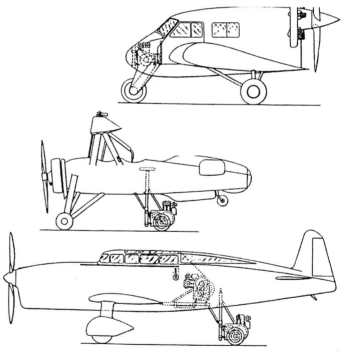

Top: Phoebe F. Omlie's roadable aircraft model (Memphis Pink Palace Museum). *Bottom:* 1930s French designs for transforming aircraft for ground travel (*l'Aeronautique Magazine*).

A second plane was built later in 1937 with a larger Pobjoy 140-hp engine, which provided a top speed of 137 mph and a cruising speed of 123 mph.

Gwinn Aircar on cover of *Popular Aviation*, November 1937.

Gwinn hired two pilots, Frank Hawks and Nancy Love, to tour the country demonstrating the aircraft. On the 23rd of August, 1938, Hawks failed to clear high-tension power lines shortly after taking off from East Aurora, New York. He and his mechanic died in the resulting crash. Gwinn suspended production and closed the Aircar plant.

From 1937 to 1950 aviation aerodynamic engineer Theodore P. "Ted" Hall, at times chief development research engineer for Consolidated Vultee Corporation (later Convair and General Dynamics), devoted his time to designing several different versions of modular roadable aircraft. All were successfully flown. His styling partner was Henry Dreyfuss, an industrial designer.

Top: Convair No. 3 Aircar (San Diego Aerospace Museum). *Bottom:* Convair Model 116 (San Diego Aerospace Museum).

Convaircar 118 maiden flight, November 15, 1947 (courtesy Johan Visschedijk, 1000aircraft-photos.com).

His first design used the same flathead 98-hp Mercury V-8 engine to power both the car (off the rear of the engine through a three-speed transmission and rear wheel differential) and the airplane (through a shaft leading to the propeller mounted at the front of the car). The wheelbase of the three-wheel car was 63 in. while the overall length of the airplane was 29 ft. The 30-ft. wing, twin boom and tail assembly weighed more than 300 lb. and was at least a two-man operation to attach and detach; this led to the installation of built-in struts.

With a gross weight of 2,200 lb. and four passengers, the vehicle later included a 130-hp, aircraft flat-six, Franklin aircraft engine and projected a cruising speed of 110 mph, service ceiling of 10,000 ft., cruising range of 280 miles and road speed of 60 mph.

His next design approach, the Convair Model 116, combined a four-place, fiberglass-body car with a single rudder with its own 26.5-hp, water-cooled Crosley automotive engine rear mounted and a flight module that incorporated a 190-hp Lycoming 0-4350 aircraft engine for aerial power and a 34.5-ft. detachable wingspan.

The Convair Model 116 had a cruising speed of 128 mph, a service ceiling of 11,500 ft, a range of 400 miles, and could travel 45 miles on a gallon of gas.

His idea, to which Consolidated Vultee agreed, was to sell the car and have flight modules available to rent at various airports. First given the designation Convair Model 118, this vehicle was later named Stinson Aircar (after the division that was to produce it) and finally ConvAIRCAR. In November 1947, after several successful flights, the plane apparently ran out of fuel and crash-landed. Though the body was crushed, the pilot and passenger survived. The ConvAIRCAR reportedly flew again in February 1948, but Consolidated Vultee, having spent an estimated $800,000 on research and development on five different designs by that time, abandoned the project and dissolved its Stinson Division.

Hall's patent application outlined problems for flying cars and his approach to solving them:

> The utility of flying automobiles is well recognized and in striving to effect a vehicle of this type having a maximum of efficiency both as an aircraft and as a land vehicle troublesome structural problems are encountered by reason of the fact that the design criteria for aircraft are radically different than for automotive vehicles. In the design of aircraft it is particularly essential to minimize gross weight and reduce overall dimensions in order to obtain optimum performance. It has been found necessary in prior proposals of this type of flying vehicle to compromise the characteristics and design of the automotive vehicle in favor of the airborne unit. The present invention contemplates a combination automobile and aircraft in which the gross weight of the vehicle is kept within practical limits as a useful airplane, and the characteristics of the automobile component meet conventional automobile specifications while being considerably lighter by reason of a novel arrangement of load distribution and structural members.
>
> The present invention also contemplates the complete independency of the flight component and its controls from the automotive unit. Earlier proposals have combined their flight and automotive controls and instruments in such a manner that operation of the vehicle as an automobile or as an airplane has been complicated by the presence of unfamiliar or unnecessary controls when in one situation or another. At the same time, the inter-dependency of the control systems in prior designs complicates the conversion of the vehicle from an airplane to an automobile or vice-versa and obviously increases the possibility of failures and accidents due to improper rigging or malfunctioning of the controls.

In 1937 William F. Gerhardt designed a single-engine, roadable vehicle with three wheels and one driven, a pusher propeller, no wings and one rotor.

That same year aviation pioneer Waldo Dean Waterman, often referred to as the "father of America's flying automobiles," flew his first integrated Arrowbile. It was an outgrowth of his small, tailless, single-engine Arrowplane built for a U.S. Department of Commerce contest in 1935.

The Arrowbile had a streamlined, compact, two-passenger cab mounted on three wheels and a pusher propeller. It used a 100-hp, six-cylinder, 1937 Studebaker Commander automotive engine modified to the extent that it was fitted with special intake and exhaust manifolds, three carbs, a high-compression head and a large oilpan.

The engine stood above and just behind the two main (rear) wheels so that landing loads were taken by these wheels and not by the craft's framework. Drive to the overhead pusher prop came via six V-belts, and a clutch pulley tightened these belts for flight. On the ground, the engine drove the two rear wheels through chain belts for one forward speed and through a friction clutch for reverse.

The 38-ft. detachable wing locked on by a safety device inside the cabin, which housed all airborne controls. The steering wheel hung from the roof. It used a Studebaker dashboard, seats, radiator, cabin hardware, small parts, knobs, hood grille, trim, self-starter, generator, battery, etc. There was also a compass, altimeter and airspeed indicator.

Length overall was 19 ft. The Arrowbile had a 25-gallon tank, air speed of 125 mph, range of 400 miles and ground speed of 70 mph.

Pilot Jerry Phillips with Waldo Dean Waterman's Arrowbile No. 3, "Miss South Bend" (National Air and Space Museum, Smithsonian Institution, SI Neg. No. 78-1875).

Conversion from air to road took three minutes.

The first public demonstration was at Bendix Field, in South Bend, Indiana, on February 20, 1937. Then in 1938 pilot Jerry Phillips took Arrowbile No. 3, "Miss South Bend," on a cross-country tour that covered 2,200 miles in 28 hours, from Santa Monica, California, to Floyd Bennett Field, U.S. Coast Guard Air Station in Brooklyn. It used only two quarts of oil and delivered 18 miles per gallon.

Lockheed Vega Autoplane (EAA Library Archives).

The Arrowbile was intended to be sold through Studebaker dealers after travel and demonstration in every principal U.S. city.

Amelia Earhart was a very enthusiastic supporter of the Arrowbile and it enjoyed extensive coverage in the press.

An improved seventh version in 1958 was called the Aerobile, this time with a water-cooled, flat-six Franklin engine.

An Arrowbile may be found today in the National Air and Space Museum, where it was placed in 1957.

Waterman summed up his opinion on the future of the flying car as follows:

> The more that I thought over the situation, the more convinced I became that the idea of a "flying automobile" was of little potential — elusive and unrealizable. Sure the concept was fascinating and the public eagerly took to it, but simple practicability foretold an impossible goal. Even today I believe that the flying automobile is a dream forever doomed.

In 1938 John A. Johnson designed his Autoplane. It had seven wheels with two driven and a detachable flight section.

In 1939 B. L. Beals, Jr., designed a flying automobile with a single engine, pusher propeller, four wheels with two driven, a detachable flight section and a twintail boom.

In 1939 a Lockheed Aircraft Corporation subsidiary built the Vega autoplane. It had two in-line engines placed side by side and tricycle landing gear. The cabin shell was mounted on steel-tube truss construction. Automobile-like accommodations were provided for six persons. It weighed 5,750 lb. and was 32 ft. 5 in. overall and 41 ft. from wingtip to wingtip. It could fly on one engine, could fly at 210 mph, and had a 1,060-mile cruising range on 160 gallons of gasoline.

In 1939 Juan de la Cierva introduced a roadable variation of his autogiro design, the Pitcairn P-36 Whirlwing.

1940s

Four different vehicle designs are detailed for 1943.

F. F. Frakes, using a commercial automobile, designed a roadable airplane with three engines, two tractor propellers, four wheels and a detachable flight section.

Robert C. Reed and Ernest W. Schliber designed a combination aerial and land vehicle. It had three engines, two tractor propellers, seven wheels with two driven, a detachable flight section and twintail booms.

George G. Thompson designed an aerial and land vehicle with a single engine, tractor propeller and four wheels.

Nathaniel B. Wales, Jr., designed a control mechanism for helicopters having two co-axial, center-rotating rotors and three wheels with one driven, yielding complete roadability to the vehicle.

Three vehicle designs from various inventors are listed for 1944.

Edgar A. Clark designed a single-engine aircraft having power-driven, adjustable, retractable and steerable front wheels, a tractor propeller and a detachable flight section.

John Harlin Geisse designed a roadable, single-engine airplane with folding and detachable wings, ten pusher propellers and twintail booms.

Alex Tremulis, while a U.S. Air Force Master Sergeant in charge of design and illustration at Wright-Patterson Field in Ohio, responded to the government's looking ahead to the type of personal transportation that mustered-out service people might turn to after World War II.

He had two similar designs consisting of teardrop-shaped, aluminum- or fiberglass-body four- or six-passenger cars with removable wings that could be stored at one airport while the car was driven to the next airport to pick up another set of rented wings. The powerplant was to be a four-cylinder, air-cooled, 400-hp aircraft engine that in one model would drive a pusher prop and in the other would drive twin props through a differential. Top speed estimates were 160 mph on the ground, 140 mph in the air. The wheelbase was 100–105 in., the overall length was 14 ft., and the wingspan was 40 ft. An interesting safety feature in case of engine failure was a large parachute to bring the car/plane safely to earth.

Six designs from inventors are described for 1945.

Lt. Col. Ercolano Ercoloni of the Italian Air Ministry designed the Erco-Spider automobile-airplane. It had a four-wheel cab/fuselage for two, detachable wings and, depending on the version, one or two tail booms. For flight it was to use an air-cooled, four-cylinder aircraft engine in the nose with a two-cylinder engine for ground power. It flew at 110 mph and was driven at 40 mph in 1946 but never went into production.

Herbert D. Boggs, assistant to the vice-president and general manager at Glenn L. Martin-Nebraska Co., introduced his single-engine Airmaster as a four-place, low-wing monoplane with a two-door cabin. It had spinproof wings, a 145-hp, gear-drive, air-cooled pusher Continental engine, twintail booms, twin rudders and tricycle landing gear. The nose wheel was fixed, while the main wheels were semi-retractable. It had a two-control system with ailerons and elevators only and wheel brakes. Top speed in the air was 150 mph, cruising speed was 130 mph and stalling speed was 53 mph, with a range of 500 miles.

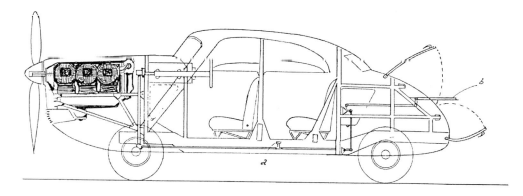

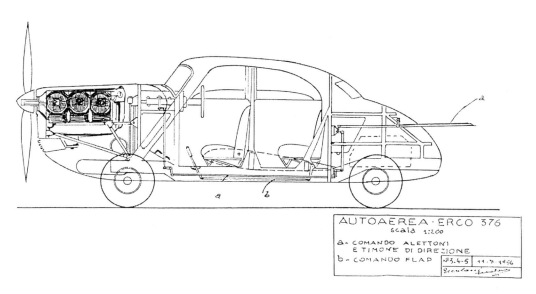

Original drawing of Lt. Col. Ercolano Ercolani's Erco-spider 376 (courtesy Gianclaudio Polidori).

Land speed was 105 mph. The detachable body containing the powerplant was designed to be used on either a plane or a car chassis. Five minutes was required to change.

Agencies would provide rental services of car chassis for transit trade, and also rental of airplane chassis in some cases. In the beginning, these 50–70 agencies would be located in about 47 cities throughout the 38 economic or geographic centers of the U.S.

Curtiss-Wright Industries called its two-place aircraft the Flymobile, a helicopter powered by a four-cylinder, 90-hp Franklin opposed engine. It was of metal construction with wood fairing strips and fabric covering, and used a three-wheel landing gear. Gross weight was 1,100 lb. The engine turned a 25-ft. diameter, four-blade, co-axial rotor. Top speed on land was 56 mph; air speed was 95 mph.

Designed by Dr. E. E. Kay and Curtiss-Wright, the Flymobile had a gimbal ring system for the tilting rotors and differential pitch control actuated by foot pedals. The fuselage measured 40 in. wide and 150 in. long. The adjustable seat, curved instrument panel and upholstery were in a dark cherry color.

Lt. Col. Ercolano Ercolani's Erco-spider (courtesy Gianclaudio Polidori).

Control in transferring engine power from roadability to flying or neutral was accomplished by swinging a lever located just behind the seat. Simultaneous change of pitch for ascending or descending was achieved by a separate lever located just below the cockpit ceiling. Devices on the steering wheel and steering gear permitted coordinated movements between the steering wheel and rotor shafts. The fuselage was shaped like a small car and was mounted on three 16 × 14 in. wheels — two in front and one in the rear.

Norman V. Davidson designed his Roadplane. He was an engineer employed by Consolidated Aircraft Company. It had a tricycle wheel pattern with the front steerable, a 75-bhp air-cooled engine, 36-ft. wingspan and detachable flying surfaces.

Edward M. Nye and Alphonse Poisson designed a modular combined single-engine aircraft and automobile with twintail booms. The unique feature of the invention was their method of joining a self-contained, three-wheel road vehicle to an airframe which had its own engine, complete with pusher prop. Once you had landed and parked your aircraft on the ramp, all you had to do was unlatch the wing struts where they joined the fuselage and pull them down so they stood vertically. They then served as support to hold up the wing. Additional supports for the rear of the airframe were telescoped out of the rudder fins. They could be cranked down to hold up the tail section. The action of disconnecting the struts automatically disconnected the automobile from the airframe, and you could now drive away.

Edward H. Page designed a helicopter with a folding rotor, pusher propeller, and four wheels with two driven, yielding complete roadability.

In 1946, the year after the end of World War II, ten designs were outlined by different inventors, an all-time high number!

Charlette in Montreal designed a flying car that could be converted into a skiplane.

Russell H. Fish, Sr., designed a single-engine land and air vehicle with a pusher propeller, six wheels with two driven, a detachable flight section and twintail booms.

Robert Edison Fulton, Jr., descendant of the inventor of the steamboat and Thomas Alva Edison, introduced his single-engine, Model FA-3, modular Airphibian. He was a self-taught pilot.

Robert Edison Fulton, Jr.'s Airphibian (FA-2 roadable monoplane) (National Air and Space Museum, Smithsonian Institution, SI Neg. No. 91-13262).

The vehicle had two sections: a wing and tail unit that came off in one piece and stayed at the airport between flights and a narrow, two-seated, aluminum-bodied, 7 ft. × 4.5 ft. convertible coupe with a fabric top and four airplane-sized, semi-enclosed wheels sticking out on struts. For highway driving the Sensenich three-blade tractor propeller was unbolted with a built-in wrench and stored on the side on the fuselage.

The same controls were used for both flying and driving. The hookup of the flight controls was automatic when the wings and fuselage went on. The right rudder pedal became the foot brake of the car.

The engine was an air-cooled, valve-in-head, horizontally opposed, 150-hp Franklin up front for hydrostatic climb.

SPECIFICATIONS

Brakes . . . . Discs with spot
. . . . contacts
Suspension . . . . Independent rubber torsion
mounts on four wheels

Fulton's Airphibian on the cover of *Popular Science*, July 1952.

IN THE AIR

Length . . . . 16 ft. 9 in.
Wingspan . . . . 34 ft
Height (vertical tail) . . . . 7 ft. 8 in.
Gross weight . . . . 2,100 lb.
Empty weight (flight unit) . . . . 400 lb.
Useful weight (81% of gross) . . . . 1,700 lb.
Wing area . . . . 152 sq. ft.
Wing loading (per sq. ft.) . . . . 13.9 lb.
Power loading (per hp) . . . . 14 lb.
Maximum speed . . . . 120 mph
Cruising speed . . . . 110 mph
Landing speed . . . . 50 mph
Rate of climb . . . . 600 ft./min.
Ceiling . . . . 12,000 ft.
Fuel consumption (3½ hr. range) . . . . 8 gal./hr.
Baggage . . . . 50 lb.

ON THE ROAD

Length . . . . 11 ft.
Width . . . . 6 ft.
Height . . . . 5 ft. 6 in.
Wheelbase . . . . 72 in.
Gross weight . . . . No specified limit
Empty weight . . . . 1,200 lb.
Useful weight . . . . No specified limit
Maximum speed . . . . 50–60 mph
Fuel consumption . . . . 20 mpg
Turning radius . . . . 22 ft. 8 in.
Baggage . . . . No weight limitation

CONVERSION TIME
(One person, no tools)

Road to flight operation . . . . 5 min.
(Engine starter would not work unless units were properly secured)
Flight to road operation . . . . 4 min.

Fulton had designed the conversion process to use a series of failsafe interconnecting rods that locked when the two correct components linked and then automatically engaged the electrical elements. These same interlocking mechanisms would prevent the engine from starting unless the units were properly secured.

In all there were six prototypes built by U.S. Continental Inc. and they logged over 200,000 miles driven or flown in the late 1940s in demonstrations, starting with the maiden flight from the Danbury, Connecticut, airport in 1947. Marketing was planned, with aircraft and automobile sales outlets. In 1950 the aircraft type certificate was awarded.

Examples of the first roadable plane said to be certified by the CAA may be found in exhibits at the National Air and Space Museum of the Smithsonian Institution and the Pate Museum of Transportation.

Fulton succinctly summed up the problems inherent in flying cars:

When a pilot leaves the aircraft at an airport and takes a cab to town he leaves behind 90 percent of the basic elements of an automobile — an expensive and unnecessary procedure which has done more than any other thing to stifle aviation.

Others have recognized this fundamental problem and have made efforts to solve it by accomplishing a transition from airplane to car and back. But the problem has many aspects — mechanical, aerodynamic, practical, safety, economy, comfort, service, and maintenance, public reaction and acceptance. Of the several suggested solutions which have been offered to date, all have failed due to neglect of one or more of the above features. Most have been so radical in conception and based on such untried principles that they have failed to hold public interest. Others have made contributions which, unless supplemented by many additional features, were of little practical value.

Fred Guardine designed a composite, single-engine vehicle with a tractor propeller and a detachable flight section.

Bruce K. Hallock, a professional pilot and aeronautical engineer, built and flew a four-place roadable integrated autoplane, the Road Wing (originally the Road-A-Plane). It was a blue and yellow tailless vehicle with a wood pusher propeller with a reverse pitch. The folded wings with small casters on the tips were pulled behind the fuselage and the prop spun between them to propel the vehicle. Folding took about 15 minutes. The body and wings were made of wood and covered in fabric. While the basic airframe was built from scratch, some of the smaller trim pieces like wheel parts, prop spinner and control wheels came from other small planes. Most of the parts were made by hand.

The Road Wing had a 145-hp Continental 0-3000 aircraft engine. The registration number on the outside of each vertical fin was N2721C.

Bruce Hallock's Road Wing (courtesy Don Hallock).

Top: Bruce Hallock's Road Wing, showing the wing folding process. *Right:* Road Wing cockpit. Note Erocoupe control wheels (both photographs courtesy Don Hallock).

A production plane would have required a folding prop to clear the wings when on the road.

SPECIFICATIONS—IN THE AIR
Experimental Model

Wingspan . . . . 34 ft. 0 in.
Length . . . . 15 ft. 8 in.
Weight empty . . . . 1,470 lb.
Useful load . . . . 830 lb.
Gross weight . . . . 2,300 lb.
Power . . . . 145 hp Cont.
Cruise speed . . . . 125 mph
Stall speed . . . . 48 mph
Seating capacity 4

Production Model

Wingspan . . . . 28 ft. 6 in.
Length . . . . 16 ft. 0 in.
Weight empty . . . . 1,525 lb.
Useful load . . . . 1,325 lb.
Gross weight . . . . 2,850 lb.
Power . . . . 230 hp Cont.
Cruise speed . . . . 160 mph
Stall speed . . . . 53 mph
Seating capacity 5

ON THE ROAD
Experimental Model

Length . . . . 24 ft. 6 in.
Width . . . . 7 ft. 2 in.
Height . . . . 9 ft. 0 in.
Gross weight . . . . 2,300 lb.
Power . . . . 145 hp Cont.
Propulsion method . . . . Propeller
Reverse . . . . None
Seating capacity 4
Top Speed . . . . 50 mph

Production Model

Length . . . . 23 ft. 4 in.
Width . . . . 7 ft. 2 in.
Height . . . . 8 ft. 6 in.
Gross weight . . . . 2,850 lb.
Power . . . . 230 hp Cont.
Propulsion method . . . . Propeller
Reverse . . . . Reversible pitch
Seating capacity 5
Top speed . . . . 50 mph

The prototype is on display at the Pioneers of Flight Museum. Fulton's sons are writing a book about their father and his work called *A Sky Full of Dreams*.

Jozef Hendrik Hanssen designed an auto-airplane combination with two engines, a pusher propeller, and three wheels, with one driven, detachable flight section and twintail booms.

George H. Hervey designed his Travelplane with a four-place cabin, pusher propeller, three-wheel landing gear and steerable nose wheel. A 200-hp Ranger engine drove both the propeller and wheels. Minus wings and tail it was 16 ft. long by 6.5 ft. wide.

Engineer Luigi Pellarini in Italy designed the three-seat, monoplane Aerauto, built by Aernova Costruzioni Aeronautiche. It had a pusher propeller, a tail on a boom, twin fins and tricycle landing gear with a steerable nose wheel. It was powered by a 125-bhp Lycoming 0-240 AP air-cooled engine. The fuselage and wings were metal and the ailerons fabric-covered.

By folding the half wings at the sides of the frame and retrocessing the back wheels, the Aerauto could be turned into a screw propeller land vehicle. The wingspan was 31.5 ft., the length 20 ft. 7 in. and the loaded weight 1,562 lb.

The prototype was shown first at the Milan Fair in 1948 and its first flight was on May 9 that year. It was taken on an Italian tour in 1950 of more than 4,000 kms., about half in flight. It was later destroyed by fire in airfield storage.

The Southern Aircraft Division of Portable Products, Inc., developed a roadable plane, the Southernaire, built and flown by Willis Brown, a two-place with removable wings and tail structure. It used the auto's rear-wheel drive along with the propeller's power for speedier take off as an airplane. Once the plane was airborne, the gears driving the rear wheels were disengaged. It had all the conventional automobile controls and the steering wheel operated the aileron and elevator when in the air. The 30-ft. wing, tail and tail boom were in one section and, with the propeller, could be removed in about five minutes. Driven both in the air and on the ground by a 130-hp air-cooled, six-cylinder Franklin engine, it cruised at 110 mph and had a range of more than 600 miles. It had three wheels and weighed 1,800 lb.

The firm flight-tested it but did not proceed further.

Daniel R. Zuck and Stanley D. Whitaker, aircraft engineers, designed their two-passenger, high-wing monoplane, the Plane Mobile.

It used a 40-bhp Continental at the rear but production plans called for a modified 125-bhp Lycoming 0-290 engine. The single rear wheel gave ground traction via undetermined drive that included reverse. The wings pivoted from a center point above the cockpit, folding back over the car roof. A wing-carrying frame was built into the tail, which used trifoil vertical fins. Two men could convert the craft either way in three minutes. An innovation was the ailerator, a combination of ailerons and elevator.

Specifications: wingspan 31.5 ft.; overall length 15.5 ft.; height 5.75 ft.; wheelbase 8.42 ft.; gross weight 1,150 lb. With wings folded, length was 16.8 ft. and width was 5.9 ft. Cruising speed was 80 mph.

Some five designs from various inventors emerged in 1947.

Kenneth R. Bailey designed a single-engine roadable aircraft with two pusher propellers, four wheels and a canard.

Engineer William F. "Bill" Chana, president of William F. Chana Associates consultants, and at the time flight test engineer at Consolidated Vultee, built a series of models of roadable planes and helicopters. The former had separate rigid flying modules with engines that could be rented at the airport.

He advanced careful observations on flying automobiles: "The biggest challenge is to end up with an attractive, comfortable, cost efficient and reliable automobile and a com-

William F. "Bill" Chana (courtesy William Chana).

bined car and plane that is certifiable with the FAA and approaches the flight performance of a contemporary aircraft."

Adolph R. Perl designed a single-engine, integrated roadable aircraft with a pusher propeller, four wheels, two of which were driven, folded multiple wings into the body of the fuselage longitudinally and a retractable tail boom. It had an airscoop in connection with the doors of the fuselage thereof for directing air backwardly into the engine at the rear of the fuselage.

Charles B. Smith designed a convertible automobile-airplane with seven wheels.

Aeronautical engineer Moulton B. ("Moult") Taylor produced his single-engine, modular high-wing monoplane, the Aerocar. The fuselage was used as a two-seat (side by side), front-wheel-drive sports coupe whose interior resembled a typical 1948 automobile.

It had a fiberglass body over an all-aluminum frame, monocoque fuselage and tail section, four retractable wheels, white sidewall tires and aluminum wings.

The Aerocar used a conventional steering wheel and gearshift stick from the floor, a toggle switch for the turn signal lights and a horn button on the steering wheel. The car instruments were located on the left side of the dashboard while the aircraft instruments were round gauges across the upper part of the dashboard.

There were padded bucket seats, a deep-dish steering wheel and a padded dash. It had a three-speed Borg Warner automatic transmission and torsion bar suspension.

Top: Model of William F. Chana's flying auto-helicopter. *Bottom:* William F. Chana's car and plane canard version (both photographs courtesy William Chana).

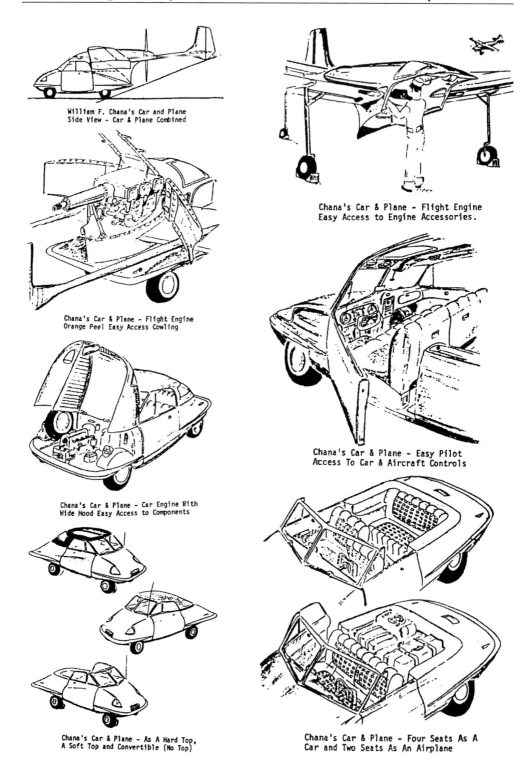

William F. Chana's Car and Plane
Side View – Car & Plane Combined

Chana's Car & Plane – Flight Engine
Orange Peel Easy Access Cowling

Chana's Car & Plane – Flight Engine
Easy Access to Engine Accessories.

Chana's Car & Plane – Car Engine With
Wide Hood Easy Access to Components

Chana's Car & Plane – Easy Pilot
Access To Car & Aircraft Controls

Chana's Car & Plane – As A Hard Top,
A Soft Top and Convertible (No Top)

Chana's Car & Plane – Four Seats As A
Car and Two Seats As An Airplane

William F. Chana's car and plane designs (courtesy William F. Chana).

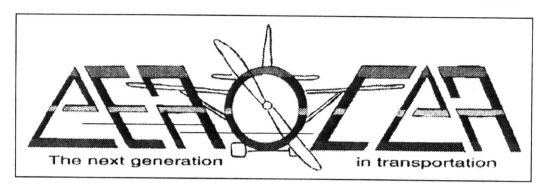

Top: Moulton B. Taylor's Aerocar logo. *Bottom:* Moulton B. Taylor in 1950 with a wind tunnel scale model of his Aerocar (Detroit Public Library, National Automotive History Collection).

A self-contained trailer, whose wheels popped out of compartments in the wing's leading edges, carried the wings, tail, and pusher propeller, available either for towing or parking on a temporary basis.

Aerocar I, which first flew in 1949, won federal CAA certification on December 13, 1956. Six were built.

Aerocar on cover of *The AOPA Pilot*, May 1959.

Top: Aerocar on cover of *Sport Aviation,* January 1990. *Bottom:* Advertisement for Aerocar
model (courtesy Historic Aviation).

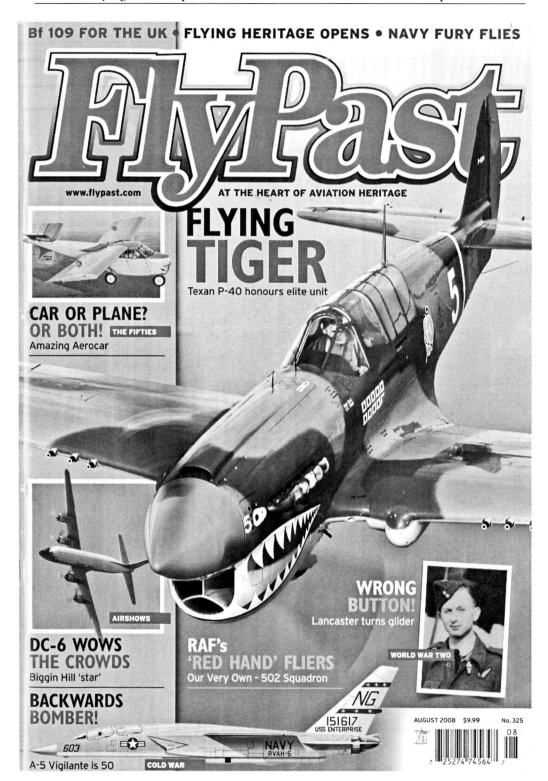

Aerocar on cover of *Flypast*, August 2008.

Specifications

Wingspan . . . . 34 ft.
Wing area . . . . 190 sq. ft.
Wing loading . . . . 11 lb./sq. ft.
Power loading . . . . 14.7 lb./hp
Car empty weight . . . . 1,100 lb.
Trailer weight . . . . 400 lb.
Design useful load . . . . 600 lb.
Allowed baggage weight . . . . 100 lb.
Pilot and passenger weight . . . . 340 lb.
Fuel weight (24 gallons) . . . . 144 lb.
Maximum gross weight . . . . 2,100 lb.
Car-trailer length . . . . 26 ft.
Wheel and tire size . . . . 4.50 in. × 12 in.
Engine — Lycoming 0-320 (derated) . . . . 143 hp
Trailer wheel size . . . . 10 in. × 3.50 in. × 4 in.
Seat width . . . . 3.67 ft.
Trailer width . . . . 8 ft.
Height (aircraft) . . . . 7.5 ft.
Height (car) . . . . 5.33 ft.
Height (trailer) . . . . 8 ft.

Performance

Top speed . . . . Over 110 mph
Cruising speed . . . . Over 100 mph
Rate of climb at full load . . . . Over 550 ft./min.
Service ceiling at full load . . . . Over 12,000 ft.
Cruising range . . . . Over 300 miles
Landing speed . . . . 50 mph
Landing run (with normal braking) . . . . 300 ft.
Take off run . . . . 650 ft.
Distance to clear 50 ft. obstacle . . . . 1,225 ft.
Designed road speed (engine red line) . . . . 67 mph
Road range . . . . Over 400 miles
Fuel consumption (cruising) . . . . 8 gal./hr.
Road fuel consumption . . . . 18 mpg
Time to change from plane to car . . . . 5 minutes

It was equipped for crosswind landings and was said to be spinproof.

Subsequent improvements and refinements over the next 20 years produced a re-engineered car body: Aerocar IV with a Honda CRX and later the Geo Metro.

The vehicle appeared in numerous air shows, fairs, tours, and car meets. In a flight to Cuba Fidel Castro's brother was taken for a ride. It accumulated more than 200,000 miles of road time and more than 5,000 hours in flight.

Robert Cummings used the Aerocar in his 1960s television comedy series, *Love That Bob*, painted bright yellow and green to match colors of vitamins being sponsored. It also appeared on the program *I've Got a Secret* and Portland, Oregon, radio station KISN featured it in its traffic reports.

Taylor envisioned several conversions from his basic Aerocar, mainly for the military. These included versions for amphibious operation, tracked vehicles, a Jeep vehicle, a helicopter and an electric-powered vehicle. The Ford Motor Company displayed quite a bit of interest in Aerocar III.

An Aerocar may be seen at the Silverwood Museum and models for home assembly using the body of a Honda CRX were produced. A complete history of the Aerocar is contained in Jake Schultz's book *A Drive in the Clouds*.

Ed Sweeney in 1996 created Aerocar 2000, a modern and high-performance version of the original, using the new Lotus Elise, a lightweight 1,510-lb., two-seat roadster. The flight module is powered by a separate Lotus, liquid-cooled, twin-turbocharged, 2.5-liter V-8 engine producing 350 hp and weighing 491 lb.

The weight of the vehicle is 2,500 lb., its maximum loaded weight 3,450 lb. and its wingspan 36 ft.

It has a maximum cruise speed of 108 mph, empty take off and landing speed of 65 mph and range of 300 miles.

It has two control systems: the car system essentially unchanged and a primary electronic flight control system.

Taylor had cogent comments on many aspects of flying cars:

> *Image*: "Flying cars will never become fully popular until they have the broad appeal of modern automobiles. The image of sportplanes, the association with discomfort, the need for technical ability, any association with overt risk will turn most people away"
>
> *Financing*: "Despite the fact that the problem can only be solved directly by engineering effort, it must be first solved by financial backing. Finance, therefore, holds the key."
>
> *Conversion*: "The changeover from plane to auto can be made by a woman in a fur coat with high heels on."
>
> *Market*: "The ultimate market is obviously as great as the present day auto market. Who wouldn't buy an airplane if it came along with his own car at no appreciable extra cost? There is scarcely a person with any imagination who hasn't at one time or another dreamed of owning his own flying automobile."
>
> *Trailer Advantages*: "A trailer can be easily unhitched from the land automobile portion of the assembly and either towed along the highway, temporarily parked at any convenient spot along the highway or stowed in a garage, at the same time meeting existing vehicle codes and regulations."

From 1948 to 1974 Leland D. "Dewey" Bryan designed, built and flew three versions of his integrated pusher prop monoplanes, variously referred to as Autoplanes or Bry-Cars, 8 ft. wide, 7 ft. 10 in. high and 17 ft. long, with a 22-ft. wingspan. There were three control flight systems: rudder, aileron and elevator.

The Bryan I Special used a basic fuselage pod propelled by a pusher mounted aircraft engine both on the road and in the air. Unlike later models, its tail was supported by a three-tube open structure similar to that of modern ultralights. It was a high-wing, single-place design with a fuselage pod of welded steel tubing, fabric-covered. The center section of the three-piece wing was permanently mounted to the fuselage. The outer wing panels detached completely and switched to the opposite sides of the ship, where the wing struts formed part of the mounting rig and propeller guard. Headlights and license plates were also mounted. Air speed was 90 mph.

His second roadable, the Bryan II, was first flown in 1957. He cannibalized the cantilever aluminum wing, rugged landing gear, and other parts of a standard Erocoupe. He also used the Erocoupe's no-rudder pedal control system for its compatibility with road

Leland D. "Dewey" Bryan's Autoplane II (EAA Library Archives).

use. The wing was modified to fold up manually and over the engine area, a ten-minute operation. The basic design was a single-place, twintail boom pusher of all-aluminum construction. The combination of a pusher propeller inside the tail booms, plus the box formed by the folded wing, was considered to be a sufficient safeguard to allow using propeller thrust to move the Bryan II down the road.

Construction on the Bryan III, an all-aluminum delta wing configuration, was started in 1963. It followed the same basic layout, with refinements. The five-piece wing was replaced by a three-piece delta wing. This maintained wing area while simplifying the conversion process and improving ground visibility.

Bryan was fatally injured in a crash of the Bryan III. The wing folded in flight after he failed to insert securing pins to lock it in the extended position.

Three designs are detailed for 1948 from various inventors.

Adelard J. Geo, Jr., designed the Roadmobile, a tailless convertible airplane with a pusher propeller and four wheels.

James Wismer Holland, a pilot and flight instructor, designed a roadable Erocoupe, an easy-to-fly model of the 1930s and 1940s for the mass market of weekend pilots. He intended it as a homebuilt kit modification with a folding wing on a standard two-place vehicle.

Its wings could be readied for flight or detached and stowed on top by two persons in 30 minutes. The wings were attached to the center section by two bolts on each side, at the landing gear strut and the rear spar. The propeller was used for motive power on the ground, but a separate hydraulic drive to the landing gear was considered. Road speed was 35 mph.

He also designed a folding-wing Vagabond.

S. C. Rethorst designed several roadable aircraft with tractor propellers in both three- and four-wheel models.

For 1949 three designs are listed from different inventors.

Henry Clark designed a two-control vehicle with the entire aircraft component (wings and tail) carried locked to the roof of the fuselage and spoilers atop the wings.

Aircraft engineer Richard G. Naugle designed a vehicle with an aircraft engine, folding wings and tail stored inside the fuselage when on the road, where a 26-hp engine was employed.

Reginald Reid built an aluminum scale model of a roadable aircraft whose wings folded back atop the fuselage insect-fashion.

1950s

In 1950 aviation pioneer Dr. Lewis A. Jackson designed, built and test-flew his J-10, an integrated, four-place roadable light biplane. It was constructed of metal with some fiberglass. There were two jump seats in the rear. Only one stick existed.

Subsequently some ten versions were designed and the first test flight was for Versatile I in 1956.

It had a foldable flair pivot wing control so that it could be either taken off or folded back to make a car within 15 seconds. By unlocking a single pin, the 18 ft. 4 in. wing was rotated spanwise above the fuselage, reducing overall width to 7 ft. 6 in.

The prototype was built from Piper J-3, J-4 and Aeronca components.

Dr. Lewis A. Jackson's J-10 Roadable Airplane (courtesy Dr. Robert L. Jackson).

SPECIFICATIONS

Engine .... 85 hp Continental
Empty weight .... 720 lb.
Gross weight .... 1,150 lb.
Length .... 18 ft.
Wingspan .... 22 ft.

PERFORMANCE

Air speed .... 100–150 mph
Road speed .... 50 mph
Cruise .... 85 mph
Climb rate .... 2,000 ft./min.
Fuel consumption .... 40 gal./hr. at 90 knots
Touchdown .... 52 knots

Spill plates on lower wings and tubular fence guards around the nose reduced propeller hazards while the vehicle was on the ground.

In 1950 Andre Michel of France designed a craft combining features of an autogiro, a helicopter and an automobile. He patented the completed model. It was to run 50 mph on the ground and, rising almost vertically, fly with the speed of a normal touring plane. Secret trials were made with a tiny motor and he planned a full-sized prototype.

In 1951 William E. "Bill" Horton and Wallace R. Johnson designed and flew an integrated, roadable wingless plane or lifting body, Horton's Wingless.

With the airfoil section serving as the passenger compartment, the fuselage was eliminated. The plane weighed 2,000 lb. and was 12 × 22.5 ft. Power came from a 215 hp Franklin engine, which drove a Hartzell constant speed propeller.

For road purposes the power was converted to the front wheels by a conventional, chain-driven gear box and differential. Ground steering was accomplished by the tail wheel and controls were of the Erocoupe type, except for brakes and throttle.

In 1951 industrial designer Henry Keck designed a two-place, front-wheel-drive car with twin helicopter blades mounted on the roof. They came apart in sections to be stored inside the car. It was powered by a four-cylinder, 25-hp ram jet engine.

In 1952 Fred A. Carpenter designed a convertible, single-engine airplane and highway vehicle with three wheels, one driven, and a tractor propeller.

In 1953 Harry E. Novinger designed a combined air-ground vehicle with three wheels, two driven, a pusher propeller, a single engine and twintail booms.

In 1954 Elmo E. Aylor designed a roadable aircraft with one engine, a pusher propeller and four wheels.

In 1955 Charles Pritchard designed a stub-wing craft.

In 1957 engineer Igor B. Bensen, president of Bensen Aircraft Corporation, flew for the first time in his model B-8M prototype Gyrocopter. This was followed by the first production model later that year. This was a single-seat roadable, also known as an autogiro, gyroplane or rotaplane.

The rotor provided lift like a helicopter, but unlike a helicopter, the rotor was made to spin by aerodynamic forces rather than being powered by an engine which propels it forward like an airplane.

Horton Wingless lifting body on *Science and Mechanics* cover, February 1951.

Top: Bensen B-8M Gyro-copter (EAA Library Archives). *Bottom:* Igor B. Bensen in his Gyro-copter (San Diego Aerospace Museum).

Bensen B-8M Gyro-copter "Spirit of Kitty Hawk" with (left to right) Lewis S. Casey, NASM staff; Bensen; and Brooke Empie Allen (National Air and Space Museum, Smithsonian Institution, No. 2008-8046).

This version of the original Gyrocopter had a more powerful engine and could be equipped with a mechanical rotor drive which could accelerate to flying speed while the aircraft was stationary. Then, by transferring power to the pusher propeller, it was possible to take off in only 50 ft. (15.25 m.) with the rotor autorotating normally.

The pilot had an open seat with an overhead azimuth stick and rudder pedal controls.

Bensen also developed the B8 Gyro-Glider, B-9 Little Zipter and the B-10 Flying Platform. All were in kit form.

Model B-8M Gyrocopter — Specifications

Dimensions

Height	6 ft. 3 in.
Length (less rotor)	11 ft. 4 in.
Width	5 ft. 6 in.
Rotor diameter	20 ft.
Tread	60 in.

Weights

Normal gross	500 lb.
Empty	247 lb.

Useful load . . . . .253 lb.
Overload U. L. . . . . .353 lb.

Rotor

Airfoil . . . . Bensen G 2
Thickness ratio 010
Chord . . . . 7.0 in.
Solidity 037
Normal disc loading . . . . 1.59 psf
Rotor speed . . . . 420 rpm

Construction

Laminated plywood with steel spar
Design load factor 9.0

Suspension

Teeter hinge, no lag hinges

Power Plant

Engine . . . . .McCulloch 4318 E
Cooling . . . . Air
Cylinders 4
Cycle . . . . 2 stroke
Horsepower . . . . 72 hp
Rated speed . . . . 4,100 rpm
Fuel capacity . . . . 6.0 gal
Fuel cons. at cruise power . . . . 4.5 gal./hr.
Weight dry . . . . 77 lb.
Compression ratio . . . . 7.8 to 1
Displacement . . . . 100 cu. in.
Dimensions . . . . 15 in. × 27 in. × 28 in.

Propeller

Make . . . . Banks-Maxwell
Model 45–24
Type . . . . Pusher
Material . . . . Birch
Rotation . . . . CCW
Pitch . . . . 24 in.
Diameter . . . . 45 in.
Normal speed . . . . 4,100 rpm

Controls

Cyclic — overhead azimuth stick (joystick optional)
Collective . . . . None

Fuselage

Main structure — 6063-T6 aluminum tubing
Landing gear — tricycle with auxiliary tail
Main wheels — general tire, pneumatic wheel
All primary structure is assembled with AN-4 bolts.
There are no welded, brazed, glued, riveted, or bonded joints
    in the primary structure.

Equipment

(a) *Standard*
Airspeed indicator

1000-lb. safety belt
Kapok seat cushion
Wheel-type landing gear
Tow hook 1000-lb. capacity
(b) *Optional*
Hi-thrust propeller
Altimeter
Compass
Auxiliary fuel tank
Conventional joystick control

Performance — At Normal Gross Weight

Cruising speed at S. L. . . . . 60 mph
Max. speed . . . . 85 mph
Min. level speed . . . . 14 mph
Take-off speed . . . . 18 mph
Landing speed . . . . 7 mph
Max. economy speed . . . . 45 mph
T. O. run in calm air . . . . 1,300 ft.
Landing roll in 15 mph wind. . . . . 0 ft.
Range . . . . 100 miles
Endurance . . . . 1.5 hrs.
Service ceiling . . . . 16,500 ft.
Max. rate of climb . . . . 2000 ft./min.
Min. rate of descent . . . . 1,800 ft./min.
Ferry range . . . . 300 miles
Landing roll in calm air . . . . 20 ft.

In 1957 engineer David T. Dobbins constructed and piloted the homebuilt Simcopter auto-helicopter, combining the Simca car with a 300 hp Lycoming aircraft engine and a welded superstructure. It rose to a height of five feet.

He was a resident of Guadalajara, Mexico, at the time and the August 15, 1957, newspapers, including the *El Sol de Guadalajara* and *El Occidental* featured it on front-page photographs and articles. It was later displayed at the Watsonville, California, airshow. Currently it is on display at the hangar of the Wings of History Museum.

In 1957 Thomas E. Sturgeon designed a convertible, single-engine airplane with a tractor propeller and three wheels.

In 1958 Richard Allen Strong designed a four-wheeled automobile-type, integrated, single-engine ground and air vehicle, the Magic Dragon Aircar. It included a wing structure which folded from operative position to inoperative position within the body of the aircraft. It had a warp action spoiler plate aileron and a full span flap which, with the wings, could be swung into overlapping positions in the fuselage. Folding could be done merely with the push of a button.

In 2005 Strong established a not-for-profit scientific research and education charitable organization, the Air-Car Research Association (TACRA), to insure the continuation of his inventions.

Opposite, top: Mexican newspaper report on David T. Dobbins' Simcopter. *Bottom:* Simcopter on display at the Watsonville, California, airshow (both photographs courtesy Wings of History Aviation Museum).

¡UN HELICOPTERO!— El Ing. David T. Dobbins, un americano residente en esta ciudad, ha inventado este singular helicóptero que a su vez, en tres minutos, se convierte en un flamante automóvil. Ayer se hicieron las primeras pruebas y el artefacto cuando menos se levantó del suelo. Se tiene la seguridad de que con nivelar bien las aspas, pronto volará raudo y veloz. Habrá que ver la maquinita, que no deja de ser algo muy especial.
Gráfica de Ornelas.

Joseph L. Halsmer's Aero Car Model F on the cover of *Air Progress*, February-March 1964.

In 1959 Herbert L. Trautman designed the Rodair, a small, sleek, single-passenger, integrated three-wheeler. It had a lifting body design, an 85-hp Continental engine and a pusher propeller driven by a 75-hp airplane engine which was placed directly aft of the pilot to promote additional lift.

As an airplane the retractable wings folded out from the body to create a 25-ft. wingspan. The wings were stored in the lower portion of the fuselage. Small doors on each side were opened to access the wings, which were pulled out and then locked in place.

Twin rudders and an elevator were located in the rear. The body was 15 ft. long and 7 ft. 10 in. wide. As an auto it rode on tricycle gear, the single rear wheel driven by a small gasoline motor.

Speeds were 90 mph in the air and 70 mph on the ground. The pilot gained access by lifting the front hood and climbing into the cockpit. The Rodair completed flight tests in 1960 and received an FAA experimental license. It now resides at Kermit Weeks' Fantasy of Flight Museum.

In 1959 Joseph L. Halsmer designed and flew an integrated, roadable aircraft, the Aero Car, with a 25-hp Continental tandem engine, tractor and pusher propeller, folded back high wings, four wheels, twintail booms and an open cockpit.

1960s

In 1960 David R. Dodd designed a combination land and air vehicle with a single engine, pusher propeller and three wheels.

In 1962 Walter B. Mills designed a combination road and air vehicle. It had a single engine with one rotor, four wheels with two driven and a detachable flight section.

Beginning in 1962 Canadian Paul Moller, Ph.D., mechanical and aeronautical engineer and college professor, started developing levitation-powered lift aircraft. Some 43 patents contribute to his Volantor evolving designs.

His first one-passenger VTOL saucer, the XM-2, was completed in 1966. It demonstrated hovering ability and was followed in 1968 by the two-passenger XM-3, which used a single fan powered by eight engines. The first flight of the XM-3 achieved an altitude of three meters (10 ft.) and it could make a 360-degree turn. The next in the series, the XM-4, was powered by eight air-cooled rotary engines. A two-piece fiberglass airframe acted as a lifting body, while the thrust modules provided lift to hover and the impetus for forward flight. In test flights, Moller himself attained an altitude of over ten meters (32.6 ft.) and sustained it for several minutes before setting back down again.

According to Moller, the new two-man, eight-engine M200X Volantor has proven the technical feasibility and reliability of the Volantor design.

Subsequently his company has built a radically different four-passenger Volantor, called the M400 Skycar, to meet the needs of the commuter of the future. This composite VTOL aircraft, like the M200X, uses Moller rotapower engines and company-developed electronic stabilization and fly-by-wire control systems. The Skycar combines the high-speed perform-

Top: Paul Moller's M400 Volantor Skycar (courtesy Moller International). *Bottom:* Paul Moller's latest Skycar, updated from the original model in the 1960s (courtesy Moller International).

ance of 500 kilometers per hour with VTOL capability and the practicality of a commuter vehicle. Specifications call for cruising speeds up to 350 mph, a top speed of 390 mph, a ceiling of 30,000 ft., a range of 900 miles and over 20 miles per gallon on standard gasoline.

The M400 Skycar features a Moller-patented system of variable-camber exit-duct vanes that direct thrust from seven-blade, variable-speed fans mounted on each engine to produce lift for vertical takeoff and hovering. Three on-board computers adjust the stability for hovering and the vanes in flight for lift or forward motion. Each of the four nacelles surrounding the fuselage contain two engines, with synchronized counter-rotating fans that face each other to confine prop-tip noise to the center of each nacelle. Another Moller invention, the Supertrap Muffler, keeps noise down to less than 30 percent of that from a light aircraft at takeoff.

With plastic construction, the Skycar is also designed for safe and simple use. Computer-enhanced flight controls are based on a lever, which is used to select altitude and rate of climb, and a control column for direction.

The estimated sticker price is $95,000 to $145,000.

The bullet-shaped M400 Skycar has three small wheels, a small propeller and a teardrop-shaped plexiglas canopy. It is hot-rod or candy-apple red. The engine can run on alcohol, kerosene, gasoline, ethanol, diesel, or unleaded. It is joystick driven and a six-person version is on the drawing boards.

Various humorous descriptions of the M400 Skycar include iron canary, giant hummingbird, batmobile and the flying saucer. It has received almost as much publicity as Moult Taylor's Aerocar and was offered in the 2005 79th annual Nieman Marcus Department Store Christmas catalog.

Moller succinctly sums up the present status of his operation: "All of the technical problems have been solved and product liability and production money are the only limiting factors left."

In 1963 Carl Kelsey designed his Skycar for use as a commercial crop duster.

In 1964 James G. Sawyer designed an air car with three engines, a ducted fan or channel, a pusher propeller and four wheels with two driven.

In 1964 Erwin Stockwell, a retired toolmaker and veteran pilot, converted a 1960 Corvair into a modular flying car. It had a detachable airframe (wings, tail assembly), prop-driving engine (an 80-hp Corvair powerplant like the one in the car), gas tank, electrical system, and flight controls that mounted on top of the automobile and were secured by special brackets and guy wires. The airframe construction was all wood except the engine compartment, which was aluminum. For road travel the plywood-covered wings folded up along the sides. Wingspan was 29 ft. and the gross weight, including the standard Corvair, was 3,500 lb.

Before flight trials began the prop-driven Corvair engine was to be replaced by a 300-hp aircraft powerplant.

In 1965 the German firm Helicopter Technik Wagner flew its four-seat roadable helicopter, also labeled Aerocar. In flight the machine used two counter-rotating blades, which folded back and anchored behind the cabin when the helicopter was on the road. Highway power was provided through a hydraulic drive to the wheels from the main engine. It made the rounds of the air shows in Germany during the late 1960s.

In 1966 Robert O. Schertz designed an integrated, single-engine aircraft adapted for

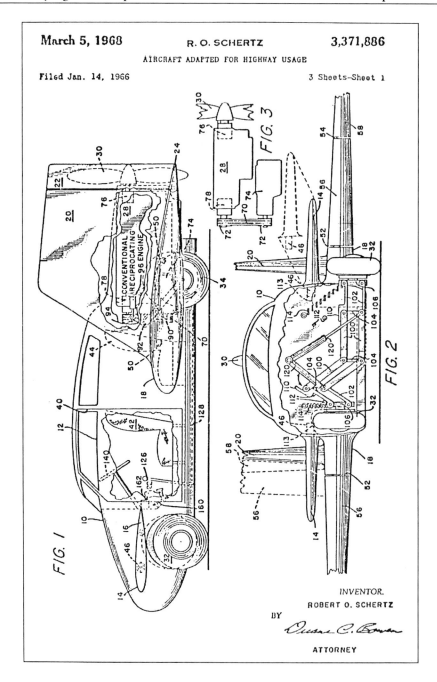

March 5, 1968   R. O. SCHERTZ   3,371,886

AIRCRAFT ADAPTED FOR HIGHWAY USAGE

Filed Jan. 14, 1966   3 Sheets-Sheet 1

INVENTOR.
ROBERT O. SCHERTZ
BY
ATTORNEY

Patent for Robert O. Schertz aircraft adapted for highway use.

highway use with four wheels and two driven, a pusher propeller and a Continental reciprocating 96 engine.

The machine had a canard configuration with removable forward horizontal stabilizers and rear foldable wings. It also had a side-opening cabin door between the stabilizers
and the wings. The purpose of this arrangement was to allow access in the normal manner

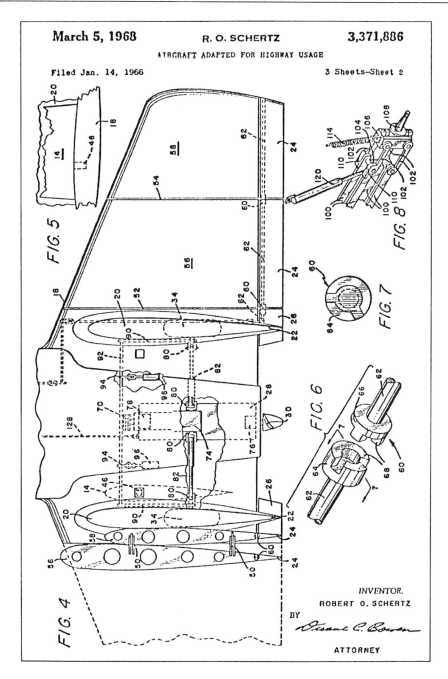

March 5, 1968   R. O. SCHERTZ   3,371,886

AIRCRAFT ADAPTED FOR HIGHWAY USAGE

Filed Jan. 14, 1966   3 Sheets—Sheet 2

INVENTOR.
ROBERT O. SCHERTZ
BY
ATTORNEY

Patent for Robert O. Schertz aircraft.

of a two-door car, rather than requiring people to climb over the wing structure. The engine was at the rear over the wings and was to provide power to the prop for flight and to the wheels for road travel. Controls were also designed for use in both flight and highway driving. The vehicle had powered rear wheels for highway use, and all four wheels could be retracted when the vehicle was in flight.

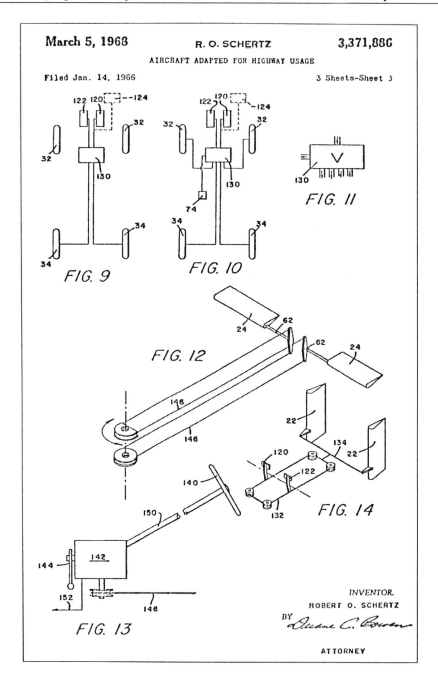

Patent for Robert O. Schertz aircraft.

Wing design was unique. Each of the wings extended from a wing-root structure at the rear of the fuselage where a vertical stabilizer and rudder were mounted on each side. Outboard from that assembly each wing consisted of two panels. The first step in folding the wings was to unlock the panels and fold the outer one in on top of the inner one. Next, the two were folded up beside the vertical stabilizer to create a kind of panel sandwich. One of the removable canards could then be stowed inboard of each of the vertical stabilizers or, if preferred, the canards could be stowed behind the rear seats in the cabin.

Schertz had this astute analysis of the economic advantage of a drivable aircraft:

> Owning a light plane may be difficult to finance in the family budget and may be foregone partly because of inconvenience, extra expenses for surface transportation away or at home, or even the purchase of an additional car to avoid the situation outlined. The economic importance of dual air and highway usage will be understood as to a family that can substitute such aircraft and a single automobile for a conventional aircraft, a first car and a second car. Many business light plane owners, large or small, will have similar considerations of expense and convenience.

In 1966 was announced the unveiling of the Autocopter, made by the Aeronautical Research and Development Corporation. It had folding rotor blades and was able to travel along the ground. Apparently the project never was completed.

In 1967 Henry A. Smolinski, president of Advanced Vehicle Engineers (AVE), in conjunction with fellow engineer Harold Blake of the firm, announced plans to launch the AVE Aircar. It involved integrating an FAA–certified airframe and aircraft engine with a conventional automobile such as a Pontiac, Ford, Chevrolet, Volkswagen or various others.

The wings and tail boom section of an airplane such as a Cessna 337 Skymaster, combined with an aircraft engine such as a Pratt & Whitney or Continental, formed the AVE airframe system which attached to a modified car. The automobile steering system was arranged to control the ailerons by turning the wheel, and to control the elevator by moving the wheel backward and forward. Retractable rudder pedals were mounted under the steering column. The Aircar was flight-controlled from the driver's seat and all controls, instruments and structure were connected with six high-strength pins which were inserted and locked in a self-aligning track assembly on the car roof and in the wing support connections.

The automobile engine was used during takeoff and for taxiing. In flight the car engine was off and power was supplied by the aircraft engine, a turboprop with 500–700 hp, operated at the rear of the car. Aircars with 700-hp engines had a maximum speed of 150 mph, while those with lesser horsepower had a top speed of 130 mph. Range was 500 miles with reserve fuel. The Aircar climbed at the rate of 750 ft. min. The takeoff roll was 500 ft. at a freeway speed of 65 mph. The landing roll was 550 ft.

In addition to the dash panel for aircraft controls, modifications to the automobile included a special roof structure for attaching the airframe, rear suspension, special paneling under the car, relocation of the fuel tank and battery and installation of better grade tires on some models. The car had disc brakes and there were several minor modifications to reduce weight. The steering column had the same angle for driving or flying the Aircar and the same steering wheel was utilized.

The Aircar had a gross weight of 6,000 to 7,000 lb., of which 3,700 lb. was the maximum for the automobile. Wingspan was 38 ft., length was 30 ft. and height was 7.5 ft. Larger, heavier cars such as Cadillac or full-sized Buicks or Oldsmobiles could not be used at first because of weight restrictions. A more powerful engine would be needed. But there were 55 cars that did meet the standard. The AVE Aircar was powered for flight by an aircraft engine and a propeller selected to match the weight of the automobile. Economy class

Ave Mizar (courtesy Mathew Smolinski).

vehicles used a 250–350 hp reciprocating engine, while intermediate and luxury-class cars used turboprop engines of greater horsepower.

A tour of 40 major U.S. cities was planned for a year and the first model was a Pontiac Firebird.

But in 1973 the AVE Mizar was produced, named after the dual star in the handle of the Big Dipper, with room for four passengers and their luggage. The "Flying Pinto," as it was known, also had an optional 60-ft. parachute.

On a second taxi test flight it crashed when the wing came off, killing both Smolinski and the test pilot. The Pinto had been selected because of its excellent aerodynamics.

1970s

In 1970 Samuel H. Arbuse designed a combined land and air vehicle using a commercial automobile and an engine for travel on land and a detachable air structure. The automobile was adapted to be connected with this structure, which included wings, tail assembly, and an airplane engine for air travel.

To ready the automobile for flight the steering wheel was disconnected from the front wheels and connected to the elevator and aileron controls. A rudder-steering pedal trolley system had pedals that were removed when driving on land and connected for flying. A power transmission system permitted the automobile engine to rotate the propeller in case of failure of the airplane engine.

In 1976 K. P. Rice, a former Marine fighter and bomber pilot, designed the two-passenger, modular, three-wheel Volante flying car. It had a fiberglass body and a removable, canard-style low wing to be carried in a trailer. The air-cooled, four-cylinder, 75-hp Volkswagen engine was aft of the cabin. The Volante reached speeds of 130 mph cruising and 70 mph on the ground.

K.P. Rice's Volante flying car (courtesy K.P. Rice).

The vehicle was intended as a homebuilt kit. Rice used the General Motors Astro III prototype of the 1960s as his model. Gross weight was 1,250 lb., overall length 15.5 ft., wingspan 225 ft. and the car width 4 ft. Conversion time was five minutes for one person.

Rice, CEO of Volante Aircraft, has designed and built a second vehicle. The original made some 300 flights and the car portion was driven frequently. That machine was dismantled to provide components for the new design. The same car was much modified for use in the current version, which is a two-place, composite machine with an empty weight of about 1,200 lb. and a gross weight of 1,850 lb. Conversion time, either way, is less than ten minutes and the job can be done by one person. This version will cruise at 150 mph with a Lycoming 0320 engine and drive at highway speeds as a car. Speed with the flight section trailer attached will always depend on a crosswind.

This concept prototype has completed just over 17 hours of successful flight tests.

Rice's rationale for choosing a modular design is expressed in some detail:

> I chose this for the Volante for several reasons. I didn't think the world was ready for the integrated machine on an economic basis. It may well be that unit production costs at 100,000 vehicles or more per year will be low enough for a large number of pilots to own, but it will be some time before the market develops to that point. In fact, I chose the kit route for initial introduction, because I think the flying car has to demonstrate its projected value before any entrepreneur will invest the magnificent sum required for automotive type serial production which is the only other route I can see to really low cost airplanes. We really need to learn the "real world" contribution a flying car makes within the aviation spectrum before we know what it should look like, how it will operate, what are its economies, all of its pros and cons, considered within an evolutionary framework which simultaneously deals with necessary regulatory and facility changes. Incidentally, with all of these uncertinties, my hat is off to the current group of entrepreneurs working on such machines. We each think that we know what the market needs and we may all be right for the segment to which we cater.

His observations on the question of affordability are also of interest:

The Volante Flying Car Conversion process

This is the Volante as it arrives at a parking place at the airport.

With the trailer wheels and tail support lowered and locked In place, and the flight component released from the car.

The car drives away to the final destination, leaving the flight component at the airport

OR

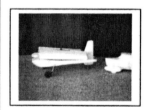

The car drives to the trailer connection position, and the pilot folds and locks the wings in position for highway travel.

Lock the built-in trailer hitch to the car —retract the tail support- connect the trailer electrical plug and the Volante is ready for the road.

Reverse the process to go back to flight configuration.

Note 1: With wings folded, the flight component can be parked in one side of a standard garage with or without the car.
Note 2: The car can be driven without the trailer as well as with it attached.

Volante flying car conversion process (courtesy K.P. Rice).

With an airplane only, you can tie it down outside and pay increased maintenance costs, or you can hangar it, and over a 5-year period, in California you pay as much for the hangar as you initially paid for the kit itself. However, a flying car you can keep in your garage and use the car a lot more than the 100 hours per year the average pilot flies his aircraft. Also with the Volante's separate flying and driving engines you do not accumulate expensive aircraft engine hours in driving around town as you will with a single engine for both air and ground use, and when used as a car alone you do not need to expose the aircraft parts, which are very expensive to repair, to traffic damage.

Finally his car/aircraft/flying car comparison puts it all in perspective:

What do you want	Car	Aircraft	Flying Car
Door-to-door convenience	Yes	No	Yes
Operable in any weather with low cost/training/proficiency	Yes	No	Yes
High speed with safety	No	Yes	Yes
Minimum transportation system investment	No	No	Yes
Minimum storage and upkeep	No	No	Yes
Minimum operating costs	No	No	Yes

In 1977 George Spratt II designed his Model 108 roadable with a Subaru engine.

George Spratt's Model 108 Aircar (courtesy Mid-Atlantic Air Museum).

In 1979 Harry R. Miller designed the Avi Auto, a combined road vehicle and aircraft. The wing and tail assemblies as well as propelling structure were movable outwardly for the flying form and inwardly into stored position for the road vehicle form. All of the parts remained intact in both forms. Storage for the wing and tail assemblies and the propeller structure was in the side and end compartments, and the wing and tail assemblies had foldable sections for this purpose. There was a pair of front wheels and a pair of rear wheels, the latter being movable between a narrowed rearward position for road use, which allowed storage for the wings in the side compartments, and a widened forward position for aircraft use. The tail assembly was supported on a slide mechanism, which extended downward in a forward longitudinal direction, whereby the tail assembly was lowered as it moved forward for storage in the rear compartment.

A propeller assembly was between the front and rear wheels and faced the rear. The rear axle was moved forward to place the center of gravity in a more favorable position for takeoff rotation. The pilot pushed a button to convert to ground mode or vice versa.

In 1989 Miller started collaboration with J. Robert Smurthwaite and a second engine was added.

Currently work is ongoing at the University of California's Irvine Campus, at Florida Institute of Technology and at Iowa State University to develop a spherical mechanism design to deploy and retract the wings on the Avi Auto. Previously two planar hinges, each activated by a stepper motor and gear head, were used.

1980s

In 1980 Bill Schugt of the IDM Company, a design engineer and pilot, began designing aircars, airvans and mini roadable aircraft.

In successive years and with continuing refinements he produced designs for eight aircars, culminating in 1984 in his Ultra-Flite Car.

It was a single-place with a pusher propeller, twintail boom, and tricycle landing gear. There was a single engine for both modes.

The outboard wing section retracted by first being jacked above the center section wing panel and then pivoting on the combination jack or pivots location on the wing joint near the rear spar.

Looking ahead, he commented: "I foresee the day when any small or medium sized community is accessible via a 1500 foot long paved airstrip with nothing more than a windsock for ground facilities."

In 1980 Roger W. Williamson, a former fighter pilot, designed the low-wing Roadrunner, a land vehicle and aircraft combination. It was a modular, two-place monoplane.

The auto component contained an engine, torque converter, automatic transmission, prop reduction unit, forward reverse gear box, three wheels with air suspension, brakes and rack and pinion steering.

The aircraft component consisted of an airframe and tricycle landing gear. The auto

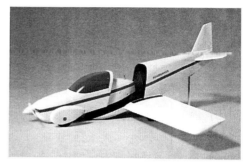

Top: Roger W. Williamson's Roadrunner (courtesy Roger W. Williamson). *Bottom:* Cutaway view of Williamson's Roadrunner (courtesy Roger W. Williamson).

component sat on a fuselage extension and was attached with four center hooks. The aircraft controls were mounted on a folding stalk attached to the top side of the platform. The land vehicle had a central opening in its body through which the control stalk could be elevated to a vertical position.

The wings could be removed and stowed in the fuselage, allowing the airframe to be towed behind the auto.

Specifications of the Latest Version

Wingspan .... 25 ft.
Length overall .... 20 ft.
Height .... 6 ft. 7 in.
Wing area .... 100 sq. ft.

Empty weight . . . . 900 lb.
Useful load . . . . 500 lb.
Power loading . . . . 11.2 lb./hp
Wing loading . . . . 14 lb./sq. ft.
Fuel capacity . . . . 15 gal.
Seats 2
Maximum power . . . . 125 hp
Prop . . . . 72 in.

Performance

Cruise . . . . 130 mph
Stall . . . . 45 mph
Top speed highway . . . . 80 mph
Takeoff roll . . . . 1,000 ft.
Landing roll . . . . 1,000 ft.
Range . . . . 500 miles

Conversion time was five minutes and no tools were required.

Williamson has some interesting observations about the flying car potential:

Is a really good flying car even a possibility? I think so but first let's set some criteria: (1) The car must be capable of safe operation at freeway speeds, say 70 to 80 mph. (2) In the flying mode we want a 130 mph cruise speed. (3) Conversion from one mode to the other should take five minutes or less and be easily accomplished by one person. The fear of a road accident will keep the mileage low on any flying car. Only an experimental home built design has any chance of reaching the marketplace.

In 1983 Elbert L. Rutan designed and flew a tandem or multi-winged, high performance aircraft with two engines, two pusher propellers and three wheels.

In 1984 Harry Einstein, a mechanical engineer, registered professional engineer, former Air Force engineering officer and glider pilot, designed Air Vans in two integrated formats to accommodate two or four passengers at fully laden weights of 2,030 and 2,640 lb., respectively, including luggage. As homebuilt experimental aircraft kits of metal construction they had two engines, three wheels and twintail booms.

The fuselage was shorter than many automobiles.

In the air mode, the craft had a 21-ft. wingspan supplemented by a 17-ft. canard, with a total wing area of 114 sq. ft. to support a 60-gallon fuel tank and 320-lb., 180-hp engine (the two-passenger model). This package was expected to deliver a maximum estimated speed (at sea level) of 165 mph, with an estimated cruising speed of 155 mph at 75 percent power.

The four-passenger model had similar flying characteristics, but would require a 225-hp engine. This model would be roughly 18 in. longer and the wing loading would be increased from 18 lb./sq. ft. to 23 lb./sq. ft.

The aircraft's main wing consisted of three sections: center, right and left. From the flying configuration, the outer wing sections rotated horizontally, one section rotating forward and the other rotating to the rear, thus forming a "canopy" of wing sections above the fuselage. Rotation was assisted and guided by pairs of struts which also supported the outer wing sections in both flight and land uses. The main wing's outer section did not have any movable wing panels (e.g., ailerons, flaps) when used in conjunction with a canard wing with movable panels at the trailing edges, which served as both elevators and ailerons.

(One minor design modification would permit the main wing to contain ailerons and the canard movable surfaces would be used only as elevators for pitch control.) The center section of the main wing could incorporate a spoiler for increased descent rate and decreased landing roll. The spoiler could be used in land travel to compensate for any possible lift due to the wing extensions over the fuselage. This would also increase the load on the nose wheel for better land control. Additional yaw control was provided by the straight vertical sides of the rear of the fuselage. The low "high life" wing stubs along and the fuselage shape would provide additional lift, along with the ground effect, resulting in a lower stall speed.

The canard wing also consisted of three sections, with the center section affixed to the fuselage and the outer sections removable. For land operation these outer sections would be removed and attached to the sides of the fuselage. The unusually large span of the canard was intended to provide good roll and pitch control as well as enough lift to move the aircraft's center of gravity forward, thus increasing the load on the steerable nose wheel for good driving control.

The aircraft could be converted for ground operation about as fast as one can lower and secure an automobile's manual convertible top or remove and store a sunroof.

Einstein has made some interesting comments on the image and market for flying cars:

> What flying car proponents failed to recognize is that these hybrid air-land vehicles must be operated by *pilots*, not *motorists*. Like the observation that "all cats have four legs, but not all four-legged animals are cats," one must recognize that almost all pilots can drive, but few motorists can fly. In order to arrive at a practical design, one must change the usual concept of an "auto-plane." A practical autoplane is a plane that can travel on land rather than an automobile that can fly. A lowered flying efficiency must be accepted as well as the obvious limited land use and drop in driving comfort. The flying car may still have its place in the annals of aeronautical history and may capture the imagination of motorists and car designers for decades or even centuries to come. But the roadable aircraft is a concept whose time has certainly come. And with our highways and streets far more crowded than our airways, it has come not a moment too soon.

In 1984 Nick de'Acquisto, a mechanical engineer and retired Navy officer, designed the lightweight Piranha Flying Cycle at Piranha Aircraft.

It was a two-place VTOL that used two 200-hp, two-cycle internal combustion engines with a three-wheel undercarriage. Two 12-volt batteries and alternators provided electrical power for engine starting, lights and other devices. Two 35-ft. canopy parachutes could be deployed. It could travel at 65 mph on the road and had an airspeed of 300 knots and a service ceiling of 12,000 ft.

In 1987 Karl Eickmann developed an airborne vehicle with hydraulic drive and control.

It had at least four propellers arranged as a front propeller pair and a rear propeller pair having vertical or forwardly inclined axes driven by hydraulic motors. A pumping device supplied two pairs of separated flows to the motors. One pair of the flows had fixed delivery and equal flow quantities per revolution of the pump while the other pair had variable flow-rates. The flow quantities of both flows of the variable flow pair were also equal relative to each other. One of the flow pairs drove the front propellers at equal speeds and the other pair of flows drove the rear propellers at equal speeds. But the variability of the rates of flow of one of the pairs of flows allowed one of the propellers to run with a different rotary velocity than the other. The difference of rotary speeds of the propeller pairs was

Sky Rover (courtesy British Aerospace).

utilized to incline the vehicle and control its forward speed. The variable flow pair had a common control means which assured an equality of the rates of flows in the variable flow pair, whereby a forward flight path of the vehicle was assured and departures to the right or left of the desired flight path prevented.

For 1988 five different designs are described from various inventors.

Right after British Aerospace bought England's Rover Group (Austin Rover and Land Rover) the new owners conducted secret tests in Norway with a radical Land Rover Whirligig/Personnel Carrier, the Sky Rover.

Gary M. Bullard of Land-Air designed his GB 2000, an integrated, two-place, single-engine, ultralight convertible airplane with a fuselage and four wheels with two driven.

It had three wings, including a forward canard wing, a foldable main wing and a secondary left wing. The foldable wing was capable of folding to a size which allowed the automobile to be driven safely. All wings were used as ground effect airfoils for roadway use.

A single engine provided power for both ground and flight operation. For ground use the pusher propeller was disengaged from the engine by a clutch assembly.

It had standard yoke-type aircraft controls along with ground mode controls and was intended for the kit plane market.

Specifications
Ground Data

Length . . . . 17.5 ft.
Width . . . . 8.5 ft.
Steering . . . . Rack and pinion
Brakes . . . . Hydraulic disc front and rear
Transmission . . . . Motorcycle type with reverse
Engine . . . . 100–180 hp
Fuel capacity . . . . 50 gal.
Fuel consumption . . . . Up to 30 mpg
Maximum speed . . . . Over 100 mph
Cruise speed . . . . 60 mph

Flight Data

Wingspan . . . . 23.5 ft.
Wing area . . . . 113.25 sq. ft.
Wing loading . . . . 4–15.9 lb./sq. ft.
Empty weight . . . . 1,100 lb.
Useful load . . . . 500 lb.
Rate of climb . . . . 1,000 fpm
Range . . . . 1,000 miles
Stall speed . . . . 55 mph
Maximum speed (100% power) . . . . Over 225 mph
Cruise speed (80% power) . . . . 200 mph

Dr. Branko Sarh designed his Advanced Flying Automobile, with the help of automotive engineer Merkel Weiss, as a four-passenger single module system concept in which all

AFA

Sokol A400

Sokol A400 designed by Dr. Branko Sarh (courtesy Advanced Flying Automobile Company).

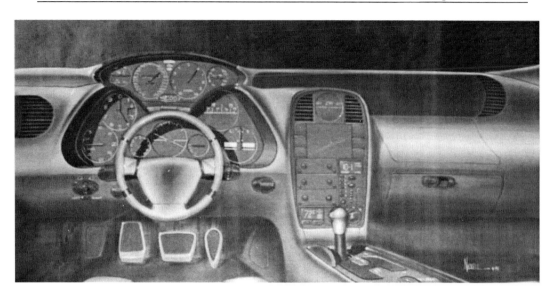

Cockpit of Sokol A400 (courtesy Advanced Flying Automobile Company).

components for automobile and flight configuration were permanently attached and carried all the time with the vehicle. Wings and horizontal and vertical stabilizers were of telescopic design and could be retracted or deployed in a short time using motor drives without any manual intervention.

It had a generally rectangular platform fuselage with four wheels and telescopic wing which retracted into a housing in the roof of the fuselage. Telescopic horizontal and vertical stabilizers were provided at the rear end of the fuselage, as well as a retractable pusher propeller that was driven by an engine mounted on the front end of the fuselage. Both the propeller and the rear wheels were connected by a transmission box to the engine, so that either could be driven to operate the vehicle as an aircraft or as an automobile. On takeoff, the rear wheels were partially retracted so as to place the aircraft at a proper angle of attack at the same time that the elevators were raised by pulling back on the control wheel, which was also connected to both the front wheels and the ailerons. When turned 90 degrees to the left or right while in the flight configuration, the control wheel caused the ailerons to move to their extreme angular positions while the front wheels were turned only a minimal amount. Further turning of the control wheel caused the front wheels to turn to their full angular position, without causing further movement of the ailerons. The wing was also movable longitudinally with respect to the fuselage so as to trim the aircraft for shifts in the center of gravity with varying load conditions.

Sarh expressed the need for a flying vehicle and its required support structure:

> Analysis of intercity travel characteristics and transportation systems in use today shows that there is a clear potential and need for a fast and convenient door-to-door transportation system. The Advanced Flying Automobile would enable travelers to cut existing travel times using airlines in half or better for certain distances. What is needed is engineering excellence in pursuit of such a sophisticated transportation system, vision, and long term commitment by the industry to sustain development, production start-up, and introduction of the AFA to the market, and foremost, mobilization of financial resources and adequate support by the business community, entrepreneurs, and government agencies for these efforts.

Joe Yasecko and Martin Hollman designed the Airtrike. The original conceptual work on this vehicle stretched back 20 years and included four different designs. It was a light, single-place homebuilt style roadable aircraft with a canard pusher. Its main wings would hinge upward to form a triangular guard around the propeller for ground travel. Also considered was a small helper engine to drive the front wheels for limited ground travel at low speeds.

SPECIFICATIONS

Empty weight . . . . 400 lb.
Gross weight . . . . 640 lb.
Engine . . . . Rotax 503
Prop . . . . 4.7 ft.
Length . . . . 15.4 ft.
Wings . . . . 64 sq. ft.
Span . . . . 20 ft.
Chord Root . . . . 31 in.
Tip . . . . 20 in.
Strake root . . . . 64 in.
Airfoil . . . . Epler 1053 MOD
Canard . . . . 8 sq. ft.
Span . . . . 8 ft.
Chord . . . . 11 in.
Winglet area . . . . 27.9 sq. ft. total

Aerospace FSC-1 designed by Mitch La Biche (courtesy La Biche Aerospace).

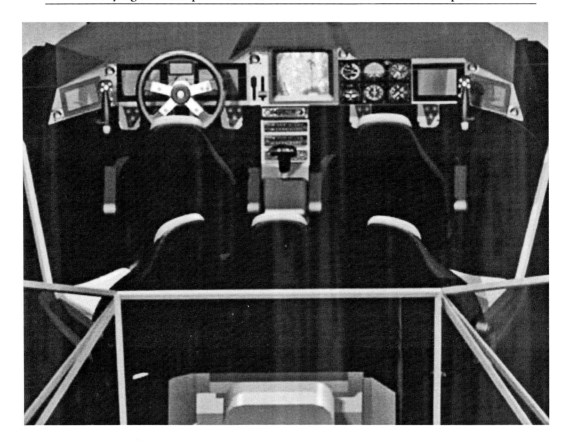

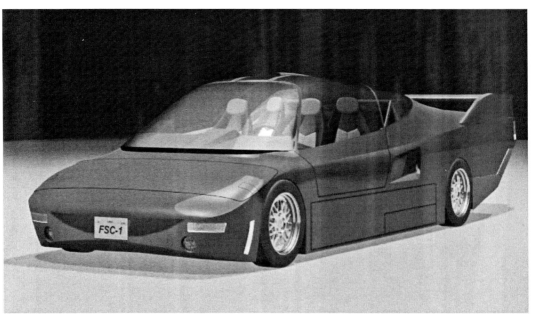

Top: Cockpit of Aerospace FSC-1. *Bottom:* La Biche Aerospace FSC-1 (both images courtesy La Biche Aerospace).

PERFORMANCE

Stall .... 4 mph
VMAX .... 30 mph
Cruise................................ 120 mph
Rate of climb .... 608 ft./min.
Range .... 240 miles

Another design from this source was called the Airkar.

Don Parham of Rotary Flight International designed the RFI Model GC100 Gyrocar roadable aircraft in a homebuilt kit mode. It was a rotary wing with several different power configurations, including a Honda Goldwing motorcycle engine, a water-cooled Subaru engine and a Volkswagen Rabbit engine. Conversion time was ten minutes.

In the late 1980s Mitch La Biche started work on Aerospace FSC-1. It was an integrated combination of a high performance aircraft and a sports car. It was designed after extensive marketing research to take an 800-lb. load and have an air speed of over 275 mph and a range of 800 miles.

Conversion time was 30 seconds from car to airplane.

1990s

In 1990 North American VTOL was founded to design, develop, manufacture and market personal vertical takeoff and landing automobile-sized aircraft.

Projects included 3D computer flight navigation control systems, efficient ducted fan designs, thrust vectoring systems and aerodynamically stable composite airframe structures with 4 × 4 hybrid power systems.

Three new designs from different inventors were outlined in 1991.

Joachim E. Lay designed a hybrid electric vehicle. It provided for movement over the ground by means of wheel motors mounted at each end of four ground-engaging wheels. Electric power was supplied by a battery pack or an electric generator powered by a combustion engine geared to vertically oriented ducted fans and a horizontally oriented ducted fan or a propeller for providing travel through the air. Pressure jets supplied with air from a compressor driven by the combustion engine augmented the lift of the ducted fans and provided steering. The vehicle could also be provided with photo-electric cells for supplying a portion of the electric power.

Joseph J. Szakacs designed a combined aircraft and road vehicle with two pusher propellers and three wheels.

Donald Howard Wooley, a research scientist, aeronautical engineer and commercial-rated pilot, designed an integrated, single-engine craft with a pusher propeller, canard and three wheels. His articulated fuselage concept was to hinge the tail cone horizontally from the main fuselage. The rudder and vertical fin were below the tail cone. Fast conversion was his prime objective.

Then in 2007 he came up with a fly-drive airplane design with a single-dual hybrid propulsion system. This was said to be adaptable to other aircraft, including commercial transports. He also developed an improved method to fold and store the main lift wing and configure the front canard that allowed ample wingspan and vehicle control for greater aerodynamic efficiency.

In 1992 three designs from other inventors were proposed.

Dr. Steven Crow designed the integrated Starcar, a roadable airplane which used electric power on the road and a gas turbine in the air. It was a single-place three-wheeler that could be licensed as a motorcycle but carried two wing panels on the sides that could be attached for flight. A modified Subaru engine supplied power to the rear wheels on the road and to a pusher propeller aloft.

The vehicle was turned by joy stick steering, both when driven as a motorcycle and when used as an aircraft. The aircraft tail surfaces were used for flying and driving; the driver/pilot used the rudders to compensate for side loads and the elevator to adjust vertical loads.

Bruce Crower designed an airplane with three wheels of spun aluminum. Two Geo engines powered twin pusher propellers for both air and ground propulsion.

A. J. Smith of Aerosmith Consulting Engineers, Inc., designed and built the Aero Caballo, a two-place, three-wheeled (two in front) vehicle with an airfoil-shaped fuselage. Two vertical stabilizers, together with a horizontal stabilizer on top and the trailing edge of the fuselage, formed a box enclosing two small, overlapping three-bladed propellers. Each prop was powered by a small auto engine through a long drive shaft. Two small, high wings pivoted backward in a horizontal plane for storage on top of the aft fuselage.

In 1993 five designs by different inventors were detailed.

Flight Innovations, Inc., designed a vehicle using vertical ducted fans, with canards for increased lift.

Nicholas Geranio of Geranio Aviation designed the Flyer, a compact VTOL roadable aircraft. The airplane portion had a single vertical ducted fan in a package that was eight feet wide and had no folding parts. As an automobile it was complete with wheels and transmission.

A single engine provided power for both modes of operation: aerial and ground. The propulsion system while on the ground was a single gear torque converter which worked like an automatic transmission but weighed less than ten pounds, achieving speeds up to 90 mph.

The propulsion system for flight used a rotor assembly very similar to that of a helicopter, minus the cyclic control. Instead a yaw vane assembly was used for directional control. The amount of thrust provided depended on the horsepower of the engine and the blade diameter, which varied from one model to the next. The engine was a conventional four-cylinder, four-stroke, 152-hp, water-cooled Rotorway helicopter engine. It had its own separate fan and cooled in the air and on the ground.

Other products planned included a flying scooter, and a one-, two-, five- and seven-seat Flyer.

Steve James designed a car/airplane, the Hon Doc 4-place, which combined an ultralight with a Honda 600 coupe.

Engineer Jeffrey J. Spitzer of Aeromaster Innovations designed the integrated, single-engine Synergy roadable kit aircraft with a hydraulic wing-folding system, cockpit acti-

Jeffrey Spitzer, designer of the Synergy (courtesy Jeffrey Spitzer).

vated, away from the fuselage. It had a pusher propeller and a twinboom tail. There were two front seats for the crew and two smaller rear seats for baggage with split gullwing doors. It was constructed mostly of fiberglass and carbon/epoxy.

SPECIFICATIONS

Empty weight . . . . 1,250 lb.
Gross Weight . . . . 1,950 lb.
Length . . . . 19.0 ft.
Wingspan/folded width . . . . . 28.4 ft./7.5 ft. folded width
Height . . . . 5.3 ft.
Wing area . . . . 103 sq. ft.
Powerplant . . . . MAZDA 13B rotary; custom
                            turbocharged/intercooled,
                            fuel injection, dual electronic
                            ignition, 220 hp at 6,500
                            rpm, flat rated to 10,000 ft.
                            + custom muffler
Propeller and drive . . . . 72 in. variable pitch custom
                            HV chain reduction drive,
                            2.28:1, selected only
                            in flight mode
Ground drive . . . . Main wheels drive through
                            stock VW bug transaxle and
                            clutch adapted through
                            selectable cogbelt drive
Top speed . . . . 235 mph at 10 miles/gal.

A version with four full-size seats was envisioned.

Aeronautical engineer Kenneth G Wernicke, president of Sky Technologies Vehicle Design and Development Co., designed his narrow, sleek, integrated prototype four-place Skycar with an 8.5-ft. fixed wing, requiring no airframe re-configuration conversion except selecting propeller or wheel power. He used a stumpy, fractional aspect-ratio wing with winglets on the ends for aerodynamic efficiency. The cockpit included both air and road instrumentation, a dual-mode steering yoke and automobile-style pedals.

His wind tunnel and model testing indicated lift-to-drag ratios of about 7.5. He expected the range and efficiency to fall between those of helicopters and typical general aviation airplanes: 1,300 miles in the air and 2,200 miles on the ground.

SPECIFICATIONS

Chord . . . . 13 ft.
Length . . . . 21 ft.
Gross weight . . . . 1,400 lb.
Engine . . . . Mazda Rotary 180 hp

PERFORMANCE

Highway speed . . . . 65 mph
Air speed . . . . 200–400 mph

These were the planned specs for a production version. The design lacked a horizontal tail; both aileron and elevator functions could combine into a single wingtip control surface called an elevon.

Wingspan . . . . 10 ft.
Length . . . . 24.17 ft.
Gross weight . . . . 2,800 lb.
Engine . . . . 475 hp racing-car

PERFORMANCE

Maximum speed . . . . 266 mph
Maximum speed with supercharging . . . . 310 mph
Takeoff distance at gross weight . . . . 980 ft.

In 1994 five designs from various inventors were listed.

Kip Anderson designed a low aspect ratio, folding-wing roadable aircraft.

Clarence Kissell designed the kitplane, two-place Pegasus with ducted fan propulsion. Wings were stored by sliding them into the rear of the body. It was a sports car that converted into an airplane. It was accelerated to takeoff speed with the assistance of the front wheel drive. Conversion time: 90 seconds. The wings were 145 sq. ft. spanning 37 ft.; stall speed was 70 mph; cruising speed was 160 mph with retractable wheels at 2,500 lb. gross weight.

Gary Payne designed a VTOL aircar with low aspect ratio wings in a 10-ft. span with a top speed of 60 mph and a cruising speed of 200 mph. Two airframe parachutes, front and rear, guided it.

Gerry Soucy designed a Gerry-buggy roadable with a one-cylinder, air-cooled, two-cycle Honda engine. Empty weight was 400 lb.

Kenneth G. Wernicke had his Skycar on the cover of *Popular Mechanics* in August 1994.

Skyblazer logo.

Palmer C. Stiles, when a Florida Institute of Technology professor, designed a flying automobile using a conventional automobile configuration with folding canard-style wings pivoted at each corner. It had automatic conversion, even while moving. The swept rear wing and top fins dispensed with an aft fuselage or tail cone.

In 1996 aircraft designer Robin Haynes invented the integrated Skyblazer, a dual mode vehicle with a pressurized cabin. It automatically transformed between modes.

SPECIFICATIONS

Engine . . . . Williams FJ44
Wingspan . . . . 28 ft.
Wing area . . . . 143.67 sq. ft.
Gross weight . . . . 3,706 lb.
Empty weight . . . . 2,170 lb.
Useful load . . . . 1536 lb.
Occupants (four places) . . . . 750 lb.
Baggage . . . . 46 lb.
Fuel capacity . . . . 740 lb.

IN ROAD CONFIGURATION

Length . . . . 17.76 ft.
Width . . . . 5.21 ft.
Height . . . . 5.48 ft.

PERFORMANCE

Takeoff distance . . . . 1,330 ft.
Takeoff distance assisted . . . . 945 ft.
Climb rate max . . . . 1,250 ft./min.
Range . . . . 725 nm
Cruise speed . . . . 270 ktas
Max speed . . . . 350 ktas
Stall speed . . . . 60 ktas
Best L/D . . . . 9.1 at 105 ktas

It had no propeller and was powered by a fan-jet engine when aloft. When used as a car the same engine drove an electric generator to power the wheels.

2000s

In 2000 Aero Copter, Inc., produced the Humming, a VTOL design with a mono-tilt rotors system which could be scaled up or down to provide a range of aircraft sizes. The larger edition could have a capacity of up to 50 passengers; the smallest could be a two-place aircraft. The version with two- to four-passenger capability had potential as a flying car.

The system consisted of a single disc, blades and engines, which were horizontally mounted around the body of the aircraft. The spinning rotors provided the lift for vertical takeoff.

Once aloft, a small engine in the aft of the fuselage provided thrust for forward motion. The ring was then tilted to an upright position and the rotors were feathered to reduce form drag.

Landing could be achieved by reversing the takeoff procedure. Once the aircraft had landed, the mono-tilt rotor assembly would disassemble and/or fold up. The fuselage, now a two- or four-passenger car, could be driven away. It would use the engine in the aft of the fuselage to provide power for ground propulsion.

The design incorporated the Small Aircraft Transportation System (SATS) and the Highway-in-the-Sky (HITS) technologies developed by NASA and the FAA. It also used fuel cells, Maglev propulsion systems, artificial intelligence and the Global Positioning System (GPS).

In 2000 the integrated Pegasus aircraft was developed by students at the Virginia Polytechnic Institute and State University and the Loughborough University in England. At Virginia Tech the project was under the direction of Dr. James F. Marchman, III, professor emeritus, aerospace and ocean engineering.

It was a four-place, single-engine roadable with overall vehicle structural design similar to that of a general aviation aircraft. It used composite materials and the most significant feature was the telescoping wing with the retraction of outboard wings into the inboard section.

Power came from a five-cylinder, liquid-cooled aircraft Wilksch diesel engine. There were conventional rudders on the twin vertical tails and conventional elevators and full-length flaperons.

The spacious, modern cabin with leather seats measured 7.55 ft. long and 3.94 ft. wide. There was only one set of controls; a button was pressed to convert.

ROADABILITY COMPONENTS

Tire designation .. P165/75 R14 (front) P175/75 R13 (rear)
Wheels . . . . TSW Imola Alloys
Front suspension . . . . Double wishbone with longitudinal torsion bars
Rear suspension . . . . Trailing arm with coil springs
Damping . . . . Active
Brakes . . . . 4× disc brakes with floating calipers

Pegasus aircraft developed by universities (courtesy Dr. James F. Marchman).

and electric actuators; mechanical
handbrake to rear wheels
Steering . . . . Motor driven rack and pinion

ROADABLE PERFORMANCE

Maximum speed . . . . 160 km/h (99 mph)
0–100 km/h . . . . 11 seconds
Min. stopping distance (from 80 km/h) . . . . 43 m
Understeer gradient (at MTOW) . . . $0.95 + 0.137 + 0.79_a$, deg/g
Rollover condition (at MTOW) . . . . 0.9 g

In 2001 George Gregory designed a dual use vehicle, the integrated Solstice. It had two seats, a three-surface pusher of composite construction with a tricycle gear and detachable main wings. The driving footprint was 6.5 ft. wide by 17 ft. long by 5.5 ft. high. The main landing gear moved up and aft to lower the body for driving. It followed a curve of the longerons. The nose wheel retracted partway into the nose for driving to keep things level.

In 2001 Roger N. Pham designed several different integrated roadable aircraft, called "Plans for the Millennium."

The Excitation is the poor man's twin jet for small business, with twin engines. The name comes from the best-selling jet the Cessna Citation.

The Skyjawk is the poor man's sport jet or the cure for a mid-life crisis. The name comes from the jet-bound jock on a Cessna 172 Skyhawk.

The Skylar is named for the best-selling four-seat Cessna Skylark.

The Caesarion is named for the popular six-seat Cessna Centurion and Julius Caesar.

ArrowCar, the practical, go-anywhere roadster, was named in honor of Moulton B. Taylor's Aerocar.

Roadability features include a four-wheel undercarriage suspension; a hydraulic ground propulsion system; a simple wing rotation mechanism; a light-weight, fuel-efficient engine; and inflatable bumpers.

In 2002 Trek Aerospace came out with the Solotrek XFV (Exo-Skeleton Flying Vehicle) ducted-fan personal VTOL. In 2003 it introduced the Springtail and Dragonfly.

In 2003 three different designs were described.

Mat Fletcher designed his integrated Car-Plane or CANE with the wing split in two, making a biplane.

Macro Industries, Inc., designed the Sky Rider X2R ¼ scale model with an RC motor. Fuel capacity is 50 gallons and it flies itself by computer.

Dr. Rafi Yoeli, president of Urban Aeronautics Ltd. (Urban Aero), originally Romeo Yankee, Ltd. of Tel Aviv, Israel, began experimenting with a motorless VTOL aircraft, the CityHawk.

Ground and flight testing have now been successfully completed. An auto-stabilization system was not used and it was not tethered from above.

The CityHawk was able to carry two people, could take off and land vertically, and was estimated to be able to stay aloft for close to one hour. The maximum operating ceiling was estimated at 8,000 ft., with flight speeds of 80–90 knots.

Macro Industries' Sky Rider X2R (courtesy Macro Industries Inc.).

The most significant feature was its small footprint, merely 2.2 × 4.7 m. This is compatible with most standard urban parking spaces and garages.

It was configured as a tandem-four, turbine-powered vehicle with a center section to house the crew compartment and payload bay. Maximum payload was 1,700 lb. including the pilot and nine seated passengers (calculated at 175 lb. per person). The payload bay could also be configured to serve as a medical rescue cabin. The vehicle could also be used for police and traffic patrol and agricultural environmental monitoring.

The lift fans operated using variable pitch rotors and a rather complex system of vanes. The multiple-vane control system had a U.S. patent and would consist of four separate layers of independent movable vanes in each duct, with two layers at the top and two layers at the bottom of each duct. These could be coordinated to provide effective lift or side forces. Fore and aft movement was controlled by fully reversible variable-pitch thrusters connected to the two turbine engines. The pilot also used a "fly-by-wire" multi-channel flight control system and an automatic stabilization feature to help control the aircraft and maintain level flight without tilting the machine. These features simplified the pilot's workload, allowing him to concentrate on the kind of precise piloting that is required in situations such as rescue missions at high-rise apartments and offices. The vehicle would be fully FAA certified. Even with a full payload it could still come to a safe landing after the loss of one of the turbines.

Another interesting feature called for the ducts to be acoustically treated to reduce noise levels.

The design included such improvements as on-board computers. They simplified the complexity of piloting an aircraft, and they also reduced the weight of the machine by

Hovering CityHawk, June 2003 (courtesy Dr. Rafi Yoeli).

replacing heavy mechanics with electronic controls. Advanced composite materials also made the vehicle lighter and stronger. Modern turbine engines were used that are significantly lighter and more powerful than those available in the 1960s. The military derivative is TurboHawk.

In 2004 the Boeing Company reported that it was studying an integrated, hybrid flying car, a sporty red helicopter/car. The goal was to make a vehicle that costs the same as a luxury car, is quiet, fuel-efficient and easy to fly and maintain. They created a miniature model and sent out a news release. Phantom Works, Boeing's research arm, was involved in the project.

In 2004 Mirror Image Aerospace and the TCB Composite Company, Inc., produced a prototype experimental VTOL, the Skywalker, as a homebuilt kit.

In 2005 Jesse James on the season finale of his *Monster Garage* program on the Discovery channel converted an aluminum and carbon-fiber, two-passenger Panoz Esperante sports car into a flying car.

To lighten it 1,000 pounds were removed from the car, resulting in a 3,800-lb. final vehicle, now a ground effect machine with a custom airfoil shape. Over the rear was fabricated an articulated frame out of steel square tubing. Two engines were provided: a 4.6

CityHawk cockpit (courtesy Dr. Rafi Yoeli).

On August 19, 2004, Lynne Wenberg, Boeing senior manager, is shown with a hybrid helicopter in a news release sent out nationwide (AP/Wide World photo by John Froshaver).

liter Ford V-8 coupled to the rear wheels and the 0-320, 200-plus-lb., flat four-cylinder Lycoming aircraft engine on top with 520 cu. in. and 160 hp that drove the pusher propeller. It took five people to put on the wings, 16-ft. long, 5-ft. wide and a foot thick. There was a vehicle stabilizer but no rudder.

In 2005 Butterfly LLC introduced its Super Sky Cycle gyroplane. At least six kits have been sold so far. Some 42 kits for the predecessor Butterfly have also been sold. The designer of the three-wheeled, two-engine craft is Larry Neal.

In 2005 Milner Motors began development of its AirCar, a four-door, four- or five-person, four-wheel, completely self-contained, highly aerodynamic, advanced composite roadable aircraft. It is about the same size as the Toyota Corolla or Honda Civic.

Two rotary engines drive 28-in. ducted fan units. It has a 28-ft. wingspan and in ground mode the wings fold to 7 ft. wide in the rear with a canard in the front.

SPECIFICATIONS

Empty weight . . . . 1,800 lb.
Maximum weight . . . . 3,000 lb.

Top: Experimental Skywalker VTOL. *Bottom:* Mirror Image logo (both photographs courtesy Mirror Image Aerospace).

Cruise speed in air . . . . 200 mph
Power in air . . . . 300 hp
Range in air . . . . 1,000 miles
Power on ground . . . . 40 mph
Speed on ground . . . . 85 mph
Useful load . . . . 1,200 lb.

It will have modern instrumentation with two flat-panel displays for air and ground mode, and it will eventually be pressurized, have normal de-icing equipment and operate up to 25,000 ft.

The initial prototype is being built as an experimental aircraft with the goal of getting it certified for commercial production. The vehicle went on display at the 2008 New York Auto Show March 21–30.

Jesse James' flying car project was featured on the cover of *Popular Mechanics* in July 2005.

The U.S. market is estimated to be in the range of 1,000–2,000 units per year. The firm feels an effectively designed flying car or roadable aircraft must

- Be light enough to fly yet strong enough to be crashworthy
- Be roomy enough for practical everyday use yet aerodynamic enough to fly at 200 mph
- Have adequate constant airborne power (300 mph) with appropriate variable ground power (120 mph)
- Have controls and instrumentation that provide adequate and normal control on the ground and also in the air.
- Carry 150 sq. ft. of wing area yet allow the wings to fold while on the ground so the vehicle meets highway standards and can drive safely in side winds
- Adjust the weight on the wheels so in air mode, the rear wheels lift about 90 percent of the weight, and in ground mode the rear wheels lift about 50 percent of the weight.

In 2006 Terrafugia, Inc., was formed by a team of pilots and engineers in Cambridge, Massachusetts. The name is derived from the Latin for "escape from earth." The organization is made up of graduates of the Department of Aeronautics and Astronautics at the Massachusetts Institute of Technology and is developing the integrated Transition, a roadable aircraft which is the idea of Carl Dietrich, the company's CEO.

The Transition looks a lot like a small Cessna, except that it is closer to the ground and has wings that fold up for driving and down for flying. It seats two people side by side and is intended for travel between 100 and 500 miles.

The Transition is normally limited to an altitude of 10,000 ft. above sea level and can go to 14,000 ft. It requires only a few hundred feet to land, and the only feasible place to operate will be the 6,000 public-use, smaller, relatively uncrowded local airports near home and destination.

The firm wants the FAA to place it in the Light-Sport Aircraft Classification (LSA). Drivers will need a pilot's license as well as a car license.

On March 5, 2009, the Transition successfully maintained flight for 37 seconds at Plattsburg, New York. The price is set at $148,000.

SPECIFICATIONS

Gross takeoff weight	1320 lb. (600 kg)
Maximum payload	430 lb.
Useful load	550 lb. (250 kg) with cargo space of 20 cu. ft. (0.6 cu. m) and enough length for skis
Engine	100 hp (engine fuel consumption based on Rotax 912 ULS), four-stroke
Vs	(51 mph, 83 km/hr.) 45 knots
Vr	(80 mph, '70 kts) (130 km/hr.)
Vh	130 mph
Maximum wingspan	27.5 ft. (8.4 m)
Maximum length	18.75 ft. (5.7 m)
Maximum height	6.75 ft. (2.1 m)
Width when folded up	6.5 ft. (2.0 m)

Transition by Terrafugia, Inc. (courtesy of Terrafugia, Benjamin Schweighart).

Cabin width . . . . 4.17 ft. (1.3 m)
Fuel . . . . Super-unleaded autogas or 100LL

PERFORMANCE

Fuel capacity . . . . 20 gallons (120 lb./54 kg)
Fuel consumption (75% power) . . . . 4.5 gal./hr.
Cruise speed (75% power) . . . . 120 mph; 100 kts
(185 km/hr.)
Gas mileage . . . . 30 mpg (air) 40 mpg (hwy)
30 mpg (city)
Minimum takeoff distance . . . . 1,500 ft.
Range . . . . 460 miles
Takeoff distance over 50-ft. obstacles . . . 1,700 ft. (520 m)

Several special safety features are listed:

- Ground mobility facilitates good pilot decision-making when faced with inclement weather
- Patented FMVSS-compliant aerodynamic bumpers on front and rear
- Protected propeller
- Integrated safety cage and crumple zones
- Preflight safety assists: tactile and visual wing lock confirmation; damage-evident tell-tales for road damage with potential airworthiness impact; PIN, weight on wheels, and engine off interlock for wing stowage and deployment
- Airbags standard
- Full-vehicle parachute pending final approval

Chief operating officer Anna Mracek Dietrich has some very interesting thoughts on the market potential:

A team reviewed a great deal of information that showed Americans take 370 million trips per year between 100 and 500 miles, to places that airlines service is not practical and are locations that trains and mass travel generally don't service.

At the present time the following five designs are among those under development by other inventors.

The Hiller Helicopter Corporation is developing a helicopter car weighing less than 1,000 lb., employing the ducted fan principle with a sleek, streamlined design. It is said to be capable of doing 100 mph on the ground or in the air.

Kestrel Aerospace, Ltd., of England is designing VTOL vehicles with a patented propulsion system powered by a new type of lightweight rotary engine, situated internally, which uses a new technique for distributing power to the lift units.

The airframe has gear similar to that of a Blackhawk helicopter. Two retractable landing gear units (one on each side of the airframe) are built in, and a tail wheel is built into the base of the tail strut.

Steve Nichols is working on the Fusion, a roadable lightplane. It is a conventional, low-wing tail dragger which uses a pneumatically adjustable suspension in concert with a two-blade feathering propeller. It also uses variable-geometry wings to convert the machine into a Morgan-style trike with an active leaning chassis for improved cornering. The current model is the Vindicator, a three-seater version. It will be followed by longer, more capacious models in the years to come.

Bill Snead's latest design for an integrated, roadable aircraft, No. 6, featured a forward engine position, pusher propeller, four wheels and a retractable fifth wheel that is only used for takeoff and landing. This fly wheel is mounted on the vehicle's center of gravity and is used to lift the aircraft at airspeeds greater than 10 mph so that it can rotate to higher angles of attack for takeoff and landing. To take off it will accelerate on all four wheels. After about 20 mph is achieved, the fly wheel will be extended. Since it is located at the center of gravity, the pilot will control the attitude and direction with the flight controls. When flying speed is achieved, the pilot will rotate takeoff.

On approach to landing, the fly wheel will be fully extended. The craft will be landed on the fly wheel in a slightly nose high attitude. Once on the ground, the pilot will use flight control to balance the airplane on the fly wheel. As the aircraft slows down, the fly wheel will be retracted and the nose will be lowered on the front wheels.

Snead envisions that the wings will be constructed of carbon fiber and should weigh about 60 lb. apiece. The transition from the aircraft to road mode will be done manually. The wings can be taken off and stowed over the split tail by the pilot working alone.

George Vraneck has designed the modular Porsche Skymaster.

In January 2009 the CBC News featured a segment on the Parajet Skycar, probably considered more a recreational vehicle than a utility one. A group of adventurers led by Neil Laughton set out from London on January 14 for Timbuktu in the bio-fueled flying car, which looks like a dune buggy with a huge fan and a paragliding wing attached. It was designed by self-taught engineer and inventor Giles Cardozo.

UNCONVENTIONAL ROAD-AIR VEHICLES

In addition to passenger cars a very wide variety of other land vehicles have been taken airborne.

Roughly in descending order of incidence these vehicles are:

- motorcycles
- bicycles
- buses
- motor scooters
- motorbikes
- tricycles
- motor homes
- tanks
- trucks
- sleds

Two watercraft are also listed: submarines and ocean liners. There is the convertible aircraft that can also travel along a railroad track, and, finally, we must not forget the road-able hot air balloon.

Motorcycles

Jess Minick first put wings on a motorcycle in 1919.

In the 1960s and 1970s daredevil Evel Knievel used a thin Skycycle with bolted wings and a steam-powered rocket engine that enabled the chopper to go airborne. It could go 350 mph in eight seconds. He used it to leap over school buses, live sharks, cars and 1,000 ft. over canyons.

In 1985 the Mainair Company in England developed the Skybike, a cross between a motorcycle and a flex-wing microlight trike. It was derived from Mainair's Gemini Flash, a fairly conventional flex-wing bike, with the front of the trike unit replaced with a conventional Yamaha YZ80, a small off-road motorbike, to provide ground transportation.

Daredevil Evel Knievel sails over seven Mack trucks in Toronto, August 20, 1974 (AP/Wide World Photos).

The pilot's feet were used on the cycle handlebars when flying or maneuvering on the ground. The motorcycle could be detached in two minutes.

SPECIFICATIONS

Empty weight . . . . 386 lb.
Gross weight . . . . 761 lb.
Useful load . . . . 375 lb.
Span of flex-wing . . . . 34.6 ft.
Area . . . . 168 sq. ft.
Airborne powerplant . . . . 40 hp 747 Rotax

Another machine was also developed which used one engine and a gearbox to switch between propeller drive and the wheel drive.

In 2001 Al Bragg designed a flying motorcycle, the integrated Flite Bike. It combined a Honda 2001 reflex motorcycle with a Buckeye Ram Air Wing. It was powered by a 582 Rotax aircraft engine using a four-blade propeller. The buyer must acquire the motorcycle. The flight kit consisted of a custom frame for the Honda, the Buckeye chute, the Rotax engine and the propeller.

Douglas Malewicki, an engineer-designer, and two others have created a hang-bike motorcycle, mating a motorcycle with a hang glider, designed for jumps beyond 200 ft.

Trans Air Systems has designed a TAS 102 Flying Motorcycle.

Pat Yearic designed his integrated, three-wheel motorcycle, Cycleplane, as a dual use, roadable aircraft with a single seat. It had a fixed nose gear as a single driven wheel, simple flaps, a turbofan engine, and a ducted propulsion system. The wing did not require any folding mechanism. In the transition the tail surfaces were moved from a protected position in the road vehicle mode to an extended position for flight. It was 8 ft. wide.

PERFORMANCE

Top speed . . . . 250 kias
Takeoff speed . . . . 100 kias
Rate of climb . . . . 180–200 kias

Wolff Aerocycle developed two modular designs which incorporate a conventional, lightweight motorcycle with a removable, fixed-wing flight module equipped with engines dedicated for flight and completely separate from the motorcycle propulsion. Power from the motorcycle drive train could be used to assist in the takeoff. Flight control used a single handlebar.

Wolff Aerocycle logo.

Larry Neal's Super Sky-Cycle (courtesy Larry Neal).

One model was a Special Light Sport Aircraft with maximum gross takeoff weight of 1,320 lb. The model had a maximum stall speed of 51 mph (45 knots); a maximum speed in level flight with maximum continuous power (Vh) of 138 mph (120 knots); a two-place maximum (pilot and one passenger); a single, non-turbine engine; a fixed or ground adjustable propeller; and fixed landing gear.

The other model was a General Aviation model in kit form, having a high performance, aluminum/composite construction and twin engines.

Allied Aerotechnics developed an AirBike VTOL personal aircraft. It used a vectored thrust from a directed fan to achieve both vertical and level flight. The proportions, size, shape and configuration were based on the dimensions of the proposed powerplant.

The latest flying motorcycles came out in 2008 from designer Larry Neal.

Top: Larry Neal's Turbo Golden Butterfly motorcycle. *Bottom:* Larry Neal's Monarch Butterfly motorcycle (both photographs courtesy Larry Neal).

Larry Neal's Golden Butterfly motorcycle (courtesy Larry Neal).

Bicycles

Bicycles on the wing have been spurred on since 1935 by a substantial award offered by the Royal Aeronautical Society in London to teams of aeronautical engineers. These contraptions with propellers are driven by leg power alone. Dozens of efforts have come from Germany, France, Italy, Great Britain, Japan, Australia and the United States.

In 1976 Paul MacCready, Jr., and Peter B. Lissmann, both professional aerodynamicists, designed the flying bicycle the Gossamer Condor, which was oversized, had a single blade and was fabric covered, with a propeller driven by leg power alone.

It was built of super lightweight aluminum tubing, balsa, Styrofoam, piano wire and corrugated paper and weighed 70 lb. (30 kg). The whole structure was 30 ft. long and 18 ft. high with a wingspan of 96 ft. It flew a mile and a half at 10–11 mph.

Clyde D. "Daring" Gohring designed a flying bicycle. It relied on leg power and air lift. The wingspan was 43 ft. and it was designed to fly a mile at a height of 10 ft., lift off at 17 mph and fly at 20 mph.

The Para-Cycle was an integrated powered parachute and a recumbent bicycle that became an ultralight aircraft.

Buses

In the 1930s famous industrial designer Norman Bel Geddes envisioned a Helicopter Community Bus which would require a floating airport.

In 1966 Moulton B. Taylor looked to an Aerobus with 30–50 passengers. At the airport the road vehicle would be quickly attached to an awaiting airframe at a conversion station. Servicing would take place at night or during off hours. It looked like a cargo transport.

In 1974 it was proposed that the Surtan bus-copter be used for a new transportation system connecting the Dallas/Ft. Worth Regional Airport with the two cities. Crume and Associates created it.

Motor Scooters

In 1956 Antonio E. Pellarini, an Italian, designed a flying motor scooter with a tractor propeller.

Motorbikes

John Bakker, a Dutch entrepreneur working with Spark Design Engineering and other partners, has designed PALV. This was basically an integrated gyrocopter built on a motorbike with a patented tilting system. The single rotor and propeller were folded away until the vehicle was ready to fly.

Because it flew below 4,000 ft. it could take off without filing a flight plan. Lift was generated by the forward speed produced by the foldable push propeller on the back. The autogiro technology means that it could be steered and landed safely even if the engine failed.

Trucks

Luigi Pellarini in 1970 designed his P. L. 12 Airtruk, which was built in Australia by Transavia Corp. Pty., Ltd. It won the Prince Philip prize for Australian design and was called the Skyfarmer.

Watercraft

A flying submarine was developed by engineer Walter Reid in the 1950s. He claimed that it could submerge or fly wherever the pilot wished. The experimental full-scale prototype of the torpedo-like craft was 26 ft. long and in tests reached an altitude of about 75 ft. It had a 60-hp airplane engine mounted on top of a conning tower, and an electric boat propeller on the stern. It was designed to submerge and travel 4 knots about 5 ft. beneath the surface, and to fly at 65 mph at an altitude of 20 ft.

When it was placed on display at an inventor congress in New York City it became the "star of the show" due to possible further development for the military.

Top: John Bakker's PALV gyrocopter built on a motorbike in the Netherlands (courtesy John Bakker). *Bottom:* Walter Reid's flying submarine (courtesy Walter Reid).

In the early 1960s the Convair Division of General Dynamics explored the feasibility of flying submersibles by developing a jet-powered subplane that would be able to dive beneath the water and cruise. The two-person craft was intended to have an aircraft range of 300–500 nautical miles at speeds of 150–225 knots, with an underwater range of 50 nautical miles at five knots and a 75-ft. depth. After landing the operators would seal off the jet engines and flood the hollow wings, tail and sides of the hull, causing the vehicle to submerge. Underwater propulsion would be provided by battery-run propellers.

In the 1930s Norman Bel Geddes, along with German aeronautical engineer Otto A. Kuhler, designed a luxury vehicle, the V-winged Transoceanic Airliner. The mammoth, nine-storey hybrid of ocean liner and airplane would have accommodations for more than 600 people with staterooms, suites and a two-storey dining room as well as a dance floor, tennis court, library and barber and beauty shop.

Railroad

In 1976 Louis Francois Chiquet designed a convertible aircraft capable of travel along a railroad track so that it could get into the heart of a city, instead of terminating at an air-

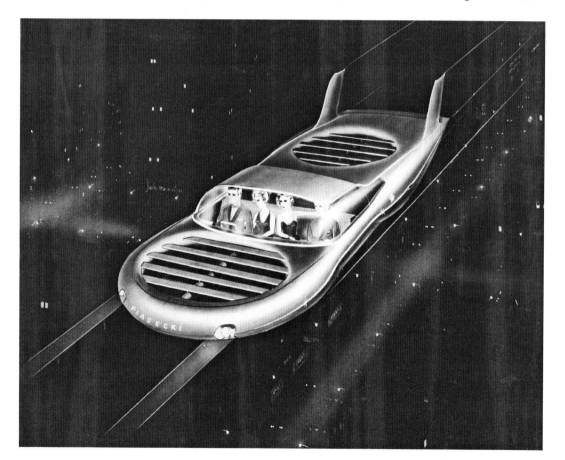

Piasecki future concept vehicle (courtesy Piasecki Aircraft Corporation).

port located some distance away from the city. The aircraft included wings that could be folded inwardly adjacent to the side of the aircraft fuselage so that it required approximately the same width of clearance as a conventional railroad train. The railroad tracks were additionally fitted with a system of channel rails welded on top of the old railroad track so that the airplane could travel on them.

MILITARY ROAD-AIR VEHICLES

The military uses of roadable aircraft and flying vehicles have always presented intriguing possibilities.

Governments worldwide have expressed interest from time to time since the 1920s, but this interest has unfortunately been sporadic and desultory.

Between 1920 and 1925 Virgil B. "Fudge" Moore's Autoplane Company in Southern California produced hybrid vehicles under the name Road-Runner.

Among these was a streamlined Navy Special Military Scout intended for combined military and aeronautical training. It had folding wings, was less than 7 ft. wide and had dual floats beneath the fuselage. It also had special facilities for taking off from the deck of a ship.

In 1921 in France Rene Tampier designed an integrated, dual-engine roadable biplane which he offered to the French army to accompany either cavalry or artillery. It was also designed to be valuable for the navy because of its folding wings. A squadron with the machines was ready to fight in less than an hour. An auxiliary gasoline engine facilitated the manipulation of bombs and torpedoes. The controls of machine guns, etc., could depend on the small engine.

In 1940 Raoul Hafner designed the experimental Rotabuggy, a standard army integrated Jeep or Blitz Buggy with rotors.

Preliminary tests in England involved loading a Jeep with concrete and dropping it from heights of up to 7 ft. 8 in. (2.35 m), demonstrating that the standard vehicle could survive undamaged from impacts of up to 11 g. A 46 ft. 8 in. (12.4m) diameter two-blade rotor was then fitted, as well as a streamlined tail fairing with twin rudderless fins. Other additions were Perspex door panels, a hanging rotor control next to the steering wheel and a rotor tachometer and glider navigational instruments.

The Rotabuggy, camouflaged, carrying RAF roundels and a prototype "P," was tow-tested behind a 4.5-liter supercharged Bentley and achieved gliding speeds of up to 65 mph (105 km/h) IAS. The first flight was made on November 16, 1943. Later some flights were made behind a Whitley bomber from Sherbourne-in-Elmet.

The combination had a height to the hub top of 6 ft. 9 in., the length was 21 ft. and the width was 9 ft. 6 in., excluding the rotors. The gross weight was 3,110 lb. (141 kg), including 550 lb. (241 kg) for the rotor unit. Maximum speed was 150 mph (241 km/h). Estimated rate of descent was 960–1,980 ft./min. (4.9–10 m./sec.).

Hafner also designed a Rotatank, a similarly modified Valentine tank.

In 1947 Theodore P. Hall tried to get the Army Air Force interested in his modular Convaircar as a convertible airplane/light armored car. It could augment the normal function of parachute troops by lowering its wings to become a motorized unit.

In 1951 Moulton B. Taylor designed several conversions of his modular Aerocar for the military. These proposals included a flying Jeep (Aerojeep), an amphibious version and a tracked vehicle. The Jeep included a kit attachment which could be fastened to any standard Jeep, making it into an airplane. A separate aircraft engine would be housed in the tailcone and be used for flight. The flight mechanism could be folded to become a trailer for ground storage and transportation of the entire machine. An aircraft carrier would be used as transport. A further refinement substituted a road component especially designed for flight operations for the standard Jeep.

In the late 1950s Luigi Pellarini, an Italian living in Australia, designed a prototype Air Jeep, a sesqui-plane design with a canard, pusher propeller and a split V-tail. The incomplete airframe is on display in Australia at the Army Museum of Aviation.

In 1959 the U.S. Army awarded more than two million dollars for research on roadable aircraft and then decided that the project would be too expensive to continue.

VTOL vehicles known as Flying Jeeps, or AirGeeps, were built and flown by the Piasecki Company and the U.S. Army and Navy in the early 1960s.

Piasecki VTOL Air Geep (courtesy Piasecki Aircraft Corp.).

Vertical lift, propulsion and control were derived from two ducted horizontal rotors in a tandem arrangement. The PA-59 could fly up to 75 mph close to the terrain and was not dependent on the aerodynamic principle of ground effect. It could also hover, land and then travel as a ground vehicle on three wheels.

The 200-hp piston engines were mounted onto the machine between the two rotor ducts. Differential collective pitch of the rotors provided longitudinal control and laterally disposed vanes in the duct assisted propulsion. Lateral cyclic pitch change of the rotors and longitudinally disposed vanes provided side force for lateral roll control. Differential movement of these longitudinal vanes provided yaw control.

The pilot was positioned on the right side of the vehicle to keep his collective pitch control lever away from the open side of the machine. This also permitted the pilot to look down over his right arm, giving him precise clues to the machine's motion relative to near obstructions. The enclosed rotors made flight close to ground personnel feasible without danger of injury. The downwash was surprisingly different than that of a helicopter and gave the pilot clear local visibility in flying over sand, water and snow, unlike the blinding recirculation characteristics of a helicopter rotor.

Continued studies resulted in the AirGeep II, otherwise known as the PA-59H. It was similar to the AirGeep, except that the aircraft was bent in the middle so that the rotors were tilted fore and aft, reducing drag in forward flight. The AirGeep II used twin 400-hp Turbomeca Artouste IIC turboshaft engines, linked so that if one failed the other would drive both rotors. One engine could also be linked to the landing wheels to drive the machine while on the ground. The increased power allowed a maximum takeoff weight of 2.2 tons.

The army also pursued a flying truck in parallel with the flying jeeps. Curtiss-Wright Corporation developed this machine under the designation VZ-7AP. It was a simple beam with a pilot up front and four horizontal propellers at each of four corners; the props were all driven by a single 425-hp Turbomeca Artouste engine, mounted underneath the central beam. Differential pitch between the propellers and a rudder in the turbine exhaust provided control for the aircraft. The flying truck was 5.2 m (17 ft.) long, 4.9 m (16 ft.) wide and weighed 770 kg (1,698 lb.), 250 kg (551 lb.) of which was payload. The VZ07 was tested in 1959 and 1960 but nothing came of the project. The Osprey has been used like a flying truck, delivering marines and gear far from live action.

In 1961 the SeaGeep was developed and tested.

In 1993 Kenneth G. Wernicke, president of Sky Technology Vehicle Design and Development, envisioned a version of his skycar for military use.

It would have nose-mounted canards for improved short-field capability and would be powered by a 450-shp turboprop engine.

In 2001 the Naval Air Warfare Center, Weapons Division, entered into a cooperative research and development agreement with Roadable Aircraft International, Inc., (RAI) for the development of a VTOL flying car.

In 2001 a joint venture by Urban Aeronautics Ltd. and LoPresti Gordon VTOL Inc. was formed to offer a military derivative of the CityHawk to the government.

Tanks

After a successful demonstration of his original model in 1931, J. Walter Christie, inventor, automotive engineer and famous automobile racing driver, produced a prototype in 1932 of his revolutionary modular flying tank in Linden, New Jersey, with a detachable tractor tread and rubber-tired retractable wheels, enabling it to speed at 100 miles an hour on a smooth highway. In order to design it to get into the air he had to cut the normal weight.

This two-man, four-ton tank with drop-off wings had an armored undercarriage and pilot's turret, a single 1,000-hp motor which drove the air propeller, wheels and tread, and 3-in. guns.

Significant construction details included:

- a chain drive to rear wheels
- a four-blade, large-diameter tractor airscrew
- controls and propeller drive shaft passed through the same housing
- thin wing sections.

Fast fighting planes were to form a convoy for flying tanks speeding into action in squadron formation.

As he landed, the pilot was to start the endless tread whirling so that he could come to earth at high speed. The tanks were projected to land almost directly on protected enemy territory. The wings could be easily shed at will by pulling a single lever to discard the entire structure. The tank unit was fully equipped to plunge into combat with guns blazing and to negotiate tough spots, maneuvering at 70 mph on caterpillar tracks and at 100 mph with them off, depending on the terrain. Unfortunately Christie apparently had continuing trouble trying to satisfy the War Department expectations.

J. Walter Christie's flying tank. This side view is in Linden, N.J. Note the undercarriage is armored.

J. Walter Christie's flying tank. Note the 1,000-hp motor to drive the propeller.

The Christie project of a mobile gun nest on land never went into production, but it is believed that the Russians bought at least one of the tanks he created and used some of his technology in World War II.

For future development he planned a different machine: a detachable airplane with its own pilot that could carry a tank to a scene of combat, deposit it while skimming the earth, and return for more tanks without stopping to land.

Hitherto planes had been unable to transport an effective battle force behind enemy lines. But with a fleet of winged tanks, a frontal attack no longer would be necessary, thus rendering traditional trench warfare obsolete, according to military experts.

It was foreseen that there would be no way of stopping a fleet of these formidable engines of war from sailing over the front lines, landing behind enemy trenches, and charging on the enemy's rear. Heavy guns capable of stopping the onslaught could not be reversed and pointed rearward in time to be of any real use.

Waldo Dean Waterman, an aviation pioneer and former Curtiss assistant, in the early 1930s designed and built a series of unconventional, integrated craft, including a radical, small, tailless monoplane, the Arrowplane, in 1934. This was for a U.S. Department of Commerce contest to make a low-cost airplane. He won first place.

Then in 1938 he turned his attention to a flying tank version of his Arrowbile flying car.

This was a veritable mobile gun nest on land with these specifications: all-metal reversible propeller and engine in the rear; wingspan of 37 ft.; steel-armored forward capsule cockpit 14 ft. 4 in. long; bulletproof gas tanks; bulletproof telescoping gun turret; and a cruising speed of 160 mph and short bursts to 180 mph. The pilot manned one machine gun while a second gunner operated in a revolving turret. The single V-shaped wing could be shed in two minutes and the vehicle could go 75 mph on roads using the pilot's wheel to steer the front wheel.

A fleet of these tiny ships could land behind enemy lines, drop their wings and operate against land troops. They could be stored compactly on an aircraft carrier and make a swift raid against inland cities, then return and stack their wings below decks compactly.

The modular Antonov KT (Kr'lya Tanka), also called the A-40 or AT, was designed in 1940 by the Russian Oleg Konstantinovich Antonov to test the idea of supplying partisan forces behind enemy lines with a light tank to harass the lines of communication.

A model AT-6 light tank provided the fuselage of the unit, while the unlocked tracks served as the landing gear. An unstaggered biplane wing of plywood and fabric was attached, together with a pair of tail booms with twin vertical surfaces and a high-mounted single horizontal surface. The aerodynamic controls comprised a single lever operating all flying surfaces from the driver's position. The flying surfaces were to be jettisoned directly on landing.

Towing speed was 99 mph (160 km/h) and landing speed was 68 mph (110 km/h). It was towed by a heavy bomber such as the Prtlyakov PE-8 or Tupolev TB-3.

SPECIFICATIONS

Wingspan . . . . 18 m
Length . . . . 12.06 m
Weight of lightened T-60 tank . . . . 5,800 kg
Final flight weight . . . . 7,804 kg

There is no official record of its ever flying, but the Russians claimed a single successful flight was made in 1941 or 1942. With only limited official support, the program was cancelled shortly afterward.

QUASI ROAD-AIR VEHICLES

There is ample evidence of a desire to achieve at least a symbolic combination of land vehicles and aircraft on a fantasy level.

The phrase "flying teapot" was affectionately given to the early Stanley Steamer; many production passenger cars have exhibited unmistakable attributes of aviation styling. One of the most striking and innovative features of the 1953 Cadillac Eldorado was its wrap-around windshield, a device straight out of the aircraft cockpit. The streamlined Lincoln Futura of 1955 was the basis for the Batmobile. The radically innovative, sporty, rear-engine 1948 Tucker Torpedo definitely had the look of a rocket ship. And just what did the names Terra*plane* or Thunder*bird* suggest?

Hood ornaments have long featured winged creatures, like Rolls Royce's Flying Lady and Packard's winged Goddess of Speed.

Saab urges drivers in its advertising to "fly home for the holidays" in its cars, "born from jets." The firm was founded by 16 aircraft engineers, it boasts. Chrysler advertises that its hydrogen fuel cell-powered concept car, the four-passenger ecoVoyager, will give passengers the feeling of riding in a private jet.

In his evaluation of the Nissan Altima Coupe, the *Detroit Free Press* auto critic Mark Phelan headlines his article "Fly the Altima Coupe" because of its sleek and sporty styling. His headline in review of the 2008 Audi TT 2.0TFSI sport coupe was "Clearing the Clouds." He characterized the Infiniti FX50 sports SUV as looking "ready to take off."

In 1947 General Motors Corporation designed a fantasy car, the Roc Atomic. It was powered by atomic energy, had no wheels and floated a few centimeters above the road.

Several years ago the Spaceship on Wheels came into view with these specifications:

ENGINE

Type . . . . four-cylinder Volkswagen
Valve gear . . . . overhead valves, pushrod operated
Displacement . . . . 1950 cc
Carburetion . . . . dual carburetors
Horsepower . . . . 110 at 5,800 rpm

CHASSIS

Body/frame . . . . fiberglass body/steel floorpan
Front suspension . . . . independent, torsion bar
Rear suspension . . . . independent, torsion bar
Number of wheels . . . . four
Wheels driven . . . . two, rear

PERFORMANCE

Maximum speed . . . . 110 mph

The following list of windblown or propeller-driven automobiles appeared in the August 6, 1992, issue of *Old Cars News and Marketplace*:

1903 Aeropinion, the 1914 Windwagon, small production run of Leyats in France (1913–1921), the 1921 Reese Aero-Car, another small production run of French Tractor Aeriennes (1921–1926), the 1922 Aeromobile, the 1926 McLaughlin Main Mobile, the 1931 Canzol, and the 1937 Menkenns trike. They were split on whether to use tractor or pusher props. Most guarded the propeller by enclosing it within a steel hoop or wire mesh cage. Weights ranged from 150 lb for the little Reese to a ponderous 1,580 lb registered by the Main Mobile. All were American one-offs with the exception of the two French efforts.

Although none of the cars were commercially successful, modern windblown surface vehicles exist today in the form of Florida swamp boats. Dave and Irene Major put together

Aircraft-oriented Saab advertisement for 9-7X SUV (courtesy Saab Automobile USA).

Mounted on a two-ton truck, a Packard aviation engine in January 1917 demonstrated its tremendous power by propelling the truck at a speed of 30 mph. With the wheels locked, it was pushed over the snow-covered ground by the action of the propeller (courtesy Fred Mauck, Packards International Motor Car Club).

their Propeller Car (Airplane BMW Isetta). It is a 1957 BMW powered by a 190-hp, six-cylinder, air-cooled Lycoming airplane engine turning a 6-ft.-diameter wood propeller. There is no transmission as the car is powered by the prop alone, like an airboat in the Everglades. It originally came with a 13-hp, one-cylinder BMW motorcycle engine.

Their other novelty vehicle is equally innovative: they transformed a small, two-door 1959 BMW 600 into their unique Rock and Roll Aerocar. It has mounted on the front door a hand-carved, wooden propeller turned by a 12-volt motor, a small tail on the rear roof and two 8-in. wings. The front tires have been replaced with Beechcraft 400A nose wheel tires and the rear tires are from the main landing gear of the Beech Starship. Special split-rims from an early Isetta were adapted to fit the airplane tires. The front parking lights and rear taillights are removed. The custom fiberglass dash holds a working altimeter, air speed indicator and aircraft compass. The front opens to allow the "pilot" to enter. It is shown in many Midwest car shows and parades.

G-whiz is what graphic expert Bill Carter in England calls his half-plane, half-car, which has a top highway speed of 150 mph. He combined engine parts from a Hawk Jet and a V-12 Jaguar to power his rocket-shaped, 21-ft. vehicle. There is a two-seater cockpit in which the passenger sits behind the driver.

Also in England some years ago the Destruction Squad, a daredevil driving troupe, put together a flying car with makeshift wings and tail attached to the top of the small sedan. The propeller was linked to the car's fan belt. It was launched at 60 mph over the edge of an 80-ft. cliff. Not surprisingly, it "flew" straight down to crash. Never daunted, they vowed to try to fit a large set of wings to one of London's double-decker buses.

Top: David and Irene Major's Rock 'n' Roll Aerocar. *Bottom:* David and Irene Major's Propeller Car; photograph by Paul McRae (both photographs courtesy David and Irene Major).

For those who seek a simplified approach to duality there is always the folding suit-case airplane. In 1989 the Pago Jet personal powered parachute by Celtech of Switzerland was demonstrated. It was small and light enough when folded to fit in the trunk of a car (empty weight 48 lb.). In 1993 Russian Victor Dmitriev designed an ultralight airplane which weighed 110 lb. and could be folded into several small packages and transported by car.

Now, turning to that strange phenomenon, an airplane that thinks it's a car, we run into the Plymocoupe Airplane which sported the portholes and side trim of the 1935 Plymouth. It was labeled a flying automobile because it was powered by an engine manufactured for use in a 1935 Plymouth. At one time Honda planned to enter the personal small jet market with its "Honda Civic of the Sky." The prototype using another company's engines was flown in a test. Other auto-engineered light planes of the time included Wiley Post's Model A Biplane in 1935 and the Arrow Sport monoplane with an 85-bhp Ford V-8 engine.

In 1926 Henry Ford supported experiments with a so-called "flying flivver," a conventional, single-place lightplane. Two were built. The first one is in the Henry Ford Museum. Both were designed by the famous Otto Koppen.

It was just 15 ft. long with a wingspan of about 23 ft. In its first version a French, three-cylinder, 35-hp Anzani air-cooled engine was used and later models incorporated a two-cylinder Ford automobile engine offering a top speed of 90 mph. The wing was not detachable nor was the aircraft intended to be converted to road use and driven. It was intended to be the everyman's aircraft, easy to fly and inexpensive.

CHAPTER II

Amphibious Vehicles

Considering the fact that about three-fourths of the surface of the earth is covered with water (1.4 quadrillion tons), it is not at all surprising that designers of land vehicles have decided to extend functions into the water.

In addition to the oceans, seas, rivers and lakes designers want to see these vehicles used in swamps, marshes, bogs, etc., and on ice and snow.

For centuries amphibious vehicles have challenged the ingenuity of designers worldwide. People have been thinking particularly about cars that can travel in water since the dawn of the automobile.

Amphibious vehicles, popularly known as amphies or amphibs, are purpose-built or converted and operate on roads, in water and on land surfaces such as ice, snow, mud, marshes and swamps. These vehicles have involved automobiles, buses, trucks, recreational vehicles, military vehicles and bicycles, as well as ATVs and air cushion hovercraft.

Those with motor car chassis are variously referred to as auto-boats, car boats, boat-cars, motor car boats, boatmobiles, vehicle-boats, swim-mobiles or land-water cars. The initials GPA designate a general purpose amphibian and GAV is for a go-anywhere vehicle.

Many designs use tracks in addition to or instead of wheels or an articulated body. Some land vehicles can be converted with a waterproof hull and propeller or a snorkel to go through shallow water.

Additional buoyancy measures include inflatable flotation devices like skirts or oil drum floats. Water propulsion is achieved by means of spinning wheels, tracks or a screw or water jet.

An amphibious all-terrain vehicle (ATV) is a smaller, lighter motor vehicle designed for use on all types of rough terrain, sandy or marshy ground, and roads. It usually has only one seat and a boatlike bottom, and it rides on soft, low-pressure rubber balloon tires or on endless rubber belts.

It has a plastic or fiberglass body with six or eight wheels. Control is by skid-steering. Engines yield a top speed of 25 mph on land. Tracks are an option, as are outboard motors and inflatable pontoon kits.

A wide variety of makes has become associated with amphibious prototypes or production vehicles. These include Chrysler, Ford, GMC, Jeep, Land Rover, Mercedes, Morris, Opel, Packard, Porsche, Studebaker, Toyota, Volkswagen and Willys Overland.

Roughly in descending order the countries generating different amphibious designs are the following:

United States	63%
Germany	13%
France	10%

England	6%
Sweden	4%
Italy	1%
Netherlands	1%
Russia	1%
Canada	1%

The introduction of new designs has produced some interesting patterns when traced by decades, as shown below.

1800–1899	1%
1900–1909	13%
1910–1919	13%
1920s	10%
1930s	23%
1940s	1%
1950s	7%
1960s	1%
1970s	13%
1980s	6%
1990s	6%
2000s	6%

Amphibious vehicles have found surprising acceptance in several different major marketing segments, especially for accessing remote sites:

- Commercial use — public utilities, agriculture, ranches, relief organizations, oil and mineral searches, large estates, expeditions, explorations, flying, photography, prospecting and surveying
- Recreational use — golfing, boating, fishing, hunting, camping, racing, and mineral and rock collecting
- Governmental use — military and paramilitary, water search and rescue, forestry, coastal patrol, paramedic units, mosquito abatement, fire fighting and mapping.

Contests sponsored by the Waterbugs of America Racing Association since the 1970s have featured boatmobiles in Portage Lake, Ohio.

Some strange amphibious journeys have taken place, some as early as 1950.

A Berlin designer in 1950 planned to cross the Atlantic Ocean in his auto, which made 40 mph in the water and over 80 on land. He tested the vehicle in the Havel River.

This same year Australian engineer Ben Carlin and his wife Elinore crossed the Atlantic Ocean by Jeep. It was the first leg of a round-the-world trip in the same vehicle, the modified GPA the Half-Safe, named after a deodorant advertising slogan. Watertight, it was an army surplus Jeep with a keel that could be removed for land operation. It also could move under sail. Their circumnavigation of the globe included 9,500 miles by sea and 40,500 by land, ending in Times Square in New York City in 1958.

In the early 1950s Frank and Helen Schreider made a trip in their GPA Toyota II from Alaska to South America. In 1951 a Chevrolet truck was used by the pilot and his family and friends to leave Cuba and cross the Florida Straits.

Then in August 1988 Giorgio Amoretti took his four children in a modified Ford from Italy to New York City on the water.

'HALF-SAFE' IN HER TRANSATLANTIC FORM

LENGTH OVERALL 18 FEET 3 INCHES: BEAM 5 FEET 3 INCHES
ENGINE: FORD G.P.A. 2180 CC
15.6 H.P. NOMINAL—60 B.H.P. AT 3600 R.P.M.

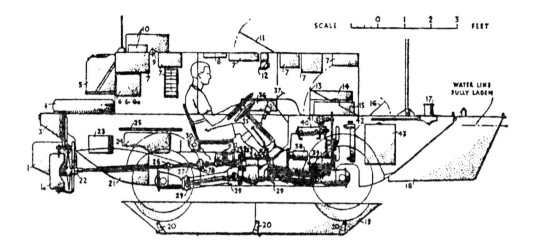

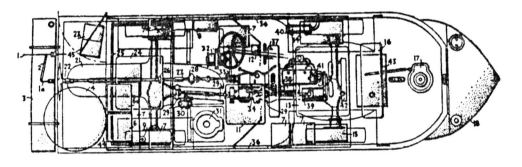

1. Primary and 1a auxiliary rudders	16. Radiator air intake (closed at sea)	31. Toilet
2. Rudder link rod	17. Capstan winch	32. Engine driven bilge pump
3. Fresh water tank	18. Nose-tank (fuel)	33. Propeller and bilge pump clutch levers
4. Spare tyre	19. Belly-tank (fuel)	34. High-low ratio & 2-4 wheel drive levers
5. Rack of five jerricans	20. Nylon straps	35. Rudder steering wheel
6. Radio transmitter and 6a receiver	21. Lubricating oil tank	36. Radiator air vents (closed at sea)
7. Shelves for stores and equipment	22. Cutless bearing	37. Hatch
8. Kleenex dispenser	23. Two 6-volt batteries in series	38. Starter
9. Antenna-lead insulator	24. Main fuel tank	39. Generator
10. Rubber raft and flares	25. Bunk frame	40. Heat exchanger
11. Upper hatch	26. Propeller shaft joint	41. Rain-water pump
12. Compass	27. Propeller shaft gland	42. Radiator
13. Engine hatch	28. Propeller shaft thrust bearing	43. Reserve fuel tank
14. Spares	29. Transmission seal	44. Canned food
15. Tool box	30. Manual bilge pump	45. After hatch

Half-Safe Jeep amphibian specifications (courtesy Ian Grieve).

In May 1999 Amoretti's son Marco, along with two younger brothers and friend Marcolino De Candia, tied together a wrecked Volkswagen Passat and a Ford Taurus filled with buoyant polyurethane to cross from the Canary Islands to Martinique on the Atlantic Ocean.

In the vehicles the driver and passenger compartment were arranged as a shelter. On top was a rubber boat with holes in the middle so that the sailors could climb in and out

Dobbertin amphibious surface orbiter Perseverance (*Toledo Blade* photograph by Greg Horvath).

of the car, and a tent, sails and solar batteries for the mobile telephone set and the desalinator. More equipment was towed on boats. The 3,100-mile journey took 119 days.

From 1993 to 1998 Karen and Rick Dobbertin logged over 3,000 sea miles and 24,000 land miles in their amphibious surface orbiter Perseverance. It was rocket-shaped, built on a 1959 Heil double-walled, standard, milk tanker body. It had six large B. F. Gooodrich T/A mud-terrain radial tires and a bullet-nosed cockpit and was powered by a Detroit Diesel 6.5-liter, water-cooled, V-8 engine and a Peninsular marine conversion when traveling through the water. With auxiliary fuel tanks and a transmission from a 1970 Chevrolet school bus, it held 260 gallons of diesel fuel and was able to get 8–10 mpg on land but only 1 mpg in the water.

Length was 32.5 ft., width was 7.5 ft., and weight was 9.5 tons. The vehicle was registered both as a yacht and as a custom home-on-wheels.

The craft took four and a half years to build, with more than 20 sponsors donating $160,000 worth of parts. The Dobbertins visited 28 countries, piloting the first amphibious vehicle through the Caribbean and the Panama Canal on their Project Earth Trek.

In 2003 11 Cubans (eight men, two women and a baby) were at sea 31 hours trying to sail to Florida in a 1950s four-door Buick converted into a tail-finned boat. They were intercepted at sea by the U.S. Coast Guard and sent back to their homeland.

Marcial Basanta Lopez and Lus Gras Rodriguez, a mechanical engineer, tried a similar stunt. They set out for Florida in a truck-raft, a 1950 green Chevrolet, 1.5-ton advanced design pickup truck with pontoons made out of empty 55-gallon drums. They welded metal to make it watertight and fabricated a pointed prow. A propeller attached to the driveshaft of the car pushed it along at about 8 mph on the 90-mile, 145-minute crossing attempt by the trucknauts.

Hovercraft

Hovercraft are a major category of amphibious vehicles.

By definition they are ground-effect machines (GEM), air-cushion vehicles (ACV) or hydroskimmers suspended 8 to 12 in. above ground or water by a thin cushion of pressurized, low-velocity air created by blowing air downward against the surface close below it.

They are variously referred to as water-air vehicles, boat airplanes, etc., and may be custom-built or conversions. Kits are also available.

A successful conversion in England involved the Vickers VA-3, a standard utility vehicle, the Land Rover, and an air-pressure system that produced 40 lb. per square foot. Several other British air-cushion vehicles have been built in recent years.

On any reasonably smooth, dense, unobstructed terrain hovercraft can carry passengers and cargo. Speeds are 30 mph over open water, 40 mph on land and 45 mph over snow and ice. They skim or float over the surface of grasslands, wetlands and sand.

Loading and unloading take place at hoverports or beaches or ramps when docking on land.

Hovercraft have earned acceptance worldwide. The number of different designs by countries of origin is roughly as shown below, in descending order:

- United States
- England
- France
- Germany

Bertelsen Aeromobile hovers over the ice in 1969 (National Air and Space Museum, Smithsonian Institution, SI Neg. No. 94-13077).

Top: Advertisement for Dobson Air Dart hovercraft kit in *Popular Science*, August 1963, by Aircars, Inc. *Left:* Advertisement for Bartlett Flying Saucer hovercraft kit in *Popular Mechanics*, February 1970.

- Russia
- Japan
- Finland
- Scandinavia
- Scotland
- Greece
- Denmark
- Sweden
- Holland
- Bangladesh

The hovercraft system reduces the hydrodynamic drag on the hull of the boat, using a propeller for propulsion and steering, and one or more lightweight separate diesel engines, or gas turbines with a double-walled flexible skirt system inflated around the edge of the vehicle.

Future designs concentrate on a more efficient propulsion unit. Very large hovercraft might even be driven by atomic power. Surface effect ships (SES) are seen as capable of crossing the ocean.

Some operational problems do exist:

- Excessive noise
- High fuel consumption
- Salt and skirt erosion
- Demanding maintenance schedules
- Limited use during rough seas
- Difficulty steering in crosswinds
- Dust
- Ability to climb hills or embankments only if the gradient is no more than one vertical foot per six feet of distance

In addition to the original, traditional hovercraft boat configurations there are several other varieties:

- hovercar
- hoverbus
- hovertruck
- hovertractor
- hoverbarge
- hover copter
- hovertrain
- hoverplatform
- hoverlawnmower
- hoverbed (for burn victims)

In the early 1970s a modular marine barge was moved with a dragline on board for use over soft, reclaimed land. Mackace (Mackley Air Cushion Equipment) produced a number of hoverbarges, such as the 250-ton payload Sea Pearl and the trim 160-ton payload Yukon Princess. In 2000 Hovertrans launched a 330-ton payload drilling barge.

These are largely used for accessing construction sites.

In 1950 Frenchman Jean Bertin, an engineer, invented the TACV air train.

Hovertrains for railways employing a magnetic Maglev levitation system combined with power supplied by a motor have been tested in the U.S., Germany, China and Japan. Prototypes have been developed and test tracks built. The concept train floats in the air on a cushion of electromagnetic repulsion created between superconducting magnets in the train and coils in the aluminum guide track, traveling at speeds above 300 miles an hour without friction.

Several dates are significant in hovertrain development:

- 1965–1977 Aerotrain in France
- 1970–1973 Earith near Cambridge, England, managed by Tracked Hovercraft Ltd.
- 1973–1985 McAlpine energy firm in England used Professor Laithwaite's Maglev train.
- 1984–1995 Maglev link of less than half a mile between the main railway station and the airport in Birmingham, England, was closed because of maintenance problems.
- 1985 Dorfbahn Serfaus, an underground air-cushion funicular rapid transit system, operated in Austria on a 4,200-ft. line and reached a maximum speed of 25 mph.

A similar system is now in Narita International Airport outside Tokyo.

Another approach to difficult terrain is airboats, swamp boats or blow boats, which have been used since 1924 in such locations as the Everglades in Florida, a marshy grassland and subtropical wilderness usually covered with water for at least part of the year. A motorcycle engine and an airplane puller propeller are mounted aft on a lightweight Penn Yann hull, generating speeds up to 30 mph. They are used for sightseeing and hunting and are steered with a rudder like an airplane.

Hovercraft users fall into three broad categories:

- Recreational—fishing, duck-hunting, racing and swimming
- Commercial—farms, ranches, passenger service, amusement parks and exploration
- Governmental—coastal patrols, police patrols, fire-fighting tenders, marine rescue and naval operations

Passenger services have operated in Japan, Scotland, and England (Hovertravel), many linking airports.

One of the benefits of this type of amphibious craft is the ability to make them large. The British-built SR-N4 Mk-3 channel-crossing ferries were 185 ft. long and 73 ft. wide. Other benefits of ACVs include their very high water speed of 95 mph and the fact that they can make the transition from land to water and vice versa at speed, contrary to most wheeled or tracked amphibians.

Drawbacks are high fuel consumption and noise levels.

The first application of hovercraft in military use was the SR-N1 through SR-N6 craft built by Saunders-Roe and used by the UK joint forces. Currently the Royal Marines use the Griffin 2000 TRX as an operational craft which was recently deployed in Iraq.

In the U.S. during the 1960s the Bell SK-5 (SR-N5) was used in the Vietnam War by the Navy as a patrol craft in the Mekong Delta. The U.S. Army also experimented with it in Vietnam.

The Soviet Union was one of the first few nations to use a hovercraft, the Bora, as a guided missile corvette.

The Finnish navy designed an experimental missile attack hovercraft, Tuuli, in the late 1990s.

The Hellenic navy operates four Russian-designed Zubr-class LCAC, the world's largest military air-cushioned landing craft.

The hovercraft's ability to distribute its laden weight evenly across the surface below it makes it perfectly suited to the role of amphibious landing craft for military purposes.

The U.S. Navy LCAC can take troops and materials (if necessary an M1 Abrams tank) from ship to shore and can access more than 70 percent of the world's coastlines, as opposed to conventional landing craft, which have only about 17 percent of that coastline available to them for landing.

An ingenious use of hovercraft technology was in an amusement park in Disneyland. There Flying Saucers made of fiberglass, weighing 100 to 150 pounds, were guided simply by shifting body weight in the desired direction. Air was provided by huge fans beneath the floor, which was covered by more than 17,000 air valves. These opened only when the saucer was directly above them; as it passed beyond range, the valves snapped shut. Eight blowers, each driven by its own motor, kept 32 saucers aloft at once.

The idea of using an air cushion for vehicles was first explored by Sir John Thornycroft, a British engineer, in the 1870s. He built some experimental models using a plenum chamber with an open bottom.

The first rigid-wall hovercraft was designed by Austrian Dagbert Muller von Thomamuhl and built by the Imperial Austro-Hungarian Navy. It was called the Versuchsgleitboot-System Thomamuhl in 1915. It was 43 ft. long, 13 ft. wide and displaced about 6.5 tons with two propellers, each of which was driven by two six-cylinder 120-hp airplane engines. A fifth four-cylinder, 65-hp engine was used to blow air under the hull. A crew of five men attained a speed of 32 knots. It was tested for anti-submarine use in 1916 as a fast torpedo boat with a machine gun and several water bombs. In World War I Russia and Germany had naval designers who built experimental prototypes.

In 1927 Konstantin Tsioikovsky was said to be the first to provide scientific descriptions of air-cushion vehicles.

In the mid–1930s Soviet engineer Vladimir Levkov put together several experimental fast craft torpedo boats.

In 1931 Finnish engineer Toivo J. Kaario designed his Surface Glider, said to be the first functional vehicle.

Experimental vehicles were developed by the Soviet Union and the U.S. prior to and during World War II. During the war Charles J. Fletcher designed his Glidemobile while in the U.S. Navy.

In 1950 U.S. Colonel Melville W. Beardsley, an automotive engineer, invented a four-foot skirt to go around the hovercraft platform that was made of a rubber and plastic mixture.

In the mid–1950s the British mechanical engineer Sir Christopher Cockrell designed the SR-N1. It had a gas turbine engine, weighed four tons with a seven-ton payload, had a

6-in. rubberized skirt and did 50 knots on calm water. Accommodating three men, it was built by aircraft manufacturer Saunders-Roe.

In 1959 Curtiss Wright displayed its Model 2500 Air-Car. The 21-ft.-long, 8-ft.-wide, 5-ft.-high hover vehicle had dual headlights and taillights, a hood ornament, chrome trim and a convertible roof. Power came from two conventional, 300-hp aircraft engines. Speed was 60 mph in the four-passenger car. It hovered 6 to 12 in. over the earth with a propeller rotating parallel to the ground.

In England in the 1960s several larger designs for carrying passengers were developed by Saunders-Roe, Hovertravel, Vickers, British Hovercraft and Cushioncraft. Hovermarine developed its Sidewall Hovercraft, in which the sides of the hull projected down into the water to trap the cushion of air.

In 1965 the first air-cushion passenger vehicle to operate commercially in the U.S. went into service between San Francisco International Airport, Oakland International Airport and downtown San Francisco. Using radar, it could operate despite bad weather. The pusher propeller in the rear drives it up to 75 mph. The seven-ton craft makes the trip in 15 minutes for up to 15 passengers. It was built in Britain. Leased from Bell Aerosystems to the Port of Oakland and operated by SFO Helicopter Airlines, Inc., it operates safely in 4-ft. waves.

In 1966 two cross–Channel passenger hovercraft services were inaugurated. Hoverlloyd ran services from Ramsgate Harbor to Calais and Townsend Ferries also started a service to Calais from Dover which was soon superseded by that of Seaspeed.

In 1968 the world's first car-carrying hovercraft made their debut in England, the BHC Mountbatten class (SR-N4) models, 185-ft. long and 305 tons. Each was powered by four Rolls-Royce Proteus gas turbine engines. These were both used by rival operators Hoverlloyd and Seaspeed to operate regular car- and passenger-carrying services across the English Channel, which took around 30 minutes.

The later SR-N4 MK III had a capacity of 418 passengers and 60 cars.

The French-built SEDAM N500 Naviplane, with a capacity of 385 passengers and 45 cars, of which only one example entered service, was used intermittently for a few years on the cross–Channel service due to technical problems. The service ceased in 2000, after 32 years, due to the advancing age of the hovercraft.

In 1998 the U.S. Postal Service began using the British-built Hoverwork AP 1-88 to haul mail, freight and passengers to and from Bethel, Alaska, and eight small villages along the Kuskokwim River. The hovercraft is an attractive alternative to air-based delivery methods and is perfectly able to operate during the freeze-up period.

In addition to the manufacturers of hovercraft previously mentioned, the following firms have been prominent in design and production:

- Ford — Levacar Mach I, Glide Air
- Scat
- Air Cars, Inc. — Dobson Air Dart
- General Dynamics — Skip I
- Cushion Flight — Rev Flite

Hammacher-Schlemmer offers a two-passenger, 60-mph hoverboat in its mail-order catalog.

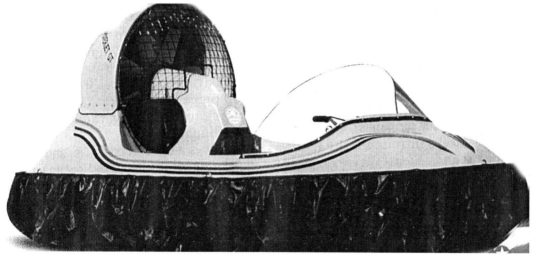

Top: Ford Levacar with Andrew A. Kucher, Research and Engineering (seated) and George W. Walker, Styling (standing) (from the collections of the Henry Ford). *Bottom:* Hammacher-Schlemmer's hovercraft.

Hovercraft, recognized as the first new form of transport since the jet plane and able to match the length of ships, are regarded as the potential motor and marine vehicle. As they grow cheaper and more efficient, wheelless dual cars may be able to leave roads and take to the countryside or water, providing that adequate hover traffic controls are in place.

In one sense hydroplanes, the nautical equivalent of the hovercraft, literally are flying when they are above the surface of the water.

Hovercraft have even found a spot in the popular Star Wars series, in which Luke Skywalker uses one. A James Bond movie has also featured one.

The following list of amphibious designs reveals some very interesting innovations and variations among amphibious vehicles.

1800s

The earliest known amphibious vehicles were carriages invented by Neopolitan Prince Raimondo de Sangro.

The Orukter Amphibolos (amphibious digger, dredge, scow or barge) has been called America's first self-propelled vehicle, designed by Oliver Evans. In 1865 the prototype 20-ton steam carriage was flat-bottomed, had paddle wheels and was equipped with axles and four sturdy but temporary wheels, driving one wheel by belt and pulleys from the flywheel shaft of the machine's twin-cylinder grasshopper beam 5-hp engine, which filled the wooden hull along with the wheels.

Evans filed the first American patent for a motor car in 1792.

Many do not realize that the majestic Conestoga covered freight wagons were amphibious. They carried supplies for the British in the French and Indian War. Later they were used by American pioneers headed over the Allegheny Mountains to the West, from the Revolutionary War to about 1850.

These "camels of the prairie," drawn by four- or six-horse teams with bells set on their collars, had high racked sides and boat-bottomed bodies that sloped to the center so that cargoes would not shift. These wagons had wooden, broad-rimmed wheels and iron tires to prevent them from bogging down in mud and were capable of carrying five tons. The upper part was usually painted red and the lower part blue. The white canvas roof was high and rounded. The name came from Conestoga, Pennsylvania, where they were first made.

A tramway-boat in 1899 was in service across two lakes north of Copenhagen, Denmark. Magrelem, a Swedish engineer, built this 11-ton amphibious steamboat with a 25-hp engine with action transmitted by a triple gear, either to the propeller or to the rimmed wheels. It accommodated 70 passengers.

1900–1909

Early in 1900 Julian P. Thomas designed the Waterland I and demonstrated it on the Hudson River in New York.

In 1905 the Frenchman Fournier produced what must have been the first true pleasure amphibian by combining an ordinary boat-type hull with a fairly conventional French automobile chassis.

The engine rested in a compartment amidships, separating the steersman in the bow from his passengers in their sideways-facing seats astern. A conventional shaft transmission drove both the rear axle and a single screw.

Also in 1905 came along T. Richmond and his three-wheeled carriage shaped like a canoe, powered by a three-cylinder gas engine. It had a set of hinged paddles attached to the wheels, which automatically opened and closed in the water.

As an ice boat it had attached spikes on the driving wheels and detachable runners under the forward wheel and inside the driving wheels. Any of these adjustments could be made in a few minutes.

At about the same time France produced the Traction Aerienne, whose chassis was its undercarriage.

In 1907 the Frenchman Ravailler developed his canoe-shaped car, also called Waterland, which resembled a small motor launch. It had a pressed steel hull to fit it for military service. A front axle was lodged in a space provided for it in the fore end. It had a two-cylinder De Dion Motor, 15 hp, which drove the screw in regular fashion or could transmit power to the road wheels merely by a change of gear through a side lever. Suspension was provided by a couple of semi-elliptical springs attached to brackets from the side of the craft. It could travel at 30 mph on land and a canvas awning protected passengers.

In 1909 Rear Admiral J. A. Howell, U.S. Navy, retired, and his young engineer son devised the vehicle they simply named Amphibian.

1910–1919

During the World War I period of 1914 to 1918 the following five amphibious designs were introduced.

In 1914 the 3,000-lb., 16.5-ft. Hydromotor was developed and promoted by William Massel and William Purcell. It drove in the same direction on land and sea and was to be made in four different models with the same chassis for each type of body:

- two-passenger roadster
- seven-passenger touring car
- light delivery truck
- seven-passenger limousine

It had a fully enclosed aluminum body and was propelled by a 6-35 Haynes engine but a Continental engine was planned for production. In the water it used a 16-in., three-bladed screw propeller which received a transmission of power from the rear axles by a special device. The rudder was mounted at the rear with the propeller. A single steering wheel operated both the front wheels and the rudder.

In the water a patented bronze sliding device locked the water out of the axle housing. All joints were made tight with two-in. brass bands riveted at the edges. Packing around the wheels and propeller kept out water. The Hydromotor traveled at speeds of 25 mph in the water and 60 mph on land. It was tested at the Panama-Pacific International Exposition in 1915 on San Francisco Bay.

In 1915 the German Zeiner designed his Monocar with a chain transmission following cyclecar practice.

In 1916 the blunt-prow Delia or motor Duck was claimed to be the invention of a machinist Michael de Cosmo. It had a compact, fully-enclosed body and the tires were Lee Zigzag. The springs were contained within the body. In the water the driver switched a lever that engaged a friction wheel which operated a prop shaft, allowing travel at 10 mph. It had a rudder attached to the rear for steering.

In 1917 George Monnot, who was a bicycle and automobile dealer, introduced his Hydrocar, part boat and part automobile. He built two prototypes.

It had a boattail back end, a Hercules four-cylinder engine, and a special propeller mounted up front near the radiator grille, which made it run backwards on the water. There were two steering wheels at opposite ends. It did 25 mph on land and 89 mph in the water.

When transitioning from water to land, the land wheels took a firm grip and the vehicle could be driven forward. If extended water travel was planned, removal of the axles and wheels was recommended. In a military application it could be used as an armored vehicle.

The Hydrometer, designed by William Mazzei in 1917, was a boat-shaped roadster on large-diameter wire wheels. It had a conventional transmission, a single screw and rudder at the rear and a Continental engine.

1920s

In 1921 the diminutive English two-passenger Cyclecar came out, with a watertight hull and paddle wheels on its rear wheels to drive it when afloat in the water. It was equipped with a 2.5-hp, two-cycle engine that propelled it on land at 30 mph.

In 1922 the Frenchman Vargoz created his aquatic Ford, its chassis extended at both ends to support two enormous lateral floats. The drive went to all four wheels, which were shod with discs incorporating paddles. Only the front ones steered.

In 1926 Dr. Thomas A. Jaggar, volcanologist, designed the Sea Turtle, a 16-ft. boat built on a Ford chassis. When it went into the water, steel paddle wheels were put on the rear axles. These kicked the boat along, while the disc front wheels served as rudders.

Also in 1926 Izzy Cholfin operated his C7270 1926 Buick as a water taxi on the Charles River in Massachusetts at a speed of 10 mph.

In 1926 the students of Wisconsin University attempted to make a floating car out of a Model T Ford.

A couple of years later there were reports of a curious, streamlined amphibian driven by a rear-mounted, 70-hp aero-engine with a pusher airscrew. Speeds of 80 mph on land and 25 mph on water were claimed.

In 1928 George Powell of Powell Mobile Boat Works built a combination auto and motorboat equipped with a Ford engine and Ford land running gear. It could go 40 mph on land or a firm beach, 10 mph on the water and 6 mph in shallow water. It could also function on snow or ice.

In 1929 the Voran amphibian was commissioned by the German Admiralty as a small fishing patrol cruiser for use on the marshy North Sea coastline, linking small islands with the mainland. It measured 22.3 ft. long, weighed four tons and had full radio equipment and four-wheel drive. It also had an all-independent suspension designed with twin rear wheels. The single screw was in the rear and a 40-bhp, four-cylinder Opel engine propelled it 15 mph on land and 7 mph in the water. It was licensed for the street.

This motor boat on wheels had the drive to the wheels designed by the Voran Automobilbau-Aktiengesellschaft in Berlin; Hoppe & Krooss built it. The front wheels had single 30 × 5 in. tires, and the rear wheels double. All the parts likely to be damaged by water were protected by leather and rubber sleeves and tallow and felt packing.

1930s

In 1931 George McLaughlin, a garage owner, built an amphibious vehicle powered by a 70-hp engine with an airplane propeller shaft. Buoyancy was furnished by pontoons under the running boards. It had a speed of 50 mph on land and 25 mph on water.

Also in 1931 Scotsman Leslie Lambert's Hydrocar joined a small wooden-hulled boat body with automotive underpinnings. It had a dead axle at the rear, a rear prop, transverse springs and front-wheel drive. Coachwork was of mahogany launch type. There were no front fenders and only basic ones at the rear. Cowl ventilators were used to deliver air to the concealed radiator. The engine in the prototype was an Austin 7 with a 4ED Meadows planned for the production model.

In 1934 in Germany Hans Trippel was recognized as one of the finest designers of amphibians.

So successful was his prototype that production began with the round-nosed SG6, an antecedent of the Amphicar, featuring four-wheel drive and a four-cylinder Adler engine, plus a propeller for use in the water. This model was later powered by a six-cylinder, 2.5-liter Opel engine. A new version appeared in 1937 with front-wheel drive and a two-liter Adler engine.

Flamboyant in his promotions and demonstrations to prove the versatility of his vehicles, he performed a number of stunts, including traveling down a flight of steps in a public building.

In 1934 came the Precursor I from Englishman Alfred Burgess, a punt onto which you drove a complete automobile. Swinging arms were then coupled to the rear tires, these being connected with twin lateral screws. Similar arms at the front linked the car steering with independent brake drums on each propeller, giving directional control akin to that of a tank. Only high and reverse gears were used on the water and the inventor's 1927 Morris-Cowley touring car could make 8.5 knots with the current and 3.5 against it.

In 1934 in Germany an inventor attached vast pontoon wheels to each corner of a stock two-liter Opel 6 sedan. The front wheels steered with paddle propulsion at the rear and propeller blades. The vehicle reached speeds of 30 mph. On the road the pontoons, of course, were removed.

In 1935 German inventor Jacob Boudig crossed the English Channel in an amphibian with paddle-wheel drive at the rear. Land speed was 20 mph.

Again in 1935 Germany introduced the Land-Wasser-Schlepper, a towing vehicle weighing 13 tons and having a crew of 20.

In 1936 Gulf Oil built a wader which used a Ford V-8 engine and had ten speeds forward and six in reverse. The wheels were hollow.

In 1937 a German inventor of an amphibious craft designed it to go from land to water and vice versa without mechanical adjustments. It had a speed of 90 mph on land and 15 mph in the water.

That same year the Donald Roebling Alligator, a unit-bodied convertible, was built. It had a rear-mounted, four-cycle, 43-bhp Triumph Herald engine which drove the rear wheels and a twin-screw propeller. It did 6.5 knots on the water and 70 mph on the road.

In 1939 the Dutch produced the DAF, which had a centrally-located engine and all-independent springing via four-wheel drive with twin citron front ends. Both driving units could steer but, of course, not at the same time.

Also in 1939 German designers built a prototype amphibious vehicle run by a motorcycle engine. When the vehicle was in the water the hinged propeller shaft was lowered below the surface and its speed was 12 mph. Steering was with motorcycle-type handlebars. It had a watertight body supported by three diminutive wheels, the single rear wheel being used both to drive and to steer the vehicle on land.

In 1939 in England there was an amphibious vehicle used at a popular South Coast town which had both road wheels and a sea-going propeller. A gearing device attached to the transmission engaged the correct method of propulsion. It had an old Model T Ford chassis and was designed for shallow water.

Also in England in the 1930s a wader was used to travel between the mainland and Burgh Island, in South Devon. It had a Caterpillar track and the passengers sat on a high platform. Power was provided by a Diesel engine which was coupled to the tracks through a conventional differential gear and chains.

In the late 1930s the Tempo had a twin-engine crosscountry trainer (each 600cc two-cycle engine drove a separate axle). It was waterproof, if not wholly amphibious.

Finally the Morris Gosling in England, tiller-steered, was an amphibious trolley designed by Sir Alec Issigonis and powered by a 2-bhp Villiers engine.

1940s

In 1940 Paul Pankotan patented his amphibious Auto-Boat with retractable wheels and undercarriage and with all the controls in the front seat of the four- to seven-passenger vehicle. Shifting levers lifted the front wheels to convert the vehicle to a speedboat in 15 seconds. It was propelled by a 90-hp gasoline engine and speeds were 35 mph in the water and 90 mph on land.

After World War II was over in 1946 the ducks (DUKW), part bus, part truck, part boat, began to be converted to civilian use. Some 225 are in use as rescue vehicles for fire departments in flood-prone towns. Hundreds were made into odd-looking dump trucks or wreckers or even shark hunters.

The major use has been for sightseeing tours. Ducks for this purpose generally have used bus seats installed. These short land and water trips are widespread on the remodeled, reconstituted and refurbished vehicles. The following locations all offer some form of sightseeing trip using these vehicles:

- Chicago
- Boston
- Seattle
- Memphis
- Branson, Mo.

Surplus amphibious duck in Branson, Mo., sightseeing (courtesy Branson Ride The Ducks Tours).

- Hot Springs, Ga.
- Wisconsin Dells
- Portland
- Toronto
- London

The Russians produced a modified duck, the ZH-485, with extra cargo space and a tailgate.

The Japanese have an amphibian sightseeing bus, fueled by cooking oil.

In 1946 the post-war German Amphi-Ranger was produced, with its hull made of aluminum alloy. Some 100 were built.

In the late 1940s Ford Motor Company created its General Purpose Amphibian (GPA), a converted 1¼-ton 4 × 4 truck, with auxiliary flotation equipment attached. It traveled the channel from England to France.

Also in the late 1940s plastics were featured on an East German amphibian, the MBB (Messerschmitt, Bolkow and Blohm), which was driven by a rear-mounted BMW two-liter engine with a five-speed gearbox. It could travel 65 mph on land and climb a 60-degree slope.

At the close of the decade in France there were experiments with hydrojet propulsion, both on the four-ton 4 × 4 Marmon-Bocquet and on a small, rear-engine, off-road vehicle with an air-cooled Panhard Dyna engine.

1950s

In 1951 the Marmon-Herrington Company produced the amphibious Rhino, invented by Elie P. Aghnides, which had been under construction and exhaustive tests since 1948. With Hydrojet propulsion deep water was no problem.

For highway operation only a narrow rubber tread touched the road. In soft places, the traction area was increased with every inch of sinkage of the wheels.

SPECIFICATIONS

Weight . . . . Approximately 10,000 lb.
Overall length . . . . 19 ft.
Width . . . . 9 ft. 6 in.
Height . . . . 9 ft. 10 in. to top of cockpit
Body . . . . ¼-in. aluminum riveted to steel
. . . . support members.
Front wheels . . . . Hemispheroidal, 6 ft. in diameter,
inclined outward at top
15 degrees from the vertical.
Each wheel weighs 1,500 lb.
Rear wheels . . . . .Hemispheroidal, smaller than front.
Drive . . . . . Either two-wheel or four-wheel drive on land.

Thornton no-spin differential may be cut
in or out as required by terrain.

Hydrojet . . . . . For power in water, pumps 1,100 gallons per
minute from intake and discharges
through a full swiveling steel nozzle
outlet at stern.

Power . . . . Ford Industrial 6-cylinder engine, 110 hp at
3,000 rpm.

Steering . . . . Gear linkage of chain drive
. . . . type leading to rear axle.

Climb . . . . . Maximum angle of climb is 65 percent grade.

Speed . . . . . . Maximum highway speed of prototype is 45
mph.

In the early 1950s Englishman York Noble came out with a Volkswagen-powered device with 20 wheels, 18 of which were driven.

At the other end of the scale in 1952 German Karl Baier introduced a tiny pontoon boat as his version of an amphibious craft.

In 1952 Russia produced a modified version of the U.S. duck, the ZH-485, 6 × 6 amphibious truck which turned out to be an almost identical vehicle.

In 1952 a German mechanic built an amphibious car with all moving parts except the wheels within the body of the hull (brakes, transmission steering system, and control cables). No changes were necessary when driving from land to water or back again.

In 1954 the GMC Truck & Coach Division of General Motors Corporation, under a Detroit Arsenal contract, developed the new Super Duck amphibian truck. It could carry a four-ton payload. Powered by a 302-cu.-in., 145-hp GMC engine, it had a plastic cab, an automatic tire inflation system and a Hydra-Matic transmission. The XM 147 vehicle was 32 ft. long, 102 in. wide and 7 ft., 5 in. high to the top of the cab.

In 1955 from Sweden came the Allskog Aquacar of fiberglass construction and a gull-wing layout.

In 1956 L. G. Wood, an English boatbuilder, constructed a three-wheeled amphibious cyclecar propelled in the water by paddle blades welded to the rear driving wheels. The single front wheel took care of the steering. The tiny two-cycle Anzani engine gave a land speed of 20 mph.

In 1957 a three-wheeled craft made from three airplanes and one jet canopy was produced. It was powered by a 65-hp Continental aircraft engine and ran on wheels, skis or floats, although it was licensed as a car. It did 115 mph on the road, 65 mph on snow and 30 mph on the water. The canopy was raised by two hydraulic cylinders.

A second prototype could reach 147 mph and was steered by the feet with hydraulic brakes for the two rear wheels and a booster-powered steel plate which dropped between the skis.

In 1959 John Brush devised his Packard boat-auto combination amphibious catamaran. He used two modified cracked-up flying boats for their hulls. Next a frame of steel tubing was designed to connect the two floats, and troughs for the car wheels were fabricated from high-tensile aircraft-aluminum sheet. Landing-gear wheels were altered and remounted, one on each float for trailing on the highway.

The 21-ft.-long, 13-ft.-wide catamaran was folded down and into itself by a hand crank. Its height when folded was 6 ft. It was steered from the driver's seat.

1960s

In 1960 in France Marcel Revers attached a motorboat propeller to his Volkswagen's engine and sealed the car so that it would float on the Seine River.

In 1960 Al Dauphin, a cabinetmaker, had his Ann Phibi, a 34- by 8-ft. amphibian with retractable wheels and a water jet for travel afloat. Inside was a galley, a bathroom and bunks for four. A 300-hp Chrysler engine with automatic transmission drove the vehicle's rear wheels on the highway. Despite its 10,000-lb. bulk, it could get up to 60 mph on land. Water speed was about eight knots. A hydrojet powered by a 60-hp engine was used for marine propulsion.

Dauphin cut frame weight by welding together 2¼-in. tubular steel. The hull was only ¼ in. thick on the sides, front and back and ½ in. thick on the top and bottom. Fiberglassed ⅛-in. plywood was used on both sides. Inside the partitions and other paneling were slabs of Styrofoam sandwiched between sheets of 1/14-in. plastic. The engine was mounted right next to the boat controls and sat over the rear wheels it drove.

Undeniably the most famous civilian amphibious vehicle was the four-passenger Amphicar. Between 1960 and 1968 Hans Trippel in Germany produced 3,300 for world markets.

It was regarded as 85 percent car and 15 percent boat, resembling a tail-finned inboard motorboat when afloat, the only mass-produced amphibious vehicle ever made for consumer use, especially for taking vacations.

German Amphicar amphibian (courtesy Marc Schlemmer).

Top: German Amphicar coming out of the water (courtesy Marc Schlemmer). *Bottom:* Amphicar amphibian sports application (Detroit Public Library, National Automotive History Collection).

Mets star Ken Boyer at Shea Stadium receives the annual Howard Clothes most valuable player award and an Amphicar from Amphibian Motors, Long Island distributor (The Detroit Public Library, National Automotive History Collection).

It was built with available components from Denmark, England, and other countries, resulting in what is probably the first "world car." The design was inspired by a German World War II amphibious military car, the Shwimmwagen.

Trippel's predecessor prototype vehicle was the 1959 Alligator, which had the steering wheel in the center and was powered by an Austin-Healy Sprite 435 engine. This was exhibited at the Geneva Salon and the name Amphicar evolved from what was originally called the Eurocar. Financial backing came from the Harold Quaandt industrial combine in Germany.

It was available in two basic series, a sporty-looking, streamlined convertible and a sedan. The 1961–1964 early versions had different sheet metal (the smooth rear fin models) with a single-piece bumper, different axle shafts and different props. The 1965–1967 cars had improved shafts and props, different body components and a two-piece bumper.

Stock colors were red, white, blue and green, with white interiors.

It had a flat bottom, an undercut front end, a small trunk in front, a full rear seat and small fins on the rear fenders.

The doors were made with rounded corners and used rubber cushions and extra locking levers to keep the water out. There was a zip-down large rear window and roll-up side windows. The manual fold-down top was plastic and vinyl-coated. The upholstery and floor mats were soil-resistant and waterproof. All seams in the body were welded.

The front wheels acted as rudders when the car was afloat. A switch on the dashboard converted from land to water propulsion and back and a tall pole with a yellow light on top was intended for night navigation.

The Amphicar proved to be a prime draw for advertisers, but owners characteristically complained of the following problems:

- sluggish performance
- lack of local service and parts availability
- uncertain ride, handling
- frequent re-greasing required
- engine, cooling and carburetor problems
- vague steering
- nonworking brakes
- leaking doors
- lack of buoyancy tanks
- failure to meet emissions requirements, U.S. Coast Guard rules
- noisy
- corrosion and rust

SPECIFICATIONS

Engine

Type	Water-cooled, OHV pushrod operated
Number of cylinders	4
Bore	2.718 in.
Stroke	2.992 in.
Compression ratio	8.0:1
Capacity	1147 cc (70 cu. in.)
Maximum hp (SAE)	43 at 4,750 rpm
Maximum torque	61 lb./ft. at 2250 rpm

Lubrication

Pump, make and type	Hobourn-Eaton, high-capacity double eccentric rotor
Oil filter	Purolator or A.C. Delco full-flow by-pass filter (replaceable unit)

Electrical

Type	Lucas, 12 volt

Fuel Consumption

On the road	Approx. 32 mpg
On the water	Approx. 11½ gal./hr.

Fuel System

Fuel tank	Located in trunk, filler also in trunk
Carburetor	Solex downdraft
Fuel pump	A. C. mechanical

Ignition System

Spark plugs–type	Lodge CNY, ½-in. reach
Firing order	1-3-4-2

Suspension

Type . . . . Fully independent on all four wheels. Coil
                 Coil springs controlled by direct-acting
                 telescopic shock absorbers.

Rear Axle

Gear type . . . . Hypoid bevel
Drive (land) . . . . Swing axle
    (water) . . . . Twin propeller shafts
Ratio 4.72:1

Gearbox

Type . . . . . Synchromesh, four forward speeds plus reverse

Water Transmission

Type . . . . 1 forward, 1 reverse
Ratio 1:3

Dimensions

Overall length . . . . 170.31 in.
Overall width . . . . 60.31 in.
Overall height . . . . 59.84 in.
Wheelbase . . . . 82.67 in.
Track-front . . . . 47.31 in.
Rear . . . . 49.20 in.
Ground clearance . . . . 10.00 in.
Weight with fuel . . . . 2292.8 lb.
Maximum permissible Payload . . . . 660 lb.
Weight distribution (app.) . . . . 38% front
                 62% rear

Performance

Gear speeds © 4,750 rpm . . . . 1st — 15.6 mph
                 2nd — 24.4 mph
                 3rd — 41.3 mph
                 4th — 70.0 mph
Maximum speed — land . . . . 75 mph
Cruising speed — land . . . . 60–65 mph
Maximum speed — water . . . . 8–10 mph
Climbing ability — fully loaded . . . . . 1st gear — 42% grade
                 2nd gear — 26% grade
                 3rd gear — 14% grade
                 4th gear — 7% grade

Brake System

Type . . . . Hydraulic internal expanding.
                 Front — two leading shoes.
                 Rear — leading and
                 trailing shoes.
Operation . . . . Foot pedal coupled hydraulically
                 to all four wheels. Handbrake
                 coupled mechanically to
                 rear wheels only.

Wheels and Tires

Tire size . . . . 6.40 in. × 13 in.
Tire pressure — front . . . . 24 psi
rear . . . . 28 psi

Steering

Type . . . . Worm and roller
Turning circle . . . . 36 ft. 5 in.
Steering wheel diameter . . . . 15¾ in.

Capacities

Fuel tank . . . . 13 gal. (approx.)
Engine sump . . . . 4.8 qt. H.D. engine oil
Gearbox . . . . 4.2 pt. SAE 90 gear oil
Water transmission . . . . 2.1 pt.
Cooling system . . . . 8.5 qt., including heater

Some units were specially equipped for the U.S. Coast Guard and police patrol duty.

At the peak of activity there were five distributors in the U.S. and 118 dealers nationwide.

The International Amphicar Owners' Club has had members in 40 U.S. states and eight foreign countries and an overall membership of 278. Activities include organizing annual conventions, producing newsletters ("Wheels 'N Waves") and selling merchandise (apparel, patches, etc.).

Promotional efforts for the Amphicar included displays at Montgomery Ward department stores and its use in TV product commercials, movies, parades and scale models. Radio and TV stations purchased them for remote programs, disaster coverage and as mobile billboards. President Lyndon Baines Johnson used one on the lake at his Texas ranch.

Several attempts were made to emphasize the versatility of the Amphicar, including the following:

- Two Amphicars crossed the English Channel from Dover to Calais
- An Amphicar drove down the Yukon River in Alaska
- An Amphicar ran 500 miles up the Trinity River in Texas from Houston to Dallas
- An Amphicar made a trip up the Hudson River in New York through the Barge Canal to Lake Champlain and on to Montreal
- An Amphicar was driven straight across the Straits of Mackinac, avoiding the bridge toll.

In 1961 the Canadian Jiger GAV prototype appeared.

Now turning to some vehicles with less publicity, in 1962 John H. Bower of Pratt Institute designed his aluminum Amphicamper, winning an Alcoa Student Design Merit Award. It seated five people, was 16 ft. long, and had a top speed of 60 mph on land and five knots in the water.

Also in 1962 the two-seater Snow Bunny was produced by the Dynamech Corporation. It had independently mounted nylon rollers that spun on the closely spaced tracks that rotated around the engine in the rear and under the seat. For making turns a combination brake and clutch called a differentiator gave brakes to one track while powering the other. A two-cylinder 18-hp air-cooled engine made by an outboard-motor maker was mounted in the rear with a louver and blower to keep the compartment at 180 degrees. The wiring system was disconnected if fumes from the fuel (gasoline or kerosene) leaked into the chamber.

In 1963 the two-man Husky Duck was created. It was from Neumann and Bennets and had a plastic and wood frame 4 ft. wide and 8 ft. long. It rode on six low-power vinyl tires with fins on the sides for propulsion. It traveled at 18 mph on land and four knots on the water.

Plans were also offered to do-it-yourselfers.

In 1966 the Lockheed Aircraft Service Company offered the Terra Star amphibian. It ran 45 mph on the road and six knots on the water using 12 wheels. It employed the major wheel/minor wheel system with triple wheel assemblies mounted on secondary axles. Both civilian and military versions were developed.

In 1969 Recreatives Industries, Inc., began producing its six-wheel-drive amphibious vehicles: Max II, Max IV and the Buffalo All-Terrain Truck. These were the choice of U.S. Special Forces in Afghanistan.

A phenomenal number of new amphibious ATVs came on the market in the 1960s. While similar to each other in some respects, each had unique features which warrant the specifications comparison which follows. Note that the tire size of amphibious vehicles is presented in a decimal format.

The Amphicat was characterized by extreme flotation and low unit load.

Max two-passenger ATV (courtesy Recreatives Industries, Inc.).

Top: Max four-passenger ATV. *Bottom:* Max Buffalo all-terrain truck (both photographs courtesy Recreatives Industries, Inc.).

Dimensions

	MAX II		MAX IV		Buffalo	
	in	cm	in	cm	in	cm
A) Wheelbase	50	127	58	147	58	147
B) Overall Height	37	94	42	107	52	132
C) Entry Height	28	71	30	76	29	74
D) Seat to Floor	13	33	15 (F) 14 (R) - 38 (F) 36 (R)		15	38
E) Seat Back to Leg Room	44	112	34 (F) 25 (R) - 86 (F) 64 (R)		34	86
F) Seat Back to Dashboard	27	69	29	74	24	61
Seat Width	35	89	41	104	41	104
Vehicle Width Inside	43	109	47	119	48	122
Overall Length	86	218	96	244	99	251

max II
TWO PASSENGER

Weight	710 lbs. (322 kilos.)	Wheel Base	50 in. (127 cm.)
Gross Vehicle Weight	1310 lbs. (594 kilos.) includes passengers, cargo and accessories	Seating	2 Persons
		Fuel Capacity	5 U.S. Gallons (19 liters)
		Transmission	T-20 Skid Steer
Gross Permissible Weight in Water	1210 lbs. (549 kilos.) includes passengers, cargo and accessories	Drive Chain	530/520 O-Ring *
		Axles	1-1/4 in. Heavy-Duty Steel (3.175 cm.)
Length	86 in. (218 cm.)		
Height	37 in. (94 cm.)	Towing Capacity	1,000 lbs. (454 kilos.)
Width	56 in. (142 cm.)		

max IV
FOUR PASSENGER

Weight	805 lbs. (365 kilos.)	Wheel Base	58 in. (147 cm.)
Gross Vehicle Weight	1805 lbs. (728 kilos.) includes passengers, cargo and accessories	Seating	4 Persons
		Fuel Capacity	5 U.S. Gallons (19 liters)
		Transmission	T-20 Skid Steer
Gross Permissible Weight in Water	1305 lbs. (592 kilos.) includes passengers, cargo and accessories	Drive Chain	530 O-Ring *
		Axles	1-1/4 in. Heavy-Duty Steel (3.175 cm.)
Length	96 in. (244 cm.)		
Height	42 in. (107 cm.)	Towing Capacity	1,000 lbs. (454 kilos.)
Width	56 in. (142 cm.)		

BUFFALO
ALL TERRAIN TRUCK

Weight	Approx. 1135 lbs. (515 kilos.)	Bed Dimension	53 in. Long (135 cm.)
Gross Vehicle Weight	2135 lbs. (968 kilos.) includes passengers, cargo and accessories		51 in. Wide (130 cm.) 10 in. High (25 cm.)
		Fuel Capacity	5 U.S. Gallons (19 liters)
Gross Permissible Weight in Water	1635 lbs. (742 kilos.) includes passengers, cargo and accessories	Transmission	T-20 Skid Steer
		Drive Chain	530/520 O-ring
		Axles	1-1/4 in. Heavy-Duty Steel (3.175 cm.)
Length	99 in. (251 cm.)		
Height	52 in. (132 cm.)	Towing Capacity	1,000 lbs. (454 kilos.)
Width	57 in. (145 cm.)		
Wheel Base	58 in. (147 cm.)	* ON MOST MODELS	

Max ATV specifications (courtesy Recreatives Industries, Inc.).

T-20 Skid Steer Transmission

The heart of the six-wheel drive ATV. Designed by the Warner-Gear division of Borg-Warner and manufactured by Recreatives, Inc.. More than 40,000 have been sold. Provides true six-wheel drive with no differential slippage. The T-20 is really two transmissions, one for the right side and one for the left. The entire transmission is enclosed in an aluminum housing with no external brakes.

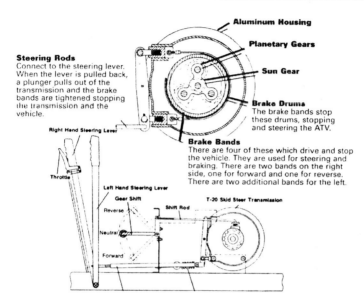

Aluminum Housing

Planetary Gears

Sun Gear

Steering Rods
Connect to the steering lever. When the lever is pulled back, a plunger pulls out of the transmission and the brake bands are tightened stopping the transmission and the vehicle.

Brake Drums
The brake bands stop these drums, stopping and steering the ATV.

Right Hand Steering Lever

Brake Bands
There are four of these which drive and stop the vehicle. They are used for steering and braking. There are two bands on the right side, one for forward and one for reverse. There are two additional bands for the left.

Throttle

Left Hand Steering Lever

Gear Shift

Reverse

Neutral

Forward

Shift Rod

T-20 Skid Steer Transmission

When the lever is pulled back, rod pulls plunger from transmission, tightening brake bands and stopping that side of the transmission and applying the brakes on that side of the ATV. All MAX ATVs are spring-loaded in the forward position. That is, when you open the throttle, you don't have to push the lever forward to go forward.

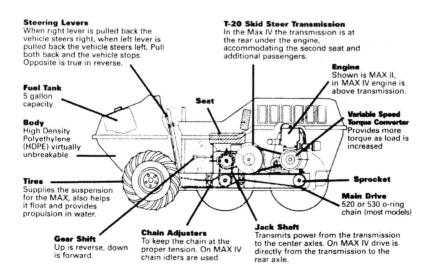

Steering Levers
When right lever is pulled back the vehicle steers right, when left lever is pulled back the vehicle steers left. Pull both back and the vehicle stops. Opposite is true in reverse.

T-20 Skid Steer Transmission
In the Max IV the transmission is at the rear under the engine, accommodating the second seat and additional passengers.

Engine
Shown is MAX II, in MAX IV engine is above transmission.

Fuel Tank
5 gallon capacity

Seat

Variable Speed Torque Converter
Provides more torque as load is increased

Body
High Density Polyethylene (HDPE) virtually unbreakable

Tires
Supplies the suspension for the MAX, also helps it float and provides propulsion in water.

Sprocket

Main Drive
520 or 530 o-ring chain (most models)

Gear Shift
Up is reverse, down is forward.

Chain Adjusters
To keep the chain at the proper tension. On MAX IV chain idlers are used.

Jack Shaft
Transmits power from the transmission to the center axles. On MAX IV drive is directly from the transmission to the rear axle.

Max amphibious vehicle components (courtesy Recreatives Industries, Inc.).

Specifications

Body material . . . . Cycolac
Frame material . . . . Steel
Starter . . . . Recoil
Engine make . . . . Sachs
Engine horsepower 16
Engine type 1-cycle, 2-stroke
Dry weight . . . . 396 lb.
Payload . . . . 480 lb.
Overall length . . . . 81 in.
Overall width . . . . 52 in.
Overall height . . . . 34 in.
Tire size 11.5.20
Number of wheels 6
Track . . . . 40 in.
Transmission type . . . . Torque converter
Transmission make . . . . Borg-Warner
Final drive . . . . Chain
Steering . . . . Disc
Ground clearance . . . . 8 in.
Braking . . . . Drums

Performance

Maximum land speed . . . . 37 mph
Maximum water speed . . . . 2 mph
Range on land . . . . 150 miles
Maximum gradient (fully loaded) . . . . 45 degrees
Amphibious drive . . . . Tire rotation

The Attex had an interesting configuration.

Specifications

Engine horsepower 20.5
Engine type 2-stroke
Dry weight . . . . 450 lb.
Overall length . . . . 82.5 in.
Overall width . . . . 53 in.
Number of wheels 6
Ground clearance . . . . 8 in.
Braking . . . . Disc

Performance

Maximum land speed . . . . 35 mph
Maximum water speed . . . . 4 mph
Range on land . . . . 5 hrs.

The Coot had extra low gearing to push its way through formidable rugged terrain.

Specifications

Body material . . . . Steel
Frame material . . . . Steel

Starter . . . . Electric
Engine make . . . . Tecumseh
Engine horsepower 12
Engine type . . . . 1 cycle, 4 stroke
Dry weight . . . . 1,020 lb.
Payload . . . . 1,000 lb.
Overall length . . . . 91 in.
Overall width . . . . 64 in.
Overall height . . . . 38 in.
Tire size 8.85-15
Number of wheels 4
Track . . . . 64 in.
Transmission type . . . . Torque converter
Transmission make . . . . Apex
Steering . . . . Worm
Ground clearance . . . . 11 in.
Braking . . . . Disc

PERFORMANCE

Maximum land speed . . . . 20 mph
Maximum water speed . . . . 5 mph with prop
Range on land . . . . 2.5 hrs.
Maximum gradient (fully loaded) . . . . 75 degrees

The Desert Rat was produced by the RAT Corporation (Who Else?).

SPECIFICATIONS

Engine horsepower 7
Dry weight . . . . 330 lb.
Overall length . . . . 86.5 in.
Overall width . . . . 48 in.
Overall height . . . . 38 in.
Tire size . . . . 16 × 15
Number of wheels 4
Track . . . . 48 in.
Transmission type . . . . Variable speed pulley

Pug Engineering was responsible for the Maverick.

SPECIFICATIONS

Engine horsepower 5.5
Dry weight . . . . 250 lb.
Overall length . . . . 76 in.
Overall width . . . . 57 in.
Overall height . . . . 30 in.
Tire size . . . . 16 × 12
Number of wheels 3
Track . . . . 48 in.
Seating capacity 2
Transmission type . . . . Centrifugal clutch

The Moto Brusso boasted a rather distinguished sounding name.

SPECIFICATIONS

Engine make . . . . Sachs
Engine horsepower 14
Engine type 2-stroke
Dry weight . . . . 475 lb.
Overall length . . . . 87 in.
Overall width . . . . 36 in.
Number of wheels 4
Ground clearance . . . . 11 in.
Braking . . . . Drum

PERFORMANCE

Maximum land speed . . . . 30 mph
Range on land . . . . 140 miles

The Muskateer had its engine mounted behind the seat.

SPECIFICATIONS

Body material . . . . Fiberglass
Frame material . . . . Steel
Starter . . . . Recoil on electric
Engine make . . . . Ilo
Engine horsepower 8–16
Engine type 1-2-cylinder, 2-stroke
Dry weight . . . . 520 lb.
Payload . . . . 500 lb.
Overall length . . . . 84 in.
Overall width . . . . 52 in.
Overall height . . . . 32 in.
Track . . . . 41.5 in.
Transmission . . . . Torque converter
Transmission make . . . . Own
Ground clearance . . . . 5 in.
Braking . . . . Disc
Final drive . . . . V chain
Steering . . . . Lever

PERFORMANCE

Maximum land speed . . . . 25 mph
Maximum water speed . . . . 5 mph with prop
Maximum gradient (fully loaded) . . . . 45 degrees
Amphibious drive . . . . Opt prop

The Scrambler tried to live up to its name.

SPECIFICATIONS

Engine make . . . . B&S
Engine horsepower 7
Engine type 4-stroke
Dry weight . . . . 450 lb.

Overall length . . . . 95 in.
Overall width . . . . 54 in.
Number of wheels 6
Ground clearance . . . . 6 in.

PERFORMANCE

Maximum land speed . . . . 20 mph
Maximum water speed . . . . 2 mph

Chevrolet's Sidewinder was articulated and had all-wheel drive.

SPECIFICATIONS

Engine horsepower . . . . 7 or 9
Dry weight . . . . 285 lb.
Overall length . . . . 80 in.
Overall width . . . . 60 in.
Overall height . . . . 33 in.
Tire size . . . . 16 × 12
Number of wheels 3
Seating capacity 3
Transmission type . . . . Drive chains

The Sierra Trail Boss presented these specifications:

Engine make . . . . Kohler
Engine horsepower 20
Engine type 2-stroke
Dry weight . . . . 665 lb.
Overall length . . . . 89 in.
Overall width . . . . 57 in.
Number of wheels 6
Ground clearance . . . . 6.75 in.

PERFORMANCE

Maximum land speed . . . . 35 mph
Maximum water speed . . . . 5 mph

The Stalker had a provocative name.

SPECIFICATIONS

Engine make . . . . Tecumseh
Engine horsepower 12
Engine type 4-stroke
Dry weight . . . . 490 lb.
Overall length . . . . 92.5 in.
Overall width . . . . 63.5 in.
Number of wheels 6
Ground clearance . . . . 8 in.

PERFORMANCE

Maximum land speed . . . . 30 mph
Maximum water speed . . . . 4 mph
Range on land . . . . 5 hrs.

The Starcraft amphibian hinted at a higher capability.

SPECIFICATIONS

Engine make . . . . Ilo
Engine horsepower 14
Engine type 2-stroke
Dry weight . . . . 460 lb.
Overall length . . . . 72 in.
Overall width . . . . 52 in.
Number of wheels 6
Braking . . . . Disc

PERFORMANCE

Maximum land speed . . . . 30 mph
Maximum water speed . . . . 3 mph

AMF produced the Sur-Trek, an articulated model.

SPECIFICATIONS

Engine make . . . . Ilo
Engine horsepower 20
Engine type 2-stroke
Dry weight . . . . 600 lb.
Overall length . . . . 126 in.
Overall width . . . . 50 in.
Number of wheels 8
Transmission type . . . . Salsbury
Ground clearance . . . . 7.5 in.
Braking . . . . Disc

PERFORMANCE

Maximum land speed . . . . 30 mph
Maximum water speed . . . . 2 mph
Range on land . . . . 6–9 hrs.

Andy Stewart's Terra Gator spoke of the swamps where danger lurked.

SPECIFICATIONS

Engine horsepower 9
Dry weight . . . . 350 lb.
Overall length . . . . 70 in.
Overall width . . . . 49 in.
Overall height . . . . 34 in.
Tire size . . . . 16 × 12
Number of wheels 6

Seating capacity 2
Transmission type . . . . Torque converter

Du Bay's Terra Kart had the following specifications:

Engine horsepower 4
Dry weight . . . . 250 lb.
Overall width . . . . 52 in.
Overall height . . . . 38 in.
Tire size . . . . 16 × 15
Number of wheels 3
Seating capacity 2
Transmission type . . . . Variable speed pulley

The Terra Tiger was produced by Allis-Chalmers. It had doughnut tires and six-wheel drive.

SPECIFICATIONS

Body material . . . . Fiberglass
Frame material . . . . Wood/fiberglass
Starter . . . . Recoil
Engine make . . . . Ilo
Engine horsepower 10.1
Engine type 1-cylinder, 2-stroke
Dry weight . . . . 400 lb.
Payload . . . . 1,000 lb.
Overall length . . . . 84 in.
Overall width . . . . 54 in.
Overall height . . . . 37 in.
Tire size 11.00–20
Number of wheels 6
Track . . . . 43 in.
Transmission type . . . . Belt
Transmission make . . . . Own
Final drive . . . . Chain
Ground clearance . . . . 5.37 in.
Braking . . . . Clutches

PERFORMANCE

Maximum land speed . . . . 25 mph
Maximum water speed . . . . 4 mph
Range on land . . . . 4–6 hrs.
Maximum gradient (fully loaded) . . . . 45 degrees
Amphibious drive . . . . Tire rotation

The Trackster was made by Cushman (Outboard Marine Corporation) and had tracks, as its name implied, not wheels.

SPECIFICATIONS

Engine make . . . . GMC
Engine horsepower 25
Engine type 2-stroke

Dry weight . . . . 985 lb.
Overall length . . . . 92 in.
Overall width . . . . 61 in.

PERFORMANCE

Maximum land speed . . . . 16 mph
Range on land . . . . 5–6 hrs.

The Wolverine was distinguished by having the largest engine of any amphibious ATV, plus eight-wheel drive.

SPECIFICATIONS

Body material . . . . Steel
Frame material . . . . Steel
Starter . . . . Electric
Engine make . . . . Ford
Horsepower 55
Engine type 4-cylinder, 4-stroke
Dry weight . . . . 1,975 lb.
Payload . . . . 1,200 lb.
Overall length . . . . 113 in.
Overall width . . . . 66 in.
Overall height . . . . 41 in.
Tire size 26.00–12
Number of wheels 8
Track . . . . 54 in.
Transmission type . . . . Transaxle
Transmission make . . . . Ford
Final drive . . . . Chain
Steering . . . . Lever
Ground clearance . . . . 11.75 in.
Braking . . . . Drums

PERFORMANCE

Maximum land speed . . . . 35 mph
Maximum water speed . . . . 3 mph
Range on land . . . . 200 miles
Maximum gradient (fully loaded) . . . . 75 degrees
Amphibious drive . . . . Tire rotation

1970s

In 1970 Allen Bartlett designed the Waterlander, a motor home/houseboat powered by a 392-cu.-in. V-8 engine.

Finally in 1970 a team of Italians floated a modified Volkswagen Beetle across the Strait of Messina.

In 1973 in England the Caraboat, a dual-purpose travel-trailer, was designed for both land and water for up to five passengers. The 16-ft. craft had fitted wheels and a collapsible tow bar built into the hull for trailing and launching and recovery from the water. Wide windows and see-through glass doors led from the open, self-draining forward cockpit. It was constructed of self-colored FRP and had a cathedral-type one-piece hull. Propulsion came from a 5-hp Lombardini 4-stroke engine, coupled to a high-power 6-jet unit.

In 1975 Bertone's amphibious vehicle was offered with a Suzuki 750-cc engine. The engine had five forward and five backward gears. Behind the two front seats was a large cargo area.

In 1976 Dick Reed of CAF Industries came up with the idea of making a recreational vehicle amphibious within 15 minutes by driving it on board a specially designed five-ton cruiser deck and securing it in place. Then the motor was started and the driver floated away on the Camp-A-Float. With 55 gallons of onboard gasoline, one could cruise up to 20 hours and up to speeds of 12 mph.

In 1978 a new amphibious vehicle with six wheels and room for four passengers was built of polyethylene. It could carry loads of up to 1,000 lb. and could climb slopes as steep as 45 degrees. Its speed was 2–5 mph on water and 20–40 mph on land.

In 1978 Karl Mayer in West Germany, who had a textile machine factory, produced his AmphiMobil with an Opel engine. It was exhibited at auto shows but never produced.

SPECIFICATIONS

General

Curb weight	3,530 lb.
Payload	1,540 lb.
Wheelbase	98.4 in.
Length	169.3 in.
Width	73.2 in.
Height	72.8 in.
Cargo length:	
Two people	74.0 in.
Six people	33.5 in.
Cargo width	64.2 in.
Cargo height	41.3 in.
Fuel capacity	15.9 gal. (U.S.)
Optional	31.7 gal.

Chassis and Body

Body/frame	Unit steel
Brake system	Discs front and rear, vacuum assisted
Suspension	Independent front, beam axle rear
Ground clearance	13 in.
Turning circle	34.5 ft.

Engine

Type	121-cu.-in. sohc in-line Four
Bore × stroke	3.66 × 2.75 in.
Compression ratio	9:1
Horsepower at rpm (DIN)	100 at 5,200
Torque at rpm, lb.-ft.	114 at 3,600
Fuel requirement	98 RON
Carburetion	2-bbl Zenith

Drivetrain

Transmission for land use . . . . 4-speed manual

Marine drive , . . . Reversible jet

Performance

Maximum speed on land . . . . 75 mph

From Canada came a two-seater recreation craft made of high-impact fiberglass that traveled 40 mph on land and 35 mph on water.

During the 1970s a rather long list of recreational amphibians came on the market, such as:

- Camper Boat
- Combo Cruiser(Ship-A-Shore)
- Land 'N' Sea
- Naut-A-Care
- Porta-Boat

Camper Boat developed a unique system for taking a trailer to water. The trailer, pulled by a pickup truck with a mounted camper, converted to a boat hull at the water's edge and a transfer device permitted switching the camper unit from the truck to the boat. Polyurethane foam in four fiberglass pontoons kept the trailer hull afloat and power could be provided by an outboard motor or oars. Camper units up to 11 ft. long could be accommodated by the trailer hull, with a walk-around gangway two feet wide.

Charles O'Hanlon's Land 'N' Sea Craft produced a 28-ft. houseboat which became the equivalent of a house trailer when fitted to its special undercarriage.

1980s

The 1980s proved to be relatively light in new amphibious designs.

In 1980 the Conte, a new amphibious passenger car, was produced by the Herzog Company in Germany. Powered by a 2.3-liter German Ford V-6 engine, it was 212.6 in. long, seated five and offered exchangeable hard and soft tops.

In 1985 the French owner of a 1950 deluxe Packard displayed his auto yacht at the old car show in Paris. It was specially manufactured.

In 1988 a modified Ford was turned into the Car-Go boat.

Then, finally, in 1989 a mayoral candidate in Detroit, Michigan, Stephen Hume, promised to invent an aqua car for the good of the people that could put skiers on the Detroit River or act as a fishing boat.

1990s

In 1990 Poncin Industries USA, a division of Poncin Industries in France, offered the ATV Poncin VP EDF for the working environments of public utilities. It had an amphibious all-steel body with a 75-hp diesel engine and could transport an 1,800-lb. payload. Of the 23 different models available, three were amphibious.

In 1991 the Otter, produced by Advanced Recreational Technology (ART), became available. This small vacation travel trailer converted into a powered houseboat. It slept four and could be towed by a compact car. Through a system of roadable wheels with retractable-extendable flotation units, it was converted when backed down a boat-launching ramp.

The mini–Tour, a very small two-passenger variation, was also available.

In 1994 the Aquastrada Delta, made of fiberglass and styled like a sports car, had wheels that retracted into watertight wheel wells in the hull. With a 245-hp Ford truck engine it did 100 mph on land and with its jet pump propulsion did 45 mph at sea.

In 1995 the Combocruiser, an amphibious motor home, was made by the IDM Company.

Finally, in 1999 in Venice, Italy sculptor Livio De Marchi had his convertible 1964 Volkswagen Beetle–style vessel carved out of pine and walnut. Known as the Beetle-boat or floating bug, it was propelled by a 10-hp inboard motor housed in the trunk. It was complete with a rearview mirror, roll-down window handles, headlights and taillights. It weighed 1,500 lb. and traveled at 5 mph.

He made a similar replica amphibious vehicle to resemble in every detail a Fiat Topolino.

2000s

In 2003 Gibbs Technologies introduced its all-aluminum frame, 3,200-lb. amphibious sports car, the Aquada. Originating in England, it is capable of traveling in excess of 115 mph on land and 40 mph in the water. It has a 175-hp V-6 gasoline engine that converts to a one-ton jet thruster. There is a single switch for transforming modes in 5 seconds.

It is in compliance with full European road and marine regulations. It has three seats, foldable wheels, a double wishbone front and a five-speed automatic transmission.

The Quadski is an all-terrain vehicle that transforms into a jet ski on water.

In 2004 the Rinspeed Splash, designed by Frank Rinderknecht, arrived from Switzerland. It is a carbon composite sports car that can be transformed into a boat or a hydrofoil in 35 seconds. It reaches speeds of up to 125 mph on land. As a boat the pop-up, three-bladed propeller takes it up to 150 mph. When its wings are lowered it can do up to 50

Top: Aquada amphibious sports car. *Bottom:* Aquada amphibious sports car on the road (both photographs courtesy Gibbs Technologies, Ltd.).

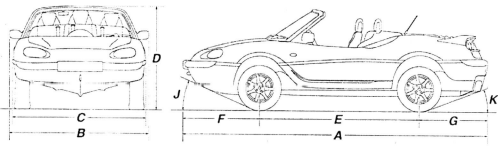

Key Vehicle Dimensions

A Overall length	4.8m	
B Overall width	2.0m	
C Track width	1.78m	
D Overall height	1.5m	
E Wheelbase	2.5m	
F Front overhang	1.2m	
G Rear overhang	1.1m	
J Front ramp angle	19 deg	
K Rear ramp angle	13 deg	

Powertrain - V6 engine delivers in excess of 175 horse power
Fuel tank - 15 gallons / 67 litres
Brakes - All round power assisted discs. Front ventilated
Suspension - Air Hydraulic self levelling with variable ride height
Steering - Power assisted on land and water
Seating - 3 Across with centre steering
Kerb weight - 1466kg
Gross weight - 1750Kg
Marine propulsion - Proprietry Gibbs Unit with almost 1 tonne thrust
Bilge pumps - 3 Independent systems
Lights - Automotive and marine compliant
Fire protection - Automatic engine compartment fire suppression

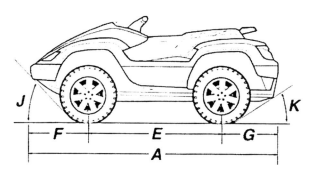

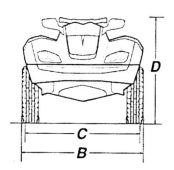

Key Vehicle Dimensions

A Overall length	3.0m	
B Overall width	1.6m	
C Track width	1.4m	
D Overall height	1.3m	
E Wheelbase	1.6m	
F Front overhang	0.75m	
G Rear overhang	0.65m	
J Front ramp angle	45 deg	
K Rear ramp angle	32 deg	

Wheels and Tyres - 26x8-12 ATV tyres
Steering - Handlebars
Brakes - Hydraulically operated discs
Suspension - Coil over springs and dampers
Drive layout - RWD
No. of Occupants - 1
GVW - 675kgs (1485lbs)

Top: Aquada amphibious sports car specifications. *Bottom:* Quadski ATV amphibian specifications (both courtesy Gibbs Technologies, Ltd.).

mph as a hydrofoil. Control instruments are fully functional in all settings. The engine: 750 cc running on natural gas.

Also in 2004 a new name, the Terra Wind, entered the list of amphibious vehicles. This 42-ft., 31,000-lb. prototype RV-yacht is from Cool Amphibious Manufacturers International (CAM). It is a mounted motor coach on an aluminum boat hull with a rigged 330-

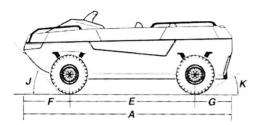
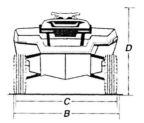

Key Vehicle Dimensions

A Overall length	4.0m
B Overall width	2.0m
C Track width	1.78m
D Overall height	1.5m
E Wheelbase	2.4m
F Front overhang	0.9m
G Rear overhang	0.7m
J Front ramp angle	45 deg
K Rear ramp angle	30 deg

Wheels and Tyres - 26x10-12 ATV tyres
Steering - Handlebars
Brakes - Hydraulically operated discs
Suspension - Hydro-pneumatic self leveling, with ride height adjustment
Drive layout - 4WD
No. of Occupants - 2
GVW - 1000kgs (2204lbs)

Top: Terraquad ATV two-seat concept specifications (courtesy Gibbs Technologies, Ltd.). *Bottom:* Terra Wind amphibian prototype RV-yacht (courtesy Cool Amphibious Manufacturers International).

hp Caterpillar 326E diesel engine to power the wheels and twin 19-in. bronze propellers. It was designed and built by John and Julie Giljam and can handle waves up to 4 ft. high.

The Hydra-Terra from CAM places the driver in the center of the cockpit and is used on cruise line tours. Options include glass windows, insulated and padded interior paneling, multiple engines, polished aluminum wheels and air conditioning. Setting it apart are a V-shaped bow and an air-ride suspension, as well as inset axles.

Hydra-Terra amphibious vehicle used on cruise line tours (courtesy Cool Amphibious Manufacturers International).

The Hydra Spyder from CAM is a sports utility vehicle 18 ft. 6 in. long, 7 ft. wide and 5 ft. high, weighing 3,600 lb. It has an all-aluminum lower hull with a fiberglass upper structure. Flotation foam makes it unsinkable. Power is provided by a Corvette LS2 fuel-injected engine with 450 hp. Other features include: full engine instrumentation package, five-speed Tremec TKO high performance manual transmission, front-wheel drive, four-wheel disc brakes, 265/70R 17-in. wheels and tires, Berkley Marine Jet power trim and steering, air-ride retractable four-point front and rear suspension system and stainless steel Sidewinder exhaust system.

Recently available is a pontoon houseboat equipped with hydraulic-controlled wheels that go from waterway to highway. A product of Mensch Manufacturing Company, it is 13 by 36 ft. and aluminum framed.

The Phibicat weighs in at 450 kg with six wheels exerting a ground pressure of just 2 psi. It was designed and built by Australian engineer Doug Waters and has three times the positive flotation needed. A 10-bhp, air-cooled diesel engine drives all six wheels and an outboard can be lowered at the press of a button on the water.

The New Zealand company Sealegs has given us an interesting system. A small boat, the Anaconda, can be launched by driving it from a storage location, down a ramp or beach, and into the water. The motorized, retractable and steerable boat wheels offer a land speed of up to 10 kmh. The system is available on boats up to 6 m and 750 kg. The wheels retract on the water, allowing the vehicle to be used normally. When returning to land, the wheels are lowered in the water and the boat driven towards shore until the wheels touch the bot-

Hydra Spyder sports utility vehicle (courtesy Cool Amphibious Manufacturers International).

tom and it can drive onto land. It can also be used as a luxury yacht tender. It uses all submersible components.

A new design was recently unveiled for a Rugged Amphibious Craft (RAC) intended for military, commercial and recreational applications. It features a 140-hp inboard engine, jet drive and a solid aluminum hull.

Monster Garage on cable TV has featured a swamp buggy or floating Fahrvergnugen. A second motor from an airboat was installed in the diminutive 2001 Beetle, which required removing the passenger seat and trunk panels. The car's factory-installed two-liter, four-cylinder motor stayed in place for use on dry land, as did its five-speed automatic transmission. The 100-hp nautical engine was mounted to a huge hydraulic arm that would pop the rear hatchback open just before thrusting the engine into the water. The engine would spin a vulcanized chrome propeller from a small aircraft engine. A set of aluminum rudders were fashioned for steering. A set of Hell Bent motorcycle exhaust pipes were fixed to the tailpipe. Mounted upside down, their sweeping lines made the car fully submersible.

Unconventional Amphibious Vehicles

The so-called normal amphibious configuration, a passenger car or truck chassis, is transcended by a range of unconventional examples, including travel trailers, school buses, motorcycles and even tricycles.

On *Monster Garage* a so-called S'Kool Bus was converted into a working pontoon boat; the show also produced a diecast replica for the toy store trade.

Way back in 1894 Beach and Harris introduced their Cycle Raft, which had twin inflatable pontoons to keep it afloat.

Then in 1912 the amphibious Hydro-Motorcycle, a single-cylinder, was perfected by Eugene Prey. It had an add-on 14-ft. flotation device made of galvanized iron that could be fitted to a motorcycle with three pontoons that could be raised or lowered, one under the front wheel and one on each side of the rear wheel.

The motorcycle engine with a detachable propeller drove paddles at the rear by a belt running off the engine. Handlebar rudders controlled the steering gear. A sail attachment was provided in case the engine was disabled. Speed was 10 mph. It was felt that the vehicle could be adapted to military use for army scouts.

In 1909 in France an amphibious bicycle was created. The front fork was linked to a rudder by a rod, and a small rubber friction wheel at the rear drove the propeller. Cylindrical floats attached to the frame could be raised when it took to land. The reversible screw was a feature.

In 1883 in England Terry's amphibious tricycle was designed. When taken apart, reassembled and covered with stretched canvas, it could be converted to a 12-ft. boat. It was demonstrated in the English Channel.

Not to be outdone, in 1896 Thore J. Olsen developed an 80-lb. tricycle which carried rigidly connected twin boats from its axle and from a yoke on the fore-wheel. It could be driven by either engine or treadle power.

Perhaps the ultimate in unconventional combinations was the boat-car-garage. Developed in England, the luxury super cruiser traveled at a speed of 40 mph. When a button was pushed, a pair of dune buggies was disengaged. Then another switch dropped up to ten berths from the ceiling. It burned 45 gallons of gas an hour.

Military Amphibious Vehicles

Military amphibians have included both original vehicles and adaptations of civilian designs.

Amphibious activities involving the military have been reported in the U.S., Germany, England, France, Japan, Russia, Czechoslovakia and the Netherlands.

In the 1920s and the 1930s experimental prototypes of amphibious tanks and other types of vehicles came under study in several countries. Most proposals were along the lines of auxiliary flotation equipment that was to be attached to existing conventional vehicles.

United States

In 1934 a new type of proposed coast defense craft came from publisher Hugo Gernsback. It traveled both on land and in the water and would emerge from the water by blowing out ballast tanks. This vehicle was envisioned as a combination tank, battleship and submarine with huge treads, yielding a distinct tactical advantage.

World War II accelerated these efforts into design development and mass production in the early years of the 1940s.

Amphibious warfare is a means of invading an enemy country from the sea. It is considered the most difficult type of modern war operation and requires long periods of plan-

Everyday Science and Mechanics featured on its October 1934 cover a gigantic coast defense craft.

ning and preparation. Amphibious attacks by U.S. forces have taken place in the Solomon Islands, North Africa, Sicily, Italy, France and Japanese outposts in World War II. During the Korean War General Douglas MacArthur also led an allied amphibious invasion at Inchon.

Anheuser Busch brewery, which produced bus bodies, barn-shaped horse vans, refrigerator truck bodies, armored car bodies and company vehicles, developed a special amphibious inboard land cruiser. It was intended as a military reconnaissance vehicle but World War I ended before it could be produced.

J. Walter Christie, automotive inventor and racing driver, in 1917 was working on an amphibious tank fitted with a 75 mm cannon.

Also in 1917 an amphibious tank was tested, designed primarily for scouting parties. It carried 12 people in a watertight body. At the front end a two-blade tractor propeller was mounted below the crankshaft, producing a speed of 10 mph. A steel bulkhead sealed the front of the engine compartment so that water could not enter it by passing through the radiator. Broad horizontal planes extended along each side, preventing water from splashing into the cockpit, and also acting as mudguards.

The first U.S. amphibian was proposed by Roger Hofheins of the Amphibian Car Company in 1940. He built a ½-ton, 4 × 4 Dodge WU Series truck named the Aqua Cheetah. It had chain drive to all wheels and a retractable propeller. A flange on the rear wheels served as a winch. Water speed was 5 mph. Changeover time was one minute. It used an 85-hp Ford V-8 gasoline engine and carried eight men.

Development of amphibious cargo and personnel transportation was initiated as a joint project in 1941 between Marmon-Herrington and New York boatbuilder Sparkman and Stevens, based on a modified Jeep chassis, known as the Seep (Sea Jeep), Duckling or Waterbug.

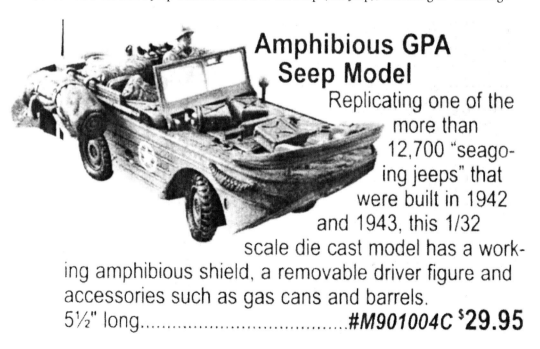

Advertisement for model amphibious Jeep (courtesy Military Issue).

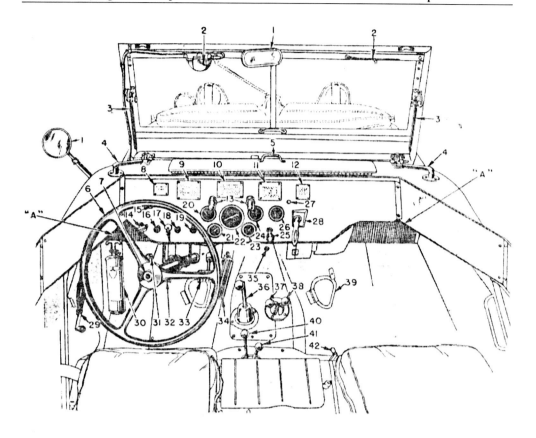

CONTROLS

1	Rear View Mirror	22	Speedometer
2	Windshield Wipers	23	Temperature Indicator
3	Windshield Opening Lever	24	Ammeter
4	Air Outlet Duct Control Handles	25	Winch Control
5	Ventilator Handle	26	Voltmeter
6	Steering Wheel	27	Voltmeter Toggle Switch
7	Horn Button	28	Hand Brake Lever
8	Nomenclature Plate (Name Plate)	29	Air Duct Control Lever
9	Caution Plate	30	Fire Extinguisher
10	Propellor and Bilge Pump Instruction Plate	31	Head Lamp Beam Control Switch
11	Transfer Case Shifting Instructions	32	Clutch Pedal
		33	Brake Pedal
12	Voltmeter Instruction Plate	34	Accelerator
13	Instrument Lamps	35	Starter Switch
14	Light Switch	36	Transmission Shift Lever
15	Blackout Driving Lamp Switch	37	Front Axle Engaging Lever (Transfer Case)
16	Carburetor Choke Control		
17	Ignition Switch	38	High and Low Shift Lever (Transfer Case)
18	Hand Throttle		
19	Panel Light Switch	39	Cover Plates
20	Fuel Gauge	40	Propellor Engaging Lever
21	Oil Gauge	41	Bilge Pump Control Lever
		42	Pump Valve Shift Lever

Amphibious Jeep controls on Ford (courtesy Ian Grieve).

Ford built them with boat-like, watertight steel hulls constructed separately from the boat chassis to make replacement easy. There were special canvas sides and a bilge pump. Road speed was 50 mph.

SPECIFICATIONS

Engine . . . . Four-cylinder side valve
gasoline(L-head),
134.2 cu. in., 60 hp,
3,600 rpm
Transmission . . . . Gearbox 3 forward, 1 reverse
transfer case 2-speed
Clutch . . . . Single plate
7–78 in., a dry disc type
Electrical . . . . 12 volt (2 × 6 volt,
15 plate, 116 ampere
hour batteries in series)
Fuel capacity . . . . 12.5 gal.(15 gal. U.S.)
Radiator . . . . Larger than standard Jeep
Springs . . . . Front 9 leaf, rear 12 leaf
Winch . . . . Capstan, Braden J2
Power takeoff . . . . . Dual control to drive both bilge pump
and propeller shaft

DIMENSIONS

Wheelbase . . . . 84 in.
Track . . . . 49 in.
Overall length . . . . 181.83 in.
Width . . . . 64 in.
Height . . . . 52.75 in. (top of steering wheel)

WEIGHT

Road weight . . . . 3,400 lb.
Payload weight . . . . 800 lb.
Gross weight . . . . 4,450 lb.

Specifications changed constantly throughout production and complaints included slowness, heaviness and clumsiness.

Some 12,778 tracked landing vehicles (LVT) were turned out under the names Water Buffalo and Alligator.

The other major amphibious vehicles were the DUKWs (ducks) in 1941 developed by the Yellow Coach Company, a General Motors subsidiary. Their hulls were designed by Sparkman and Stevens. They were 30 ft. long, six-wheel machines with dual rear axles based on a 2.5-ton GMC truck chassis. Total production was over 21,147 units. An unusual feature was the built-in ability to vary the tire pressure while on the move to suit the terrain it was covering. Speeds were 35 mph on land and 50 mph in the water. It could carry 35 men on land and 50 afloat and weighed seven tons.

The Applegate amphibian used the steering rear wheels as the rudders.

Half-track vehicles, with wheels on the front axles and Caterpillar treads on the rear axles that supply motive power, played a role in World War II. They were manufactured

U.S. Army World War II DUKW amphibian (courtesy U.S. Army Transportation Museum).

by Studebaker (Weasel), the Food Machinery Company, White Motor Company, Diamond T Motor Company and Autocar. Among them they produced 43,000 vehicles.

Two basic designs were devised. The smaller M2 carried a crew of up to seven men and was fitted with a Browning machine gun. The more powerful M3 was faster, equipped with two machine guns and carried up to ten passengers. There were open and turret-top versions.

Usage included armored infantry transport, ordnance and supply, and self-propelled mortar, artillery and anti-aircraft artillery configurations.

Most of the LVTs were powered by Continental seven-cylinder, radial engines, although the MK III version used two Cadillac V-8 engines and later MK IV LVTs could carry a payload of 6,000 lb. A total of 18,620 LVTs were produced for the American and British armed forces.

In 1944 Willys-Overland built a soft skin tracked amphibious Jeep WT-C. It had quarter-ton capacity and four-wheel drive.

The Chrysler LAV was driven by a gas turbine, with wheels which retracted into the body on the water.

In 1961 the Gamma-Goat, a six-wheeled amphibious military vehicle, was designed by Roger L. Gamaunt and built by Chance-Vought Aircraft. Its 80-hp air-cooled engine could speed it up to 50 mph and travel 1,000 miles on a tankful of gas. The rear body was detachable and could be interchanged in order to transport troops, cargo, ammunition, a missile, a flame thrower or an ambulance.

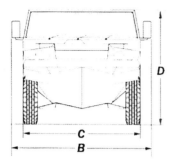
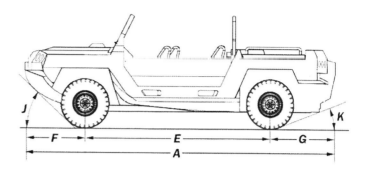

Key Vehicle Dimensions

A Overall length	5.4m	
B Overall width	2.0m	
C Track width	1.78m	
D Overall height	1.85m	
E Wheelbase	3.2m	
F Front overhang	1.0m	
G Rear overhang	1.1m	
J Front ramp angle	44 deg	
K Rear ramp angle	33 deg	

Powertrain Power unit TBD – Full time 4 wheel drive
Fuel tank - 30 gallons / 130 litres
Wheels - Front 10 x 6.5J, rear 6.5J
Tyres - Front and rear 285/75 R16. Run flat options
Brakes - All round power assisted vented brakes
Suspension - Fully retracting
Steering - Power assisted on land and water
Seating - Configurable
Marine propulsion - Proprietry Gibbs Unit
Bilge pumps - 3 Independent systems
Lights - Automotive and marine compliant
Fire protection - Manual engine compartment fire suppression

Specifications on Gibbs' Humdinga amphibian (courtesy Gibbs Technologies, Ltd.).

In 1962 Fletcher Aviation Company built the Flair, a 1,500-lb. floating military truck. The Watertight aluminum hull and rear-drive 55-hp engine carried four men and their equipment across land and rivers at speeds up to 75 mph on straightaways. It was light enough to be airlifted seven at a time by a large cargo plane or one at a time by helicopter. The company was a manufacturer of aircraft parts and light aircraft.

Gibbs Technology is currently producing the high-speed Humdinga, an off-road military vehicle. It is capable of speeds in excess of 80 mph on land and 40 mph on water and will run on diesel. Construction is aluminum monocoque.

The Max six-wheel drive amphibious ATV is in two- and four-passenger models and has been used in Afghanistan.

Germany

Back in 1934 Hans Trippel produced a new version of his amphibian, the round-nosed SG6-38 with four-wheel drive and a four-cylinder Adler engine.

During World War II he began production of his military version, which had a 2.5-liter Opel engine that could generate a speed of 50 mph on land. Some had a rear-mounted, three-liter, air-cooled Tatra V-8 engine and four-wheel drive. He built about 1,000 units.

He also designed aerodynamic 4 × 4 floating sedans with bulbous hulls, five-speed transmissions and rear-mounted pusher screws which could operate on wheels or in combination with skis and floats.

The first Schwimmwagen produced for field trials in 1940 was known as the Porsche 128.

In 1942 Volkswagen put an improved version of its four-wheel-drive amphibian into production. It featured a hinged three-blade outboard water propeller which, when in use, was driven by a power take-off dog at the rear of the body. Speed in water was 6 mph and on land was 50 mph. The air-cooled VW one-liter, flat-four was the power unit. A total of 14,265 units were produced.

In 1935 Rheinmetall-Borsig experimented with a Land-Wasser-Schlepper, an amphibious towing vehicle which began production in 1940. Typical was Sachsenberg, a massive, twin-screw machine with crawler tracks and a V-12, 30-bhp Maybach engine. A crew of 20 was carried and the machine scaled 13 tons.

The German Navy had the four-ton, four-wheel-drive Voran in 1929. It had a four-cylinder, 40-hp Opel engine and was intended mostly for marsh use, with speeds of 7 mph on the water and 15 mph on land.

England

In 1916 English military authorities experimented with the Mark IV tank suspended between two steel floats, a floating version of the 27-ton MF IX.

Britain attempted to produce an equivalent to the LVT. Most successful was the Terrapin, built by Thornycroft and Morris Commercial, but only 500 of the Mk1 version were produced. An all-wheel-drive eight-wheeler, it was powered by two Ford V-8 engines.

The full-track Neptune designed by Morris was the nearest equivalent to the LVT, with a payload of four to five tons.

The massive Morris Commercial Argosy never advanced beyond the prototype stage. Although this full-track amphibian was powered by a V-12 Liberty engine and could carry a nine-ton payload in a rough sea, it was far too heavy and was very difficult to load.

At Morris Alec Issigonias produced the Gosling, a sort of baby landing craft for the Signal Corps on which a two-cycle Villiers outboard motor drove both the rear wheels and the propeller.

Britain's main contribution to the design of military amphibians was the development of the swimming tank designed by Polish engineer Nicolas Straussler. First fitted to a Tetrarch light tank in 1941, the Straussller DD flotation equipment consisted of a flexible waterproof skirt with an inflatable rim which could be raised around the superstructure of the tank to turn it into an amphibian with propeller drive. The Straussler gear was so successful that soon it was being fitted to 30-ton Sherman tanks, 102 of which were used in the D-Day landings.

France

Alvis Stalwart amphibious vehicles in France drove on all six wheels and steered with the front four.

Also built by Berliet in France under the name Aurochs, the Stalwart had a 6.5-liter Rolls-Royce engine and, for propulsion in the water, twin Dowty pumps which jetted out water behind the vehicle to thrust it along.

Waterjet propulsion of a similar type had been featured on a light amphibian designed by the French engineer Petit in 1950, which used a rear-mounted 350-cc, twin-cylinder Dyna Panhard engine.

Japan

Japan used a limited number of a Dutch-like machines built by Toyota as well as the SD amphibious navy tank.

Soviet Union

The Soviet Union had an amphibious armored car based on the GAZ-46 (Ford) MAV chassis produced by Gorki Automotive. It had a four-cylinder engine and 7.50 × 16 tires. After World War II the Soviet Union had an amphibious Jeep GAZ-46 MAV.

Czechoslovakia

Czechoslovakia's Tatra produced an amphibian with an independent suspension and a rear-mounted, air-cooled four-cylinder engine.

Netherlands

In the Netherlands the double-ended Dutch DAF reverted to all-independent springing, four-wheel drive with two Citroen tractor front ends. Both driving units could steer, though not at the same time, of course.

Quasi Amphibious Vehicles

Several attempts have been made to produce unique quasi amphibious vehicles in a wide variety of novelty types.

Andy Saunders in England built his ambiguous amphibian look-alike on the running gear of a 1969 Reliant Regal with the boat part based on a Monbar 146.

At New York City's Guggenheim Museum Claes Oldenhurg's sculpture Swiss Army Knife is on display. It doubles as a boat when assembled and was successfully floated on a Venice canal.

For real novelty there is the 45-ft. floating milk truck made with 6,000 milk cartons by Jack O'Keefe and his family. It took 1,500 hours to create it.

For an amphibian *above* the water, not on it, we can look to the standard automobile on suspended cables operating as a passenger ferry across the Pudding River near Barlow, Oregon. Two strands support the car, which runs under its own power, while a third, through a pulley cradle, steadies the vehicle at the top. Flat rubber bands for traction replace the tires. The 120-ft. crossing can be made 1,760 times on a single gallon of gas.

Purely fictitious is Guy's Boat Mobile in Garrison Keillor's Lake Woebegon on his public radio show, *Prairie Home Companion.*

CHAPTER III

Road-Rail Vehicles

Road-legal, specially-equipped vehicles designed or converted for operation on both roads and railroad or transit tracks, using two separate sets of retractable, pivoting, flanged, steel pilot wheels, are found worldwide. They are acquired through purchase, lease or rental.

These vehicles are referred to variously as automotive rail and highway carriers, high rails, rail vehicles, and auto railer locomotives. When automobiles have been used they are listed as autorail cars, railway motor cars, rail cars and track cars.

Inspection cars were automobiles used by high-ranking company railway officers to conduct inspections of the railway's property. They were equipped with steel wheels to run on tracks and could not be used on roads. They were usually equipped with a turntable. They were attached to the rear of a passenger, freight, or mixed train.

The units may be purpose-built or temporarily or permanently converted on a regular chassis by vehicle manufacturers, specialty organizations, truck dealers or railroad maintenance shops.

In the early days numerous attempts to adapt road vehicles to travel on railroad tracks were less than satisfactory because of problems with the drive system's efficiency, maintenance service and communications, and different standards and narrow gage roads. If a friction drive system was used it also required that the vehicle be driven in reverse to achieve forward motion.

Well-known U.S. makers include Bridgewater, Case, Central, Whiting, Evans, Fairmont, Motorail, and Industrial Truck. Outside the U.S. makers are found in Italy, Canada, Great Britain, Germany and Australia.

Today makers claim conversions can be accomplished in only three to five minutes.

Gasoline-powered vehicles have been used on the rails as far back as the late 1800s. The motorcar, which replaced the handcar, was the workhorse for transporting crews, tools and supplies where needed for work on tracks, signals and communications.

Beginning in about 1920 larger gasoline-powered vehicles (passenger cars, trucks and even buses) came into use on some railroads, driven by flanged wheels in contact with the rails and employing a variety of mechanical design concepts ranging from axles which rotated with the wheels to journal bearings.

In 1937 a switch engine locomotive became available with design changes and alterations that allowed it to run on rails or road up to 70 mph.

Among the rail versions converted were the following, roughly in order of usage: Ford, Pontiac, Buick, Lincoln, Packard, Dodge, Chrysler, Willys, Chevrolet, Cadillac, Checker, British Leyland and Paige.

Opposite, top: Whiting's Trackmobile is used by such manufacturers as General Motors Corp. on the railroad. *Bottom:* Zephir road-rail vehicle (courtesy Zephir S. p. A., Italy).

Toyota four-wheel drive used on railway track (courtesy Aries-Hyrail, Western Australia).

Truck makes involved were White, Dodge, International, Volvo and Marathon. In the 1960s these were superseded by station wagons and rubber-tire rail/highway trucks. The types most commonly used were pickups, vans, dump trucks, flat-beds, and stakes, since designs of large attachment units have required just about every type of highway chassis.

Virtually all major railroads have been listed as users: Burlington Northern, Canadian Pacific, Canadian National, CST, Chicago and Northwestern, Chicago and Eastern Illinois, Erie, Hawaii Consolidated, Illinois Central, Liberian, Little River, Missouri-Kansas-Texas, Missouri Pacific, Norfolk and Southern, Northern, Ontario Northland, Pennsylvania, Queensland, Rock Island, Santa Fe, Soo Line, Southern, Union Pacific and Wisconsin Central.

These vehicles are employed for a wide variety of operating tasks as an alternative to traditional switcher work trains: inspection, maintenance, shunting, signal planting, emergency ambulance, and short-haul business trips, to name just a few.

In addition to railroads and rail contractors, users include industrial plants (chemical, steel, cement), mining companies, ports, airports and the military.

Early examples of their use are interesting.

The White Motor Company, San Francisco branch, furnished three rail cars which were put in regular service by Hawaiian Consolidated Railway, Ltd., in 1925.

The initial investigation of the equipment took place both in the East and West. General Manager R. W. Filler described the history of the purchase as follows:

> This was a decided departure from the trains previously operated. First a trial run was made from our shops at Waiakea, one mile south of Hilo, to the southern terminal of our railroad system at Kaueleau, 32 miles from Hilo. This portion of our system is laid over an undulating grade. We arrived on regular schedule time and the return trip was equally successful.
>
> The next day the same motor was operated over another branch of our system, covering

1939 Buick in use on the rail for Canadian Pacific as an inspection car (courtesy Pierre Fournier).

the 25.3 miles from Hilo to Glenwood in one hour and ten minutes. In the afternoon of the same day it ran from Hilo to Hakalau, 13 miles and return.

The following day in the presence of our president J. R. Galt, another one of the three Whites was operated between Hilo and Glenwood and made the 25.3 miles in high gear, covering the distance in 58 minutes. On another trial run in the afternoon, to Hakalau, Motor No. 2 with a trailer, performed to the satisfaction of President Galt.

On April 11th a party of 45 businessmen from Hilo were taken on a trial run to Hakalau, the performance of the motor and trailer creating considerable astonishment and exciting much favorable comment.

On April 18 the equipment was put into regular service.

Now turning to interurban and transit service, in 1918 interurban service between El Centro and Holtville, two small cities a few miles apart in the extreme southern part of California, was maintained by a bus built much like a streetcar with wheels designed for both railway and highway. The inner half of each wheel was flanged to follow a steel rail. The outer half was equipped with an ordinary solid rubber tire. It held 17 passengers and the driver as well as a rear luggage rack. Small wedges placed alongside the track permitted it to run on or off roads without difficulty.

A gasoline motorcar was used to pull passenger cars on the street railway in Apeldoorn, Holland, in 1921.

Cross-country trips also made good use of railroads.

Between 1901 and 1908 Charles Glidden of Boston took a marathon international tour by car, traveling over 46,000 miles in 39 countries. When his various Napiers ran out of road, he fitted flanged wheels on and bowled over the railroads.

Michelin rail car in France (Detroit Public Library, National Automotive History Collection).

When the first car crossed Australia in 1913 it spent much of its time thumping over railroad tracks to avoid being bogged down in sand.

In 1924 advertising executive Austin F. Bement and his partner Edward S. Evans made the first reported automobile trip in Canada from Winnipeg, Manitoba, to Vancouver, British Columbia, fitting their vehicle with flanges to allow them to use the Canadian Pacific Railroad tracks where the roads were too rough for motor travel. Both men were decorated by the Canadian Highway Association for their feat.

Other vehicles adapted to rails have been motorcycles and bicycles.

In 1900, Colorado inventor William Gillum adapted a bicycle into a railbike. It had a three-wheel outrigger design adjustable to various gauges. The wheels were 8 in. in diameter with rubber tires with wide grooves cut in so that they would fit on the edges of the rails. He founded the American Railbike Association.

Many other similar bicycle contraptions were devised in the late 1800s and early 1900s.

Military uses of road-rail vehicles have shown up in the U.S., Great Britain and Germany.

Great Britain's Armored Car Corps was formally constituted in August 1922 in Dublin, Ireland. Lancia armored cars were modified with new hulls and turrets to run on railroad tracks.

In 1943 the U.S. Army converted a 2.5-ton, 6 × 6 cargo GMC truck to a rail switch. It was virtually a three-axle version of the 1.5-ton model.

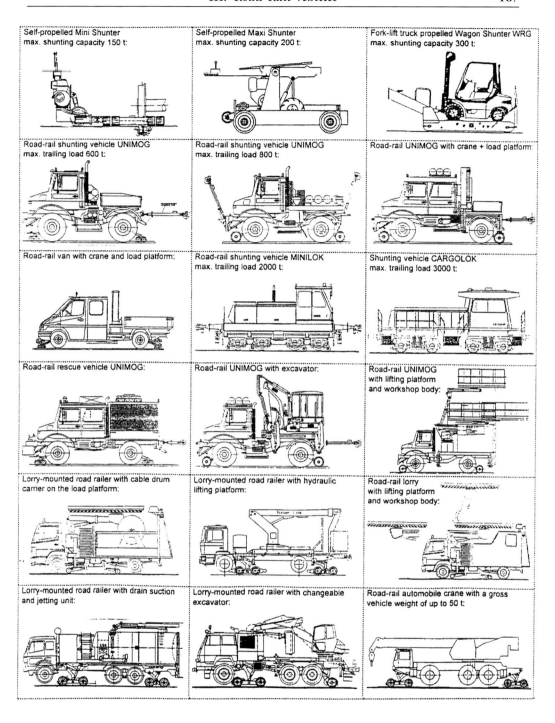

Typical road-rail vehicle variations (courtesy Brandt Road Rail Corporation).

White Motor Company rail bus in Hawaii, used by Hawaiian Consolidated Railway, Ltd. Shown is a party of 45 businessmen on a trial run (American Truck Historical Society).

It was based on the commercial GMC cab and chassis of the 6 × 4 model, and was converted by the manufacturers to a 6 × 6 type by the addition of a transfer box and live front axle. Unlike the 1.5-ton model, however, this 2.5 tonner remained in production and service until the war ended. It was built by the Yellow Truck and Coach Manufacturing Company, a subsidiary of General Motors. The cargo truck model had a steel body which was produced in both short and long body forms. The short (15 ft.) body had folding slatted bench seats for secondary use as a troop carrier. The long (17 ft.) body was for cargo only. Local modification of the short-bodied version had wheels replaced by flanged railway wheels and scrap iron ballast weights in the body section. A number of vehicles were so converted to act as switchers (shunters) at the U.S. Ordnance Corps railheads in Europe in 1944–1945. Buffing plates and support girders were added, plus an access ladder to the cab.

There was a production change when the pressed steel cab was eliminated and replaced by a canvas roof and side sheets. The appearance was then similar to the COE type which was widely used throughout the war. Some vehicles were refitted with short steel tipping dumper bodies for Engineers Corps use.

The German army has made good use of motorcycles for rail transportation.

CHAPTER IV

Water-Air Vehicles

Dual vehicles capable of operating on both the water and in the air take a variety of forms. They are numerous and have an extensive history of manufacture and use from the early days of flight through the present. In this chapter only representative examples will appear.

There are three kinds of seaplanes which can touch down and take off on water. The fuselage acts like a boat hull and provides buoyancy on the water.

- Floatplanes are equipped with one or more big floats instead of wheels that enable them to land on water.
- Flying boats have a watertight body that floats in the water like the hull of a ship.
- Amphibians are flying boats with retractable wheels attached to their floats or hull. The pilot raises the wheels when operating the plane on water and lowers the wheels on land. They are used by the government in making wildlife surveys.

Early pioneers with seaplanes were Glenn Hammond Curtiss and Henri Fabre of France in the 1910–1911 period. Curtiss is credited as the inventor of the seaplane. When he put a set of pontoons on his biplane he called it the Flying Fish. On January 18, 1911, a Curtiss plane became the first to take off and land on a ship at sea. In February he became the first person to take off and land on water in his new tractor seaplane.

In 1919 three U.S. Navy flying boats attempted to make the first crossing of the Atlantic Ocean. Only one succeeded in reaching England.

In 1920 Englishman W. Miller Metcalf created his wingless airplane, the Amphyglider. It had a three-cylinder radial engine driving a tractor airscrew, converted for the water into a twin-float hydroplane. Its chassis was an undercarriage. For marine work it could be converted in 30 minutes. Land speed was 60 mph.

In 1920 Aeromarine Airways used converted U.S. Navy HS-2 seaplanes to fly passengers from Key West and New York City to Havana, Cuba.

In 1925 Ronald Amundsen, Norwegian explorer, used a flying boat in his North Pole trip.

In 1928 Russian Igor Sikorsky introduced his S-38 as the largest and fastest amphibian in the world, seating up to 13 passengers in a cabin with leather-covered walls and mahogany trim. It had a cruising speed of 110 miles per hour. Later he came out with an even larger, more advanced amphibian, the S-40, with these specifications: length 76 ft. 8 in., height 23 ft. 10 in., empty weight 21,300 lb., wingspan 114 ft. and power was provided by two Pratt and Whitney Hornet engines of 575 hp each. The cruising speed was 117 mph.

In 1929 the German-built Dornier DO-X flying boat had a 157-ft.-wide wing stretching 28 ft. above the surface of the water. Twelve powerful airplane engines were carried in six nacelles on top of the wing. It carried 100 passengers.

Top: Curtiss-Wright CW-3 Duckling/Teal Flying Boat (San Diego Aerospace Museum). *Bottom:* Aeromarine 40F experimental flying boat (Collection of Herbert Kinsey, San Diego Aerospace Museum).

Igor Sikorsky's S-42 Flying Boat (San Diego Aerospace Museum).

In the late 1930s Bob Baier and John Fletcher constructed a prototype of their two-seater flying stripped-hull speedboat with a V-tail, the Wing Dingy. It had a steel-frame plywood hull with extra housing behind the pilot's seat. Its 22-ft. aluminum wing was fabric-covered with an odd dihedral form at the tips. Adjustable and variously pitched, it tilted and dipped, lifting the boat out of the water. At the waterway it was set in place and secured with wire cables.

On land the wing was folded back parallel to the hull and trailered, anchored in position with a toggle bar. A 100-hp Continental engine was in the hull and a 5-ft. pusher propeller was set between the tips of the tail fin.

The vehicle had a regular steering wheel, an automobile-type foot throttle, a curved windshield and leather bucket seats. Gross weight was 1200 lbs; fuel capacity was 25 gallons; range was 400 miles; ground speed was 60 mph; and air speed was 129 mph. Conversion took 10 minutes.

Baier and Fletcher envisioned a production prototype that would have a narrower two-fin tail with a horizontal airfoil between the fins for greater stability. The wing and hull would be aluminum. The cockpit would be fully enclosed.

Also in the late 1930s George Spratt designed a tiny, mosquito-like craft which consisted of a light, stripped-down hull with a wing on the tip. A small aviation engine in the rear was shafted to a pusher propeller set between tips of the tail fin.

In 1931 Consolidated Aircraft created a vehicle called the Commodore which held 20 passengers in three spacious cabins.

How to Find the **Best** Air Conditioner

POPULAR
JUNE 1962
35 CENTS

MECHANICS

This Boat Flies!

Valiant Owners Report

Two New Rotary Engines • **Build an Arc-Spot Welder**

Big Boom in Radio-Control Models:
   — Rigs for Planes • Plans for an R/C Racing Hydro

Above: Popular Mechanics for June 1962 featured the Wing Dingy speed boat of Baier and Fletcher. *Opposite, top:* Grumman Goose flying boat. *Bottom:* PBY Catalina 8026 flying boat (both photographs, San Diego Aerospace Museum).

Martin M-130 "China Clipper" flying boat (San Diego Aerospace Museum).

The Martin Aircraft Company had its M-130, a 3,000-mile long-range amphibian for 12 passengers.

Today's Martin Mars, the largest operational flying boat in the world, is a combination of airtanker and floatplane. Names include Mars Old Lady, Hawaii, Philippine, Marianas, Marshall and Caroline. Hawaii Mars can scoop up 7,200 gallons of water in less than half a minute. That's over 55,000 pounds.

The Boeing 314 Clipper was 100 ft. long and 27 ft. high and had four Wright Cyclone engines, 6,800 hp total. Its wingspan was 152 ft., cruising speed was 184 mph and maximum range was 5,200 miles. Some 74 passengers could be accommodated. Two Boeing conversions are also reported.

Also in 1931 plane designers were experimenting with a plane no wider than an automobile which could alight on and take off from land or water and be capable of vertical flight and hovering motionless in midair.

In 1944 Moulton B. Taylor designed a small, light, amphibious sport aircraft, the Duckling. It had a float-wing arrangement which allowed the aircraft to be amphibious without exterior floats. It had converted retractable tricycle landing gear.

In 1961 the Seaflight Corporation offered its stepped-hull speedboat, a two-seater with a 25-gallon fuel capacity and a range of 4,000 miles.

Also in 1961 the Evinrude Division of Outboard Marine Corporation offered its futuristic Heli-Boat, a combination helicopter and outboard boat.

Opposite, top: Boeing 314 flying boat (San Diego Aerospace Museum). *Bottom:* Heli-Boat from Evinrude (courtesy Evinrude Division, Outboard Marine Corp.).

Kirk Hawkin's Icon A5 plane-boat (courtesy Icon Aircraft).

In 2006 the four-place Airshark Amphibian kit came on the market. It had fiberglass composite construction. Its speed was 100 mph and it could cover a range of 100 miles on a 25-gallon fuel capacity.

In Russia the amphibious plane Beriev Be-200 was produced by the Irkut Corporation. This jet could land on water and scoop up 12 tons of water within 14 seconds, making it perfect for firefighting.

In 2008 former F16 fighter jet pilot Kirk Hawkins, founder of Icon Aircraft, introduced the A5, a two-seat propeller plane and recreational flying boat.

It has a red propeller behind the cockpit and a 34-ft.-long wing which can be folded and tucked behind the tail so it can be placed on a trailer. It is powered by a 100-hp engine. A parachute is optional. The interior resembles the cabin of a sports car. It can fly as slow as 50 mph or cruise at its 120 mph maximum speed. It runs on either aviation fuel or unleaded premium gasoline and takes a sport aircraft license.

In 1974 Ken London purchased a Boeing 308 airplane and turned it into a 56-ft. luxury yacht, the Londonaire. An old boat hull supported the fuselage. It moved at 30 knots. Then in 2002 Dave Drimmer acquired a 56-ft. Boeing 307 Stratoliner, the cosmic Muffin, and sheared off the wings and tail to convert it to a plane-houseboat. Both had belonged to Howard Hughes.

Sailboats

The Rohrbach flying sailboat of 1925 was hailed as the newest marvel of aviation.

It was all-metal Duralumin built by the Rohrbach Metal Airplane Company of Copenhagen with riveted girders and plates. There were two 12-cylinder engines raised above the

$10,000 Prize Contest – See Page 29

Popular Science

INVENTIONS

DISCOVERIES

RADIO

AUTOMOBILES

AVIATION

HOME WORKSHOP

Founded **MONTHLY** *1872*

AUGUST   Flying Sailboat—the Newest Marvel of the Air   25 CENTS

Rohrbach flying sailboat was featured on the cover of *Popular Science* in August 1925.

hull of the monoplane on hollow metal struts that carried the motors and propeller clear of the wing structure. Widespread cantilever wings slanted upward at an acute angle. It carried a mainsail, foresail and jib, all collapsible and serving as auxiliaries to the airplane engine.

There were two auxiliary stabilizing pontoons situated under the wings, as well as a beaching trailer. The hull was divided into watertight compartments by bulkheads and it could float with any two compartments flooded.

Submersibles

In the novel *Beyond Thirty* by Edgar Rice Burroughs, Captain Jefferson Tuck and the crew of his aero-submarine embark on an epic quest to rediscover the legendary lands of the Old World.

Military Submersibles

Seaplanes were used in World War I in training, observation and patrol. In World War II in Canada the Catalina flying boat PBY-5A was used by the RCAF and later found service as forest fire water bombers.

Also in World War II the Dormier DO-X flying boats saw service as transatlantic mail carriers and bombers.

CHAPTER V

Other Dual Vehicles

In addition to the two major dual vehicle categories of land-air and amphibious there are several other novelty pairings that occur much less frequently:

- Water–Underwater
- Road–Underwater
- Rail–Water

Water–Underwater

The two-seater Innespace Dolphin from New Zealand is a boat that can dive and make short trips underwater as a submarine.

Using a 240-hp rotary engine, the boat is shaped like a bottle-nosed dolphin but is a bit bigger at 16.5 ft. and 1,400 lb. It is capable of shallow-angle dives to a depth of about 5 ft. The crew stays dry under the same clear canopy used in an F-22 fighter jet.

Innespace Dolphin is a boat-submarine from New Zealand (***Detroit Free Press***, William Archie photograph).

sQuba shown in *Ripley's Believe It or Not* in 2008 (© 2008 Ripley Entertainment, Inc.).

The snorkel opening closes off on a dive and pitch and yaw controls adjust the front flipper (arteron) and tail fins independently. Banking, turning, climbing and descending are a lot like flying an airplane.

It has a speed of 40 mph on the surface and 20 mph underwater.

Kit models are also available. It is intended for boat races in particular.

Road-Underwater

The earliest experiments with submersible automobiles were carried out by Goubet, Gymnote and Gustave Zedi in a military milieu.

The electric-powered, all-terrain sQuba introduced in 2008 on a Lotus chassis, known as the scuba car, is a convertible that can travel at speeds of 77 mph on land, 3 mph on the surface of the water and about 1.8 mph at a depth of 30 ft. as a submersible. Occupants use scuba gear and tanks of compressed air to breathe for 90 minutes. Made by the Swiss firm Rinspeed, it is based on a James Bond vehicle and was designed by car designer Frank Rinderknecht.

Nomad, known as the upside-down car, was designed by Canadian diver and ocean engineer Doug Elsey. It is a submersible that has enough buoyancy to roll around underwater, using the bottom side of the ice sheet as a roadway. It was intended for exploration of northern Canada's polar ice pack. It requires about 5 ft. of ice to hold it down.

A customized white Lotus Esprit that could shoot bullets was used by James Bond to cruise underwater in the 1977 film *The Spy Who Loved Me*.

Rail-Water

In 1934 the Russian amphibious "Dream Train" could be converted into a boat for crossing major rivers while traveling from Siberia to Alaska.

In 1899 Swedish engineer Magelan built an amphibious tramway steamboat, designed to ply across two lakes north of Copenhagen. It was 15 m long by 4 m wide and weighs 11 tons empty and 15 tons with a maximum load. The engine had 25-hp and its action was transmitted by a triple gear, either to the propeller or to the rimmed wheels. It carried 70 passengers. Changeover was instantaneous.

CHAPTER VI

Triphibious Vehicles

Some modern Jules Vernes have mentioned in their designs vehicles which have tripartite ability to function on land, water and air. This is the next exciting possibility to emerge from science fiction into reality, and possibly to revolutionize the transportation industry.

The International Cargo Handling and Coordinating Association maintains an International Transportation Research and Technology Panel. This is devoted to establishing a global network of universities that will conduct research on all modes of transportation, including road, water, air and rail. One of the participating educational institutions is the University of Toledo in Toledo, Ohio, through its Intermodal Transportation Institute.

New designs in this category of combined vehicles that cover land, water and air peaked in the 1950s and surged a bit again in the 1980s.

In 1904 civil and consulting engineer Emery Harriman designed the radical Aerocar Sealander, a hydro-airplane with flexible wings and a canopy-parachute overhead. Its first trial run was on Dorchester Bay in Massachusetts.

The framework of the body and wing frames was made entirely of steel tubing covered with sheet brass and sheet copper. The vehicle covered a rolling drum-shaped pontoon with motorcycle tires. The rear pontoon had six compartments.

The wings on each side were pivoted in the body on the central propeller shaft in such a way that they could be held horizontal during flight.

The shaft of the motor passed entirely through the Aerocar. In front it was high enough to clear the air propeller from the water when the machine was being used as a hydroplane. It came out in the rear where there was a water propeller attached. The canopy was a flat horizontal wing with a perpendicular handle extending downward into the car in front of the operator. The Aerocar had a 125-hp motor, weighed 1,300 lb., and had a wing area of 450 sq. ft.

In 1918 Felix Longobardi designed an integrated combination vehicle: aircraft, road vehicle and gunboat.

It had airscrews and retractable wings on the front for flight. On the underside it had propellers for added lift. It had one rudder to be used for both flying and sailing, and a propeller at the stern for propulsion when on the water. Four wheels gave it movement on the ground, and three cannon protected it from intruders.

Right from the beginning Richard Buckminster ("Bucky") Fuller intended his Dymaxion Car to go by land, water and sky. He referred to it as his Omni-Medium 4D Transport.

Three handbuilt, three-wheeled prototypes were built in 1933 in the former Locomobile factory. These were similar in design to his experimental Dymaxion House. The word Dymaxion was a combination of the words dynamite, maximum and ion.

Buckminster Fuller (left) and Isamu Noguchi, Dymaxion Car collaborators (Estate of Arnold Eagle, c/o Susan Goldman).

The vehicles were brought to life with the help of famous naval architect and aircraft-builder Starling Burgess. This effort also marked the first artistic collaboration between Fuller and Isamu Noguchi, who created the first scale-sized plaster model.

The horizontal teardrop, cigar-shaped profile which tapered to a point at the end was highly streamlined and was said to resemble a light plane, an early Sikorsky helicopter, a Waco glider body from World War II or an Airstream camper frame.

Buckminster Fuller's Dymaxion Car, an innovative three-wheeler (National Automobile Museum — The Harrah Collection).

The vehicle was constructed using aircraft principles and with aviation styling. It had an aircraft-type fuselage; fixed, wrap-around aircraft windows; aircraft mechanical drum brakes; and an airspeed indicator on the dashboard.

The Dymaxion Car was mounted on two hammered aluminum frames, hinged at the front, with one frame carrying the engine and drive chain while the other carried the rear wheel mount, suspension and steering.

It used a stock, 221-cu.-in., 35-bhp, flathead Ford V-8 engine at the rear to drive the two front wheels. The single rear wheel steered like an aircraft tail-wheel or the rudder of a ship.

There were two doors on the right side only and no rear windows, just periscopes with a skylight. The roof was fabric-covered and held on by snaps.

Buckminster Fuller's Dymaxion House on display at the Henry Ford (from the Collections of the Henry Ford).

The driver sat well forward of the two major wheels up front. There were seats for 11 and the interior could be made up into a queen-size bed. Roll-over bars were provided. The insulated Formica interior was 6 ft. wide and 6 ft. long behind the front seats. To see rearward there was a panoramic mirror mounted on a spotlight stalk.

A single, central headlight was inserted into the nose and covered. The Dymaxion Car was 19 ft. long, weighed 2,300 lb. and had its center of gravity 23 in. off the ground. Its top speed was 120 mph and fuel economy was 30 mpg. Being omnidirectional, it could turn a complete circle within its own length.

At one time even inflatable rubber wings were suggested.

The third model was put on display at the 1934 World's Fair in Chicago, parked outside the 1934 New York Auto Show and later owned by Leopold Stokowski, Philadelphia Orchestra director, who bought it for his wife. Gulf Oil also used it on a publicity tour.

The second model is on display at the National Automobile Museum.

The portable Dymaxion House was conceived and designed in 1927, a round dwelling billed as "The House of the Future." Beech Aircraft Corporation produced a prototype in 1945.

The aviation motif was evident in such features as airplane doors and a stamped metal bathroom resembling an airplane bathroom. Fuller's favorite material, highly polished aluminum, was used throughout, along with steel and plastic.

The home, 1,017 sq. ft. with no basement, was suspended on a central column or mast like a giant umbrella.

Fuller gained 25 U.S. patents, authored 28 books, lectured extensively and earned 47 honorary doctorates. He enjoys a unique reputation, now being recognized as a multitasking engineer, inventor, designer, architect, mathematician, cartographer, teacher, author, poet, researcher, artist, philosopher, consultant, humanitarian and sailor.

Several other designers have attempted to invent cars like the Dymaxion, mostly in teardrop shape and aeronautically oriented.

Wallace L. Johnson has considered redesigning the Dymaxion and even building one.

In 1934 J. R. Jones designed a car using a "leaning through curves" chassis.

In 1934 industrial designer Norman Bel Geddes designed a four-wheel model.

In 1937 Paul Lewis came out with his Airmobile, an experimental sedan with huge oval doors, and he followed it up with his Fascination in 1962, the prototype propeller-driven by a rear engine. It looked like an airplane with no wings. The single front wheel had a system similar to that used on lightplane landing gears.

In the 1940s H. B. Oldfield and J. H. Norton in British Columbia designed the Aero-car with four wheels.

In 1935 Constantios H. Vlachos designed Triphibka, a three-way vehicle.

While Dr. William R. Bertelsen had been designing ground-effect Aeromobile vehicles (over 11 different models) since 1950, it was not until his eighth, the Arcopter GEM-3, that they became roadable. It was introduced in 1962 as a four-passenger production prototype with only one major moving part, the engine fan unit.

Airmobile three-wheel experimental sedan (National Automobile Museum — The Harrah Collection).

Fascination car designed by Paul Lewis along airplane lines (courtesy Keith and Eileen Carpenter).

SPECIFICATIONS

General

Empty weight . . . . 1,800 lb.
Gross weight (four passengers) . . . . 2,500 lb.
Maximum useful load . . . . 1,000 lb.
Length . . . . 20 ft.
Height to propeller tip . . . . 87 in.
    canopy top . . . . 72 in.
Width . . . . 94 in.

Engine

180-bhp Lycoming 0–360 piston engine
Fuel: automotive regular gas
Fuel consumption at cruise: 9 gal./hr.

Performance

Maximum forward speed . . . . 90 mph
Cruise speed . . . . 70 mph
Altitude without external wing panels . . . . 3 in. at zero
                                          speed; 18 in. at top
                                          speed with stub
                                          wings; 6 ft. at top
                                          speed
Grade climbing, slope depending on load 20–25%

Bertelsen ground-effect Aeromobile on display in Tokyo in 2002 (National Air and Space Museum, Smithsonian Institution, Neg. No. SI 94-13009).

Construction
Aircraft alloy tubing, aluminum sheet fiberglass

Standard Equipment
Flotation of 3,500-lb. displacement, fiberglass flotation tanks. Goodyear aircraft wheels, brakes and tires, steerable and retractable. Controllable pitch propeller.

Several different models are housed in the National Air and Space Museum.

In 1950 Al Geraci and William Simonini designed an integrated, amphibious Jeep-O-Plane with folding, variable-lift wings and two airfoils. On the road it was to be powered by the propeller. It was to take off at 30 mph, land at 25 mph, and cruise at 150 mph.

In 1951 Wilber L. Masterson designed a land, sea and air plane with a rotor and three wheels with one driven.

In 1952 Robert Z. Schreffler designed an aircraft with two engines, a pusher propeller, three wheels with two driven, a detachable flight section and twintail booms.

In 1955 J. F. "Skeets" Coleman, a professional test pilot, designed an air-sea-land vehicle, the 2,500-lb. Triphibious Aeromarine. This was a delta-wing shape arrangement that folded in two places to box in the pusher propeller. This gave the car portion a total width of 75 in. Power was a 215-hp Franklin engine that fed to the two rear wheels of the tricycle landing gear; the front wheel was steerable. A watertight hull allowed it to land on water with a pair of hydro-skis attached to a retractable airbag. Passenger capacity was four or five and the vehicle had an 800-mile range on 80 gallons of fuel. Speed was calculated to be 200 mph in the air and 50 mph on the road.

In 1956 Edward F. Bland designed a roadable aircraft and sailboat.

In 1958 Ogden L. Martin designed a triphibious, one-engine land-water-air vehicle with a ducted fan or channel and four wheels.

In 1959 Einar Einarsson designed a flying car with one engine, three tractor and pusher propellers, four wheels with two driven, and no wings. It could also be used as a boat.

In 1963 Romanian Steven Postelson Apostolescu designed a flying platform, an automobile, boat and air-suspension car combination. His helicopter version was called the Helimobile and had collapsible blades. He was associated with the rotary-winged industry from the early 1940s and had several U.S. patents for helicopters, convertiplanes and advanced aircraft systems.

In 1964 C. E. Gorton designed a triphibious vehicle.

In 1977 the Heli-Home came on the market, manufactured by Helicopter Airways and sold through the Itaska Division of Winnebago Industries. The 46-ft., eight-passenger flying camper with a cabin that provided 115 ft. of living space consisted of a surplus Vietnam War and Coast Guard dual-control Sikorsky helicopter connected to a Winnebago

Heli-Home helicopter camper (courtesy Helicopter Airways).

Heli-Home interior (courtesy Helicopter Airways).

motor home. It was powered by an 800-hp Wright Cyclone engine and carried enough fuel for a 350-mile flight at 100 mph.

It boasted an optional float for amphibious landings, a triple-threat vehicle. It was intended as a portable cabin chiefly for sportsmen, or as a field office for exploration crews and executives of oil and mineral companies.

In 1984 Joseph N. Ayoola designed an air, land and sea vehicle. The vehicle had four tires as an automobile as well as roadable vehicle structures that could be moved outward for highway usage and inward into stored position for the aircraft form or boat form. It also had storage for the wing and tail assemblies, which had a foldable section. For conversion between aircraft form and boat form, the apparatus had a retractable or extendable water propeller for use in the water, and parts arranged for steering. The wings and tail assemblies were moved inwardly into stored position, including auto and aero tires that moved into their waterproof compartments. When the boat converted to the aircraft form the wings, tail assemblies, and propelling structures were moved outward, including a winglifter to give the wings sufficient clearance from the water in order to achieve sufficient relative wind to allow the vehicle to take off. The water rudder maintained a straight forward movement. The auto and aero engines operated until takeoff on the water, then the automobile engine was turned off. The water propeller and rudder moved inwardly into their respective compartments.

In 1987 Harold I. Thompson designed a land, water and air craft comprising a lightweight body constructed in modular form and a removable lightweight engine of the motorcycle type. It had forward and rearward sections constructed in a manner that allowed in-flight or in-use alteration or molding to achieve the optimum planar or contour design as required when airborne.

In 1988 Peter J. Fitzpatrick designed a vehicle for use on land, air and water. Outer wing portions were connected to a central portion by a mechanism which allowed the outer portion to pivot into a stored position. The outer wing portions were also rotatable about a second axis in order to place them in positions where they could be used as sails for driving the vehicle without the engine. The wheels were capable of being pivoted out of the way.

In 1988 Russian designer Yuri Krassin came out with his long-range Autocraft 011. His road module was a quadricycle. It was 40 in. wide and had a 1 + 2 + 1 place configuration, or could seat three in tandem. It had a tilt steering control operated by the pilot on the road. Conversion was by push button. The flight module was removable and the cabin was pressurized. It was also available in kit form and it was possible to install two big floats and use the vehicle as a recreational trimaran vessel under sail, a veritable flying yacht.

SPECIFICATIONS

Takeoff weight . . . . As much as 860 kg
Engines . . . . Two Yanmar D 27 outboard
turbocharged diesel engines
Engine rating . . . . 800 cc, providing up
to 50 hp each
Wingspan . . . . 12.6 m
Main wing area . . . . 7.8 sq. m
Forward main wing sweep . . . . 5 degrees
Canard wingspan . . . . 4 m
Canard area . . . . 1 sq. m
Cruise CL/CD 24
Maximum cruise speed (TAS) . . . . 195 knots at an altitude
of 31,000 ft.
Maximum range . . . . 3,800 nautical miles on
160 kg of fuel
Approach speed . . . . 70 knots/hr.
Takeoff and landing distance (ISA) . . . . 300 m

In 1994 Bill Schugt, a professional engineer of the IDM Company, introduced his Air-car 7 Seagull, a roadable amphibious canard aircraft. The wings retracted into the fuselage hull and sponsons rotated up and outboard for water operation. There was an 84-in. diameter propeller over the bubble canopy which slid forward for entry to four seats. It had an air speed of 180 mph and was capable of landing on a 1,500-ft. runway or on water. It could be driven at highway speeds through the use of a hydraulic propulsion system that engaged with the 256-hp liquid-cooled engine.

Anthony Pruszenski, Jr., has designed an integrated ground–air–water craft with a box wing with a total wingspan in the range of 5–10 ft. It had a canard wing at the front to provide pitch control and the canard span was to be no greater than 10 ft. Front and rear wheels could be retractable. The body portion of the fuselage was to be watertight with a hydroplane bottom surface for reduced resistance when the craft was used on the water. The rear wheels were to be beneath the lower main wing in a longitudinal position that prevented them from contacting the ground when the craft was flying at an extreme upward pitch.

Glossary

ACV — Air-cushion vehicle

Aerodynamics — Study of air moving against objects, or of objects moving through the air

Aeronautics — Science and art of flying aircraft

Aeroplane — British spelling of airplane

Aerostation — Operation of lighter-than-air craft

Ailerons — Hinged sections near wingtips on the trailing edge used to control banking or rolling movements

The Air-Car Research Association (TACRA) — Non-profit scientific research and education organization of Richard Strong

Air speed — Speed of an aircraft in relation to the air through which it moves

Aircraft — Any vehicle capable of flight

Airfoil — Aileron wing or propeller that acts on the air to provide lift or control

Airframe — Whole body of the aircraft apart from its engines

Airplane — Vehicle with wings and jet engine or propellers that is heavier than air and is able to fly

Airport — Area where civil aircraft may take off and land

Airscrew — Propeller

Amphibians — Aircraft that can land or take off on either land or water

Articulated fuselage — Central body of aircraft that is made of two or more sections connected by a joint that can pivot

Autogiro — Aircraft that uses a propeller for forward motion and an unpowered horizontal rotor for lift and stability

Autogyro — (see Gyrocopter)

Automatic transmission — Gears that change automatically in response to the speed of the vehicle

Aviation — Design, manufacture, use or operation of aircraft

Avionics — Electric and electronic equipment in aerospace vehicles

Axle — Shaft on which wheel turns

Bay — Area divided off and used for a particular purpose

Biplane — Plane with two wings, one over the other, sticking out of each side

Blueprint — Technical drawing used as a reference before and during the building process

Boom — Span that connects the tail and fuselage

CAA — Civil Aeronautics Administration

CAB — Civil Aeronautics Board

Camber — Fore and aft curve of the surfaces of the wing

Canard — Small projection like a wing near the aircraft's nose to create a lifting force

Cantilever — Wing arrangement with no external brace

Carburetor — Device that mixes liquid fuel and air in correct proportions, vaporizes them, and transfers the mixture to cylinders

Ceiling — Maximum height to fly

Celluloid — Colorless plastic

Center of gravity — Point through which the sum of gravitational forces on a body can be considered to act

Chopper — Helicopter, motorcycle or bicycle with a lowered seat, raised handlebars and lengthened forks holding the front wheels

Climb — Move upward steeply

Clutch — Mechanism that smoothly connects and disconnects shafts

Co-axial rotors — Rotors which have a common axis

Cockpit — Pilot compartment containing instruments and controls

Cog — Projection on the edge of a gear wheel

Control Stick — Device used to control an aircraft's motion, universally mounted in cockpit

Convertiplane — Aircraft that can be converted in flight from helicopter to conventional aircraft and back to helicopter again

Coupe — Car with two doors and a hard, fixed roof that seats two people or has a small rear seat

Cowl — Part of automobile to which windshield, hood and dashboard are attached

Cowling — Streamlined, removable metal covering for an engine, fuselage or nacelle

Crop dusting — Action of dusting or spraying cotton, corn, peas, or other crops with fungicide or insecticide; action of seeding rice fields

Crosswind landing — Landing an aircraft when the wind is blowing across the direction of travel

Cruise range — Maximum distance the aircraft can travel without needing to refuel

Custom — Made to order

Delta wings — Wings with a triangular, swept-back shape

Diesel fuel — Thick oil from petroleum distillation

Direct drive — Driving and driven parts that are directly connected

Disc brakes — Brakes that work by the friction of a caliper or pads against a rotating disc

Drag — Force which resists an object's forward motion through air

Duct — Tube, pipe or chamber

Elevator — Hinged airfoil on rear edge of horizontal stabilizer which controls attitude of nose

Empennage — Tail assembly, rear part of aircraft including stabilizer, elevator, vertical fin and rudder

Erocoupe Airplane — Easy-to-fly model of the 1930s and 1940s intended for the mass market of weekend pilots

FA — Flying auto

Fairing — Streamlined wood structure to reduce drag

Fan — Aircraft propeller (slang)

Fin — Upright part of tail which gives stability and attaches to the rudder

Flair-pivot — Wing control

Flap — Airfoil under the surface of the wing near its trailing edge between the aileron and wing root section; used to change wing shape

Flivver — Small, cheap, old car

Flying vehicle — Land vehicle capable of taking to the air after modification and outfitting

Flywheel — Heavy wheel or disc that helps to maintain a constant speed of rotation

Footprint — Space occupied on takeoff and landing

Front-wheel drive — System of powering motor vehicles that uses the engine to drive the front wheels only

Fuel cells — Device that generates electricity by converting the chemical energy of a fuel and an oxidant to electric energy

Fuselage — Aircraft body containing cockpit, passenger seating, and cargo hold, but excluding the wings

GAV — Go-anywhere–vehicle

Gearbox   Transmission

GEM — Ground-effect machine

Glide path — Prescribed descent coming in to land

Glider — Aircraft with no engine that flies by riding air currents

GPA — General purpose amphibian

Ground-effect machine — hovercraft

GTV — Ground test vehicle

Gullwing — Wing that slants upward from the fuselage for a short distance and then levels out

Gyrocopter — Rotary-wing flying machine, also called autogyro, gyroplane, rotaplane

Gyroplane — (see Gyrocopter)

Hatchback — Car with a door at the back that is hinged from the roof

Helicopter — Aircraft without wings that moves by means of large blades on rotors that spin around above it. It can fly vertically and horizontally and hover

High-wing — Monoplane wing location

Home built — Plane that is built from a kit or "from scratch"

Horizontal-opposed — Type of aircraft gasoline engine with horizontal line of stroke

Horizontal stabilizer — Device that controls pitching, or up-and — down motion

Hull — Main body

Hydraulic disc brakes — Brakes that use force applied through a mechanism operated like a small hydraulic press

In-line engine — Engine with cylinders in a straight line

Integrated — Roadable aircraft that carries flight equipment

Jeep — Four-wheel-drive vehicle suitable for difficult terrain

Jet — Vehicle powered by a jet engine

Joystick — (see Control stick)

Kit — Homebuilt aircraft; set of plans for assembly

Knockdown — Kit aircraft

Landing gear — Undercarriage that absorbs shocks and supports weight

Landing speed — Minimum speed to be flying in order to land safely

Leading edge — Forward edge of wing, propeller or airfoil

Levitation vehicle — Vehicle which rises in air

Lift — Force that supports aircraft in the air, counteracting gravity

Longeron — Main structural component of the fuselage that runs from one end to the other

Low slung — Relatively close to the ground

Low-wing — Monoplane wing location

LSA — FAA light sport aircraft classification

Magneto — Small alternator in an ignition system

Manifold — Chamber or pipe with parts in an engine

Mid-wing — Monoplane wing location

Mock-up — Nonflying, full-size model of aircraft, usually made of wood or paper

Model — Small-scale accurate copy of larger aircraft

Mono-tilt rotor — System with a single disc, blades and engines horizontally mounted around the body of the aircraft

Monocoque construction — Fuselage built with ringlike bulkheads without cross bracing

Monoplane — Plane with just one wing which sticks out on both sides of the body

Multi-engine plane — Plane with more than one engine

Multiplane — Plane with more than one wing

NACA — National Advisory Committee for Aeronautics

Nacelle — Separate streamlined enclosure for crew, cargo or engines

Nose — Pointed or rounded front of aircraft

Nose wheel — Landing-gear wheel at the plane's front end under the nose

Oilpan — Lower section of the crankcase in the engine which is used as a lubricating-oil reservoir

Ornithopter — Flying machine which would flap its wings like a bird (Bacon)

Outrigger wheels — Projecting frame of spars, distance pieces and braces which supports the elevator on the tail

Parachute — Canopy attached to a harness to slow speed of drop

Payload — Quantity of cargo or load aircraft can carry in weight or volume

Pivot — Object on which a larger object turns, such as a bar or pin

Plane — (see Airplane)

Power loading — Weight per horsepower computed on full load and of power in air of standard density

Power plant — Engine and related parts supplying motive power

Prop — (see Propeller)

Propeller — Blades mounted on a power-driven shaft that changes the power of the engine into thrust; made from wood, metal, or plastic

Prototype — First full-scale, functional, piloted model

Pusher airplane — Airplane which has the propellers behind the wings

Radial — Type of gasoline aircraft engine with cylinders arranged around a central crankshaft

Range — Area within which or distance over which aircraft can operate effectively without refueling

Rib — Part of the wing crossing from the leading to the trailing edge of the wing

Roadable aircraft — Aircraft able to be driven on land after modification and outfitting

Root — (see Wingroot)

Rotaplane — (see Gyrocopter)

Rotary engine — Engine that has rotating cylinders around a fixed crankshaft

Rotary wing — Supported in flight partially or wholly by rotating airfoils

Rotors — Assembly of airfoils that rotate about a hub to give lift to a helicopter

Rudder — Airfoil, usually on the tail, that pivots vertically and controls left-to-right movement

Run up — Increase speed of engine either in stationary aircraft or on a test stand to test, check or warm engine

Sailplane — Light glider that makes use of rising air currents, used for soaring

Seaplane — Plane which lands or takes off only on water with floats or pontoons

Self-starter motor — Engine that starts using automatic attachments, rather than a crank or auxiliary turning parts

Severe staggering — Biplane with one wing ahead of the other

Ski plane — Plane which takes off and lands on snow

Skin — Wing covering

Span — Part of wing framework that runs the length of the wing

Speedster — Fast car

Spinproof — Incapable of spinning

Spiral springs — Wire coiled in a flat spiral or helix

Spoiler plate — Narrow hinged airfoil in the wing for controlling lift and drag

Stabilizer — Airfoil or combination in tail assembly that keeps aircraft aligned with the direction of flight

Stall — Sudden dive

Streamlined — Having a smooth shape which cuts wind resistance

Strut — Brace, support

Sweptwing — Slanted back from wingroot to wingtip

TACRA — The Air-Car Research Association

Tail — Rear together with surfaces attached

Tail wheel — Auxiliary wheel in light planes on which the rear of the aircraft rests or taxis on the ground

Takeoff— Process of leaving the ground and beginning to fly.

Tandem engine — Engines arranged one behind other

Taxi — To move on the ground under an aircraft's own power

Telescopic support — Collapsible parts that slide inside one another

Tethered — Having restricted movement

Throttle — Valve used to control the flow of fluid

Thrust — Force of propeller that causes the aircraft to move forward

Torsion bar suspension — Vehicle suspension in which a metal bar acts as a spring

Tractor airplane — Plane which has propellers in front of its wings

Trailing edge — Rearmost edge of wing, airfoil or propeller blade

Transaxle — Combination of the front axle and transmission

Transmission — Mechanism transferring power to the wheels, including gears and shafts

Tricycle landing gear — Landing gear with one nose-wheel and two wheels behind it

Trim — Adjust controls to give stability

Triphibian — Vehicle which operates on water, land, and air

Triplane — Plane with three main wings above one another

Tripod — Type of three-part landing gear

Turbine engine — Rotary engine with a series of curved vanes on a central spindle

Turbocharger — Specialized turbine driven by the engine's exhaust gasses that supplies air under pressure to engine for combustion

Twin-engine plane — Plane that has two engines

Two-stroke engine — Engine which completes its thermodynamic cycle in two strokes, rather than four.

UAV — Unmanned aerial vehicle

Umbilical device — Cable, pipe or tube providing a link

UMR — Unmanned, manned and/or remote

Undercarriage — Framework of struts and wheels

Van — Enclosed with rear or side doors or sliding side panels

Vane — Rotating blade

Vertical stabilizer — Device which controls yawing, or side-to-side motion

VTOL — Vertical takeoff and landing

Wheelbase — Distance between the front axle and the rear axle of a vehicle

Wing — Framework of metal, wood or carbon fiber covered with cloth

Wing loading — Gross weight of a fully loaded aircraft divided by the area of supporting surface

Wingroot — Inner end of wing attached to the body of the aircraft

Wingtip — Outside end of the wing

Wingspan — Length of the wing measured between its outermost tips regardless of intervening elements

Winglets — Wingtip-mounted angled vertical fins

Yoke — Handle of the steering mechanism for ailerons

Bibliography

Books

Cheetham, Craig. *The World's Worst Cars*. New York: Metro Books, 2005.

Chirinian, Alain. *Weird Wheels*. Englewood Cliffs, NJ: Julian Messner, 1989.

Fleming, Ian. *Chitty Chitty Bang Bang*. New York: Random House, 1964.

Gunnell, John A. *Weird Cars*. Iola, WI: Krause Publications, 1993.

Kessel, Adrienne. *The World's Strangest Automobiles*. Broxbourne, Hertfordshire, U.K.: Metro Books, 2001.

Koran, Frantisek, Ladislav Rojka, and Ivo Pospisil. *Schwimmwagen in Detail*. Prague: RAK, 2001.

Miller, Ron. *Extreme Aircraft*. New York: HarperCollins, 2007.

Schultz, Jake. *A Drive in the Clouds: The Story of the Aerocar*. Issaquah, WA: Jake Schultz, 2006.

Stambler, Irwin. *Automobiles of the Future*. New York: Putnam's, 1966.

Stiles, Palmer. *Roadable Aircraft: From Wheels to Wings*. Melbourne, FL: Custom Creativity, 1994.

Travers, Jim. *Extreme Cars*. New York: HarperCollins, 2007.

Waterman, Waldo Dean, with Jack Carpenter. *Waldo: Pioneer Aviator*. Carlisle, MA: Arsdalen, Bosch, 1988.

Zuk, Bill. *Canada's Flying Saucer*. Erin, Ontario: Boston Mills Press, 2001.

Periodicals

"Add Wings and Fly." *Motor*, December 1946, 160.

"Aerobile." *Road and Track*, August 1961, 2.

"Aerocar: Air and Water." *Flying*, August 1963, 78.

"Aerocar for Oshkosh." *Aeroplane*, June 1908, 10.

"Air Car Exhibit." *Sales Meetings*, May 19, 1961, 25.

"Air Cars." *Pilot Journal*, September 10, 1906, 78–84.

"Airboats Offer Travel Over Soggy Terrain." *Grit*, August 2003, 20.

"Airphibian Certificate." *Flying*, April 1950, 50b.

Allen, Mike. "Where the Rubber Leaves the Road." *Popular Mechanics*, July 1905, 72–77, 123–24.

Allen, Thomas B. "Odd DUKW." *Smithsonian*, August 2002, 74–77.

"America: Fly — Drive the Taylor Aerocar." *Aeroplane* (January 1999): 26–31.

"Amphibian." *Automotive Industries*, October 29, 1938, 517.

"Amphibian for Duck Hunters." *Popular Mechanics*, June 1963, 97.

"Amphibian Scout Car." *Motor*, July 30, 1941, 11.

"Amphibious." *Popular Mechanics*, July 1967, 107.

"Amphibious Auto." *Automotive Industries*, March 24, 1980, 1.

"Amphibious Auto Invented by American." *Automobile Digest*, November 1921, 25.

"Amphibious GEM Takes Swamp in Stride." *Popular Mechanics*, July 1952, 113.

"An Amphibious Motor." *Motor*, August 1907, 56.

"The Amphibious Rhino Goes about Anywhere." *Motor Age*, September 1951, 158–59.

"An Amphibious Truck." *Commercial Vehicle*, January 1, 1916, 27.

"Amphibious Truck for Land or Sea Operations." *Automotive Industries*, April 15, 1954, 19.

"Amphimobil." *Pickup, Van and 4WD*, May 1978, 102.

"Annual Roundup." *Flying*, December 1953, 52.

"Arrowbile." *Automotive Industries*, March 6, 1937, 381.

Askew, Mark. "Mark Askew Takes a Look at the Rotabuggy Flying Jeep." *Military Machines International*, August 2007, 22–24.

"Auto on Cables Is River Ferry." *Popular Science*, October 1932, 40.

"Auto Panel." *Motor Age*, November 1937, 56.

"Autogiro Company Building Flying Automobile." *Automobile Topics*, May 4, 1935, 27.

"The Autoplane for Land and Air Travel." *Scientific American*, March 24, 1917, 303, 314.

"Autoplane Nears Completion." *Automotive Industries*, May 1, 1939, 570.

"Auto-Plane Sheds Wings in Five Minutes." *Popular Mechanics*, February 1947, 152.

Baldwin, J. "Dymaxion Transports." *Automobile Magazine*, July 1968, 108–115.

"Baring the WCK Copter." *Aviation*, July 1945, 208.

Bauman, Richard. "A Different Type of Wing Car." *Autoweek*, November 24, 1978, 1.

_____. "Fantasy Flyers." *Elks Magazine*, September 1994, 34–35, 48.

Beach, Edward L. "Navy Power: A View from the Air." *American Heritage*, October 11, 1986, 66–73.

Becker, Jeffrey. "Fuels for the Future: What Will Power Your Aircraft?" *Sport Aviation*, February 2009, 38–45.

"Beetle-Powered GEM." *Popular Mechanics*, May 1967, 137.

Bilger, M. "University of Toledo Intermodal Transport Institute." *Business Advantage*, July 2004, Al–A6.

Blanchard, Harold F. *Motor*, May 1935, 40, 102.

"Boat Home." *Maxim*, March 2004, 62.

Boesen, Victor. "Fly or Drive It." *Flying Sportsman and Skyways*. September 1947, 28–29, 59.

"Bryan Autoplane." *Experimental*, September 1957, 18.

Busha, Jim. "Folding Wings." *Sport Aviation*, November 2008, 35–42.

"CAA Certifies Aerocar Flying Autocraft." *Western Aviation*, January 1957, 24.

"Car Pool." *Star*, February 9, 1988, 49.

"Cars That Fly: Swing High, Sweet Chariot." *Special Interest Autos*, April 5, 1972, 36–41, 54.

"Cars That Swim." *Special Interest Autos*, April 5, 1973, 50–54.

Chiles, James A. "Flying Cars Were a Dream That Never Got Off the Ground." *Smithsonian*, January 1989, 144–62.

Cilio, John. "Flying Cars." *Atlantic Flyer*, May 2007, 38.

_____. "Flying Cars." *Atlantic Flyer*, June 2007, 15.

_____. "Flying Cars." *Atlantic Flyer*, August 2007, 15.

_____. "Terrafugia Transition." *Atlantic Flyer*, October 2007, 10.

_____. "Traffic Is a Matter of Perspective." *Atlantic Flyer*, September 2007, 10.

"Consolidated Vultee Pioneers Revolutionary Controllable Wing." *Western Flying*, April 1945, 212.

Cox, Jack. "Aerocar: Molt Taylor's Quest for a More Useful Airplane." *Sport Aviation*, January 1990, 11–21.

"Craziest Car in the Air." *Cavalier*, May 1958, 40–1.

"The Curtiss Autoplane." *Aerial Age Weekly*, February 19, 1917, 656.

"The Curtiss Autoplane: An Aerial Limousine." *Sport Aviation*, August 1987, 32.

"CW Industries Copter Is Two-Place Roadable." *Aviation*, September 1945, 172–73.

de Glatigny. "The Amphibulous Automobile." *Automobile Magazine*, April 1899, 56–7.

"Delia Rolls on Land and Sea." *Automobile Topics*, March 4, 1916, 306–7.

Dempe Wolff, Richard F. "This Boat Flies." *Popular Mechanics*, June 1962, 67–71, 196.

"A Design in Logic." *Sport Aviation*, September 1962, 22–25, 27.

"Detachable Wings Turn Three-Wheel Car into a Plane." *Popular Science*, January 1940, 145.

"Details of "Ducks" Tire Pressure." *Control*, September 1945, 57, 158.

"The Dewey Bryan Awards." *Sport Aviation*, June 1975, 18–20.

"Does Everything but Dive." *Motor Age*, March 29, 1928, 12.

"Dream Camper." *Popular Mechanics*, December 1961, 81.

"Ducted Rotors Make Helicopter a Real Flying Saucer." *Popular Mechanics*, July 1966, 65.

Edwards, Owen, "Daredevil." *Smithsonian*, March 2008, 30–31.

"80 Years Ago Cold Fusion." *Smithsonian*, November 2007, 32.

"Evel Knievel." *People*, December 17, 2007, 142–43.

Fales, Dan. "Speeding over the Sea." *Popular Mechanics*. May 1967, 20.

"Family Bus Takes to Water." *People*, March 1960, 114–15.

"Fantastic Flying Sub." *Popular Mechanics*, September 1967, 114–15.

"Firm Modifying Firebird for Air and Land Travel." *Automotive News*, August 10, 1970, 4.

"Flying Auto Displayed." *Automotive News*, January 26, 1970, 12, 16.

"Flying Automobile Sheds Wings in Five Minutes." *Popular Mechanics*, May 1946, 87.

"Flying Automobile Uses Two Engines." *Popular Mechanics*, February 1948, 159.

"A Flying Bike That Won $186,000." *U.S. News and World Report*, October 31, 1977, 92.

"Flying Car Design." *Aeroplane*, June 1908, 80.

"Flying Car Shows Speed with Operating Economy." *Motor*, November 1937, 180.

"Flying Cars." *Scientific American*, February 1946, 73.

"Flying Corvair." *Special Interest Autos*, August 9, 1972, 6.

"Flying Penthouse, How Luxurious." *Grit*, January 6, 1974, 2.

"Flying Sailboat Newest Mode of Aviation." *Popular Science*, August 1925, 19.

"Flying Studebaker." *Southern Driver*, Winter, 1970, 22–23.

"Flying Talk." *Popular Science*, July 1932, 12–13.

"Float Camper." *Ford Times*, June 1977, 6–12.

"For Home and Away." *U.S. News and World Report*, April 10, 1978, 56.

"For Road or Airway." *Motor*, December 1936, 40.

Freeman, David. "Blacktop to Blue Sky." *Popular Mechanics*, August 1994, 33–35.

_____. "This Is Rocket Science." *Inc*, July 2000, 75–88.

Fuchs, Alice S. "Report on the Aerocar." *Flying*, September 1957, 38–39, 86–88.

Gardner, Erle Stanley. "The Case of the Agile ATVs." *Popular Science*, February 1970, 70–73, 148.

"A Genuine Flying Saucer Gets a Workout." *Popular Science*, September 1967, 119.

"German Inventor." *Motor Age*, January 1937, 48.

Gernsback, Hugo. "Monster Machines of the Next War." *Everyday Science and Mechanics*, October 1934, 536–37, 564–65.

Glines, C. V. "The Road Not Taken." *Aviation History*, September 2008, 38–45.

Grant, Bob. "Air-Cushion Vehicles." *Popular Mechanics*, December 1965, 64b.

Gross, Ken. "1967 Amphicar." *Special Interest Autos*, December 1981, 26–30, 64–65.

"The Gwinn Aircar." *Popular Aviation*, November 11, 1937, 16.

"Half Plane — Half Car." *Sun*, September 5, 1989, 21.

"Hall of Shame." *Fortune*, November 22, 1999, 140.

Hamilton, Laric. "Classic Cockpits." *Sport Aviation*, February 2007, 16.

Hampson, Donald A. "Experience Gained As a Result of Road Test of Railcars." *Automotive Industries*, April 6, 1923, 754–56.

_____. "Problems in the Operation of the Railway Motor Car." *Automotive Industries*, June 3, 1920, 1256–60.

_____. "Solving the Problems of the Railway Motor Car." *Automotive Industries*, January 1, 1920, 21–24.

"Here's What It Was." *Reminisce*, September 10, 1997, 57.

"Hervey Travelplane Is New Roadable Project." *Aviation*, April 1946, 100.

"Highway Hybrids." *Car Life*, January 1958, 43.

Hill, Herb. "Plane Talk." *Atlantic Flyer*, February 2008, 35.

"Home Built Roadable Plane Costs $250." *Aviation Week*, January 2, 1956, 55.

"Hovercraft." *Maxim*, April 2003, 162.

"How About the Next War." *Mechanics and Handcraft*, January 1937, 26–32, 107–9.

"How to Get Away from It All." *Air Progress*, February 3, 1964, 16–17.

"Hybrid." *Motor Age*, April 1937, 28.

"Hybrid Car-Airplane to Be Flight Tested." *Aviation Week and Space Technology*, June 11, 1973, 67.

"In the Air." *Independent*, February 26, 1917, 343.

"Is It Aerocar or Auroplane?" *Grit*, February 3, 1974, 40.

"Is It an Automobile or an Aeroplane? *The Horseless Age*, March 1, 1917, 40.

"Italy's Helicopter Rises, Hovers, Flies." *Popular Science*, February 1931, 55.

"It's a Bird, It's a Plane, It's History." *Inc*, June 2000, 84.

"Jeep Vehicle Developed for Rail." *Trailer/Body Builders*, June 1972, 57.

Jensen, Eric R. "Whatever Happened to Those Flying Cars?" *Mechanics Illustrated*, January 1974, 32–34.

"Koppel Rail Car." *Automotive Industries*, April 5, 1930, 559.

Kubacki, David. "Transition Vehicle Prepares to Bring Life Back to Small, Local Airports." *Business Advantage*, February 2007, 1, 3.

Lacayo, Richard. "The Big Thing." *Time*, July 19, 2008, 61.

Lamm, Mike. "Dymaxion." *Car Life*, May 1963, 49–53.

"Land and Water." *Automobile*, February 7, 1941, 18A.

"Let's Go Airpooling." *Readers Digest*, November 2007, 17.

Lindsley, E. F. "What Kind of ATV Is Best for You?" *Popular Science*, September 1969, 71–76.

Marthason, A. "Bird or Beast?" *Aeroplane*, May 16, 1947, 510–11.

McConnell, Curt. "The Plymocoupe." *Automotive History Review*, Winter 1994, 36–39.

Mellow, Craig. "When Ships Have Wings." *Air and Space*, December 1995 — January 1996, 52–59.

Naugle, R. C. "Practical Design Considerations for a Retractable Roadable Airplane." *Western Flying*, February 1949, 16–17.

"New Military Motor Truck Is at Home in the Water." *Popular Mechanics*, October 1917, 501–2.

"News in Pictures." *Motor*, January 18, 1938, 32.

"Night and Day." *Automotive Industries*, December 1, 1948, 22.

"1967 Amphicar: Split Personality." *Special Interest Autos*, February 1981, 26–32, 64–65.

"Ocean Auto." *Popular Mechanics*, April 1950, 172.

"Odds and Ends." *Air Classics*, April 1975, 74.

Oertle, V. Lee. "Buy It, Built It, Ride on It." *Popular Science*, July 1963, 54–55, 169.

"Off-Road Truck Walks on Its Wheels." *Popular Science*, April 1966, 107.

"Otter RV Converts Instantly from Travel Trailer to Houseboat." *RV Business*, January 21, 1991, 42.

Pares, Dennis. "The Autocar Takes to the Air." *Sport Aviation*, August 1987, 32.

"Paul L. Lewis's Airmobile." *Colorado Heritage*, Winter 1994 36–40.

"Paul Moller." *Esquire*, December 2003, 189–91, 210.

Petersen, Norm. "The Aerocar Restoration." *Sport Aviation*, July 1991, 41–45.

"Pitcairn AC 35." *Mother Jones*, March 4, 2000, 24.

"The Plane Mobile." *Air Trails and Science*, March 1947, 10.

"Planes That Drive, Cars That Fly." *AOPA Pilot*, August 1973, 72–75.

Poel, Jim, and Lee Sackett. "America: The First of the Great Flying Boats." *Vintage Airplane*, January 2009, 6–11.

"Pogo Pilot Designs Air-Sea-Land Sedan." *Popular Science*, November 1955, 143.

"Postwar Private Planes Begin Hatching with Three Models by Convair's W. B. Stout." *Aviation*, September 1943, 273.

"Practical Autoplane Licensed." *Automobile Topics*, September 1957, 5.

"Pusher Prop Plane Converts to Car." *Popular Mechanics*, December 1957, 100.

"Quick Change Flying Auto." *Popular Mechanics*, January 1951, 108.

"Ray Drives Autogiro 10 Miles Over Highway." *Automobile Topics*, September 14, 1935, 280.

"Report on the Aerocar." *Flying*, September 1957, 38, 87.

"Road and Rail." *Fleet Owner*, August 1972, 25.

"Roadable Airplane." *Sport Aviation*, November 2002, 10.

"Roadable Autogiro." *Automotive Industries*, October 10, 1936, 468.

"Roadable Plane." *Motor Age*, March 1946, 34.

"Roadable Plane." *Life*, February 4, 1946, 69–72.

"Roadable Plane or Flying Auto?" *AI*, December 15, 1946, 25.

"Robert Fulton and His Airmobile: The First Roadable Airplane." *FAA General Aviation News*, March 1978, 11–13.

Robin, Ben. "Fulton Airphibian. *Flying*, August 1950, 24–25, 58–60.

"The Rolligon." *Popular Mechanics*, December 1965, 68–69.

"The SAC Aerocar." *Air Classics*, September 1986, 68–71.

Sargent, Sparky Barnes. "Adyke Delta Reborn." *Sport Aviation* December 2008, 26–32.

Scagnetti, Jack. "Flying Your Own Car Now." *Science and Mechanics*, January 1971, 38–39, 91.

Scroggins, Ray, and Rich Taylor. "Cars That Run On." *SIA*, January 2, 1975, 24–27.

"Semi Amphibian." *Autocar*, April 25, 1941, 372.

Shaw, Wilbur, and Devon Francis. "What It's Like to Fly a Car?" *Popular Science*, July 1952, 72–77, 240.

"Simplified Controls." *Automobile Trade Journal*, November 1937, 40.

"Sky's the Limit." *Automotive News*, February 10, 1975.

Slattery, Chad. "Through the Lens." *Air and Space*, September 2000, 78–80.

"Snow Bunny Rides on Treads." *Popular Science*, January 1964, 86.

Sonne, Lisa. "Flying Underwater." *Aviation History*, September 2000, 13.

"Southern Roadable." *Aviation*, March 1947, 76.

"Steerable-Wing Plane." *Popular Mechanics*, June 1945, 8–9.

Stimson, Thomas F., Jr. "Your Hiller Aerial Sedan." *Popular Mechanics*, July 1957, 74–78.

"Studebaker Buys Flying Automobiles." *Motor*, July 1937, 50.

"Studebaker to Show Flying Automobile." *Automobile Topics*, May 31, 1937, 190.

"Survey: Amphicars." *Popular Science*, August 1968, 75–78.

"Swim, Car, Swim." *FHM*, June 2004, 32.

Taylor, Blane. "Militaria Report." *Militaria International*, August 2007, 51.

"Teacher Builds Roadable Plane." *Aviation Week*, December 17, 1956, 113.

"Temco to Build Flying Automobile." *Automobile*, May 1961, 11.

"Terra Star Walks, Rolls, etc." *Popular Science*, December 1968, 58–59.

"Terrible Terrain: It's Easy with Terra Tires." *Popular Science*, October 1962, 86–88.

"This Automobile Flies." *Motor*, April 1937, 54.

Tiffany, Laura. "Making Waves." *Entrepreneur*, June 1999, 97–98.

"To Fly and Drive." *Air Classics*, September 1908, 57.

"To Make Hydramotors in Los Angeles." *Outlook*, December 16, 1915, 1096.

Tobin, Pat. "It's the Aerocar: It Flies; It Drives." *Special Interest Autos*, May 6, 1994, 50–57, 70.

Tobin, Pete. "Flying Cars: From Movies to Reality." *Sport Aviation*, August 2008, 56–60.

"Tour or Cruise As You Like." *Motor*, May 1940, 38.

"Travel Trailer Cruises on Land and Water." *Trailer/Body Builders*, April 1973, 84.

Tuttle, Steve. "American Idol." *Newsweek*, December 10, 2007, 51.

"Twin Wings — Controllable and Flying." *Aviation*, May 1945, 212.

"Unreal Estate." *People*, November 11, 2002, 137.

Unwin, Dave. "Is It a Car? Is It a Plane?!" *Flypast*, August 2008, 42–48.

"U.S. to Test Hydra Automobile." *Automobile*, January 25, 1917, 210.

Vaughn, Maric. "A Wing and a Prayer." *Autoweek*, September 28, 1992, 18–19.

"Vuia." *WWI Aero*, May 1997, 4–14.

"Water Wagen." *NADA Magazine*, December 1960, 125.

"Wheeled Boat Rides on Land or Water." *Popular Science*, May 1963, 81.

"Whitaker-Zuck Planemobile." *Aviation*, March 1947, 75.

"Who Says They Don't?" *Popular Mechanics*, September 1967, 82.

"Will Cars Fly Again?" *Science Digest*, November 1984, 18.

"Will the Auto of the Future Be an Amphibious Animal?" *Automobile Trade Journal*, August 1917, 140.

"Wingless Plane — Will It Work?" *Science and Mechanics*, February 1951, 67–69.

"Winnebago Heli-Home." *Automotive News*, January 12, 1976, 8.

Woron, Walt. "Another Flying Auto in the Wings." *Automotive News*, June 18, 1973, 28.

_____. "Of Wings and Wheels: An Investigation of the Flying Car." *Automobile Quarterly*, First Quarter, 1984, 95–109.

_____. "Your Flying Car of the Future: It's Here Today." *Motor Trend*, November 1957, 35–41.

Note: All material in the *Roadable Aircraft Newsletter* vols. I, II and III from 1992 to 1994 has been carefully examined in detail.

Newspapers

"Airplane May Be Safe as Automobile Through Invention of Boston Engineer." *Boston Post*, March 24, 1912, 105.

Burgess, Scott. "Back to the Future." *Detroit News*, August 21, 1907, 1, 3C.

Carter, Elizabeth S. "Volkswagen Display of Creative Auto Collection." *U.S. Auto Scene*, June 23, 1997, 6.

Dr. Lewis Jackson Accepts OSU Aviation Assignment." *Springfield, Ohio, Sun*, August 15, 1966, 12.

"Flying Flivver." *Buffalo Courier Express*, December 15, 1946, 14.

"Ford Pinto Fitted for Flight." *Detroit News*, September 16, 1973, 11B.

"Freeway or Seaway?" *Detroit News*, February 11, 1985, 8A.

"Frey Crosses Bay in Hydro-Motorcycle." *Oakland Tribune*, May 13, 1912, 10.

Frutig, Judith. "Up, Up and Away: Car-Plane Flies." *Detroit Free Press*, November 25, 1972, 1–5A.

"Future Commuter." *San Francisco Examiner*, May 29, 1901, 16.

"Helicopter." *El Sol de Guadalajara*, June 15, 1957, 1.

"Hovertain to Be Tested by the British." *Detroit News*, November 18, 1971, 28C.

"Hydra-Motor-Bike Will Take the Bay Again." *Oakland Tribune*, May 12, 1912, 39.

"Hydro Built by Oakland Inventor." *Oakland Tribune*, February 5, 1912, 4.

Jackson, Les. "Ask Dr. Crankshaft." *Dearborn Press and Guide*, October 2, 2008, 5C.

Linn, Allison. "Flying Car Developed." *Detroit Free Press*, September 2, 1964, 8.

"Local Firm Rolls Out Odd Vehicles." *Dearborn Press and Guide*, January 11, 1990, 7A.

"Moller at Six, Boy Wonder Tried Building a House." *Sacramento Bee*, March 1, 1992, 4.

"Morphone Pickup." *Toledo Blade*, January 2, 2008, 8A.

Phelan, Mark. "Fly the Altima Coupe." *Detroit Free Press*, August 9, 2007, 1–2E.

_____. "Space Capsule." *Detroit Free Press*, June 19, 2008, 1–2E.

"Rick and Karen Dobbertin." *U.S. Auto Scene*, September 11, 1995, 3.

"Rides on Water with Motor Bike." *Oakland Tribune*, February 28, 1912, 10.

Ross-Flanigan, Nancy. "Is It a Plane? No, It's a Car." *Detroit Free Press*, October 2, 1990, 20.

Scott, Gerald. "Rare 1934 Dymaxion Visits Henry Ford" *U.S. Auto Scene*, October 29, 2007, 1, 4.

Sweeney, Ann. "Future Schlock." *Detroit News*, February 8, 1990, 1C.

"Terra Wind." *U.S. Auto Scene*, February 9, 2004, 6.

Woodward, Charles, and Sharon Silke Carty. "New Flying Car Hope." *Detroit Free Press*, August 20, 2008, 4F.

Websites

www.roadabletimes.com
www.aviation-history.com

Audiovisual

"The Flying Car Movie" by Kevin Smith

Libraries

Lewis A. Jackson Library
National Automotive History Collection, Detroit Public Library
Stanford University Library

Educational Institutions

Loughborough University, England
Harry Ransom Center, University of Texas
Virginia Polytechnic Institute and State University

Organizations

The Air-Car Research Association
Aircraft Owners and Pilots Association
American Institute of Aeronautics and Astronautics
American Aviation Historical Society
Antique Airplane Association, Inc.
Experimental Aircraft Association
International Liaison Pilot and Aircraft Association (ILPA)
National Association of Automobile Museums
National Business Aviation Association
Professional Pilots Association
SAE International
Society of Automotive Historians, Inc.
Vintage Aircraft Association

Index

Norton, J.H. 206
Norway 86
Novinger, Harry E. 63
Nye, Edward M. 5, 44

Oakie, Jack 11
Oakland International Airport 138
El Occidental 68
Ocean liner 110, 117
Oehmichen, Etienne 6
O'Hanlon, Charles 166
O'Keefe, Jack 181
Old Lady 194
Oldenburg, Claes 181
Oldfield, H.B. 206
Oldsmobile 5
Olsen, Thore J. 173
Omlie, Phoebe F. 34, 35
Ontario Northland Railroad 184
Opel engine 143, 165, 179, 180
Operation Air Watch 10
Ornamental bumper 25
Osprey 120
Otter 167
Outboard Marine Corporation 163, 194
Outboard motor 129, 166, 180
Outrigger design 186

Paddles 6, 141, 142, 173
Page, Edward H. 44, 197
Pago Jet 128
Paige 182
PALV 115, 116
Panama Canal 132
Panama-Pacific International Exposition 142
Pankotan, Paul 145
Pao Phu Tau 6
Para-Cycle 114
Parachute 42, 78, 108, 114, 119, 128, 196, 202
Parades 8, 126, 153
Paragliding wing 109
Parajet Skycar 109
Paramedic 130
Paramilitary 5, 130
Parcel delivery 4
Parham, Donald 91
Parrish, Russell 5, 19
Parrish, William 5, 19
Passenger service 136
Pate Museum of Transportation 47
Patents 4, 71, 206, 209
Payne, Gary 94
Pegasus 94, 97, 98
Pellarini, Antonio E. 115
Pellarini, Luigi 51, 115, 119
Penetralia 11
Penn Yann hull 136
Pennsylvania 32, 140, 184
Perl, Adolph R. 52
Perseverance 132
Persia 6

Petit 180
Pham, Roger N. 99
Phantom Works 101
Phibi, Ann 148
Phibicat 171
Philippines 57, 194
Phillips, Jerry 40
Photography 4, 130
Piasecki 117, 119
Pilotless plane 13
Pink Palace Museum 34, 35
Pioneers of Flight Museum 50
Piper 62
Piranha Aircraft 85
Pitcairn Autogiro Company 33; P-36 Whirlwing 41; PA-19 Cabin Autogiro 33
Plane-houseboat 196
"Plans for the Millennium" 99
Plant pollination 4
Plymocoupe Airplane 128
Poisson, Alphonse 5, 44
Polar ice 201
Polyurethane 131, 166
Poncin Industries USA 167
Port of Oakland 138
Porta-Boat 166
Portage Lake, Ohio 130
Portland, Oregon 10, 59
Post, Wiley 128
Potts, Professor 11
Powell, George 143
Powell Mobile Boat Works 143
Power take-off 1, 180
Prairie Home Companion 181
Precursor I 144
Prey, Eugene 173
Pritchard, Charles 63
Project Earth Trek 132
Propeller Car 126, 127
Prospecting 4, 130
Prototypes 5, 14, 32, 34, 47, 129, 136, 137, 142, 173, 202
Pruszenski, Anthony, Jr. 212
PTO 1
Public utilities 130, 167
Pudding River 181
Purcell, William 141
Pyramids 16

Quadricycle 211
Quadski 167, 169
Quasi Amphibious Vehicles 181
Queensland Railroad 184

RAC 172
Racing 94, 121, 130, 136, 175, 192
Radio 4, 7, 10, 30, 35, 59, 143, 153, 181, 192
RAF 118
RAI 120
Rail cars 182, 184
Rail Plane 32
Rail vehicles 1, 182, 186
Rail-water vehicles 1
Railroad track 110, 117, 118, 182, 186

Ramsgate Harbor 138
Ranching 4
Ravailler 141
Ray, James G. 32
RCAF 198
Read, Robert C. 187
Reconnaissance 5, 175
Recreation 4, 166
Recreatives Industries, Inc. 154, 155, 156
Reed, Dick 165
Reed, Robert C. 42
Regal 181
Reid, Reginald 62
Reid, Walter 115, 116
Reliant Regal 181
Relief organization 130
Rental 5, 15, 43, 182
Research grants 15
Rethorst, Scott C. 62
Revers, Marcel 148
Revolutionary War 140
Rheinmetall-Borsig 180
Rhino 146
Rice, K.P. 78, 79, 80, 198
Richmond, T. 141
Rinderknecht, Frank 167, 201
Rinspeed Splash 167
Road-A-Plane 48
Road-air vehicles 1, 3
Road-rail vehicles 1, 182, 186, 187
Road-Runner (1920s) 24, 26, 118
Road Wing 48, 49
Roadable aircraft 1, 3, 4, 13, 16, 17, 34, 35, 37, 51, 52, 62, 63, 71, 82, 85, 89, 91, 92, 94, 99, 103, 106, 109, 111, 118, 119, 120, 209
Roadable Aircraft International, Inc. 120
Roadable Autogiro 32, 33
Roadmobile 61
Roadplane 44
Roadrunner (1980s) 82, 83
Roadster 60, 99, 141, 142
Robida, Albert 6
Roc Atomic 124
Rock and Roll Aerocar 126
Rock Island Railroad 184
Rodair 71
Roebling, Donald 144
Rogers, Buck 7
Rohrbach Metal Airplane 196
Romania 5, 16, 17
Rose Bowl Parade 10
Rotaplane 63
Rotapower Engine 71
Rotary engine 71, 103, 108, 199
Rotary Flight International 91
Rotatank 118
Rover 29, 86, 129, 133
Royal Aeronautical Society 114
Royal Marines 136
Russia 5, 130, 135, 137, 147, 173, 196
Rutan, Elbert L. 84